Quentin Skinner

Quentin Skinner

History, Politics, Rhetoric

Kari Palonen

polity

First published in 2003 by Polity Press in association with Blackwell Publishing Ltd.

Editorial office:
Polity Press
65 Bridge Street
Cambridge CB2 1UR, UK

Marketing and production:
Blackwell Publishing Ltd
108 Cowley Road
Oxford OX4 1JF, UK

Distributed in the USA by
Blackwell Publishing Inc.
350 Main Street
Malden, MA 02148, USA

A catalogue record for this book is available from the British Library.

Library of Congress Cataloging-in-Publication Data
Palonen, Kari, 1947–
Quentin Skinner : history, politics, rhetoric / Kari Palonen.
    p. cm.   (Key contemporary thinkers)
Includes bibliographical references and index.
    ISBN 0-7456-2856-7—ISBN 0-7456-2857-5 (pbk.)
    1. Skinner, Quentin—Contributions in political science.   I. Title.
    II. Key contemporary thinkers (Cambridge, England)
JC257.S54 P35 2003
320.5 – dc21
                                                        2002012892

Typeset in 10.5 on 12pt Palatino by SNP Best-set Typesetter Ltd., Hong Kong
Printed and bound in Great Britain by MPG Books Ltd., Bodmin, Cornwall

For further information on Polity, visit our website:
http://www.polity.co.uk

Key Contemporary Thinkers

Published

Chris Rojek, *Stuart Hall*

Susan Sellers, *Hélène Cixous: Authorship, Autobiography and Love*

Wes Sharrock and Rupert Read, *Kuhn: Philosopher of Scientific Revolution*

David Silverman, *Harvey Sacks: Social Science and Conversation Analysis*

Dennis Smith, *Zygmunt Bauman: Prophet of Postmodernity*

Nicholas H. Smith, *Charles Taylor: Meaning, Morals and Modernity*

Geoffrey Stokes, *Popper: Philosophy, Politics and Scientific Method*

Georgia Warnke, *Gadamer: Hermeneutics, Tradition and Reason*

James Williams, *Lyotard: Towards a Postmodern Philosophy*

Jonathan Wolff, *Robert Nozick: Property, Justice and the Minimal State*

Forthcoming

Maria Baghramian, *Hilary Putnam*

Sara Beardsworth, *Kristeva*

James Carey, *Innis and McLuhan*

George Crowder, *Isaiah Berlin: Liberty, Pluralism and Liberalism*

Thomas D'Andrea, *Alasdair MacIntyre*

Maximilian de Gaynesford, *John McDowell*

Reidar Andreas Due, *Deleuze*

Eric Dunning, *Norbert Elias*

Jocelyn Dunphy, *Ricoeur*

Matthew Elton, *Daniel Dennett*

Chris Fleming, *René Girard: Violence and Mimesis*

Paul Kelly, *Ronald Dworkin*

Carl Levy, *Antonio Gramsci*

Moya Lloyd, *Judith Butler*

Dermot Moran, *Edmund Husserl*

Jim Murray, *C. L. R. James: Ideas in Social Movement*

James O'Shea, *Wilfrid Sellars*

Nicholas Walker, *Heidegger*

Contents

1

Introduction

... there is a awful lot of books, and if our books are not going to say something new, then we certainly ought not to be publishing them. Forests tremble as it is at the onset of authors.

Skinner 2001b, 21

A Revolution in the Study of Political Thought

The epigraph is a spontaneous remark made by Quentin Skinner during a debate with Yves Zarka in Amsterdam in May 1996. This remark not only expresses Skinner's attitude towards publishing books but also the proposal that novelty should be used as the main criterion for assessing the quality and significance of scholarly contributions. Historical novelty always signifies a rewriting, a revision of the interpretation of the phenomenon in question (cf. Koselleck 1988b, 37–51). The term 'revisionism' attributed to Quentin Skinner already in the 1970s rather aptly describes his project as he emphasizes the role of reinterpretation as a criterion for historical studies. The significance of the novelty may be emphasized by contrasting it with another criterion in the academic legitimation rhetoric, namely truth. In 'A Reply to My Critics' Skinner writes:

> I am convinced, in short, that the importance of truth for the kind of historical enquiries I am considering has been exaggerated. . . . Take for example . . . Machiavelli's fervently held belief that mercenary armies always jeopardize political liberty. Perhaps there is nothing to stop us from asking whether this is true. But the effect of doing so

will be somewhat analogous to asking whether the king of France is
bald. The best answer seems to be that the question does not really
arise. (Skinner 1988c, 256)

Opposing the roles of truth and novelty in historical studies is
distinctive to the work of Quentin Skinner. This contrast situates
him outside the style of analytical philosophy and empiricist
historiography and questions the frequently held opinion of him
as a typical English thinker (for example, Miller & Strong 1997).
Skinner's views on truth and novelty, rather, help us to situate him
in a wider European tradition of a perspectivist view of knowledge
and scholarship that is present, for example, in the works of
Friedrich Nietzsche and Max Weber.

In a classic account of the perspectivist view, Weber, in his article
on 'Objectivity' in 1904, takes as his point of departure the claim
that no analysis is independent of definite and one-sided perspectives (Weber 1904, esp. 170, 181). It is always possible and desirable
to propose a number of different perspectives on the study of the
'same' phenomena. The history of the human sciences is a history
of constructions, revisions and dissolutions of perspectives. There
are no 'objective' criteria for assessing research except for the competition of the perspectives themselves. The significance and the
validity of 'facts' can always be assessed differently when judged
from another perspective. Empirical analysis is a possible means of
challenging a definite perspective or changing the constellations
between concurrent perspectives, but as such it is never sufficient.
Nor, in the Weberian view, does 'approaching the truth' make sense,
and a convergence between perspectives indicates stagnation. We
cannot even define the questions and fields which should be considered to be central, because even they are determined differently
in various perspectives. Moreover, they change historically from
one situation to another (Weber 1904, esp. 184).

With this perspectivist view of the history of the human sciences
we can better understand Quentin Skinner's point about truth and
novelty. When analysing past beliefs, an assessment of their 'truth'
would tend to obstruct the understanding of their historical point
and value. Novelty-claims, by contrast, can be considered as moves
that change the current constellation through altering the positions
and perhaps creating a new 'participant' in the competition.

With Reinhart Koselleck we can distinguish three strategies of
rewriting history: new sources, new modes of reading them and
new perspectives on interpretation (Koselleck 1988b, 45–7). In his

revision of the history of political thought, Quentin Skinner has practised all of these strategies. The first point is related to Skinner's conscious use of non-canonized sources in political thought, which has also contributed to a revision of the views of such canonized thinkers as Machiavelli and Hobbes. The use of such intellectual resources as speech act theory and classical rhetoric has enabled Skinner to alter the mode of questioning, for example, by emphasizing questions of 'linguistic action' in contrast to merely asking questions about 'meaning' (Skinner 1996a, 7–8).

Quentin Skinner's distinctive mark in intellectual history and political theory lies, however, in his shifting perspective towards the entire subject matter. It is Skinner who most uncompromisingly argues for an inversion of the perspective in the study of political thought. In the Preface to *The Foundations of Modern Political Thought* he writes: 'For I take it that political life itself sets the main problems for the political theorist, causing a certain range of issues to appear problematic, and a corresponding range of questions to become the leading subjects of debate' (Skinner 1978a I, xi).

This is a paradigmatic formulation of what I would like to call 'the Skinnerian revolution' in the study of political thought. Revolution should be understood in the old literal sense of revolving the study in a new direction. The point of the Skinnerian revolution is that this very formula is reinterpreted: he does not analyse thought 'applied to the sphere of politics' but 'thinking in a political mode'. Thinking politically is an aspect of the activity of politics itself.

The history of political thought, as practised in universities of the nineteenth and twentieth centuries, still tended to start from the view that politics is a dirty subject that can be improved only by certain philosophical principles. In his classic study *Die Idee der Staatsräson*, Friedrich Meinecke presumed that for the foreign policy of a state there exists an ideal line of action that only has to be detected by the leading statesmen (Meinecke 1924, 1–2). In this view, politics is reduced to the application of some existing principles in the best possible manner.

To take 'political life itself' as the point of departure rehabilitates the political agents. They are not devalued or functionalized into bearers or representatives of some principle, but their words and deeds are taken as the first level of interpretation of the activities that, then, can be reinterpreted by scholars without devaluing the activity itself. Theorizing about politics renders explicit and reflects on the character and significance of the activity by focusing on the shifting problems of the political agents themselves. Considerable inventiveness is required from politicians in their situations of judging and struggle with one another: they are the persons obliged to face crises, the dead ends of policies, as well as threats of being played out of the situation. One condition of the study of political thought is to understand this special inventiveness of politicians.

In his *Liberty before Liberalism*, Skinner writes that one effect of the attempt to render intellectual history closer to 'real history' has been 'to make intellectual history . . . a subject of more general interest' (Skinner 1998, 106). I think the Skinnerian revolution has had similar effects in political science. If 'political life' sets the problems for the study of political thought, the explication and reflection of political activities forms the key to the study of politics. If we can make 'things with words' (Austin) or if 'words are deeds' (Wittgenstein), then analyses of the use of words, of rhetoric, is a constitutive part of political 'reality', and so is political thought.

This is also to recognize and to use the inherent contingency of politics-as-activity (cf. also Pocock 1975). Skinner insists on the heuristic value of contingency in understanding, as he remarks in retrospect about his critique of A. O. Lovejoy's style of studying the history of ideas:

> Against this contention I tried once more to speak up for a more radical contingency in the history of thought. Drawing on a sugges-tion of Wittgenstein's, I argued that there cannot be a history of unit ideas as such, but only a history of the various uses to which they have been put by different agents at different times. There is nothing, I ventured to suggest, lying beneath or behind such uses; their history is the only history of ideas to be written. (Skinner 1999c, 61–2)

Such an insistence on contingency can be traced to Max Weber's nominalist view of interpreting human actions in terms of the chances and unanticipated consequences (cf. Palonen 1998). However, the instruments of speech act theory and rhetoric lend to Skinner's view a linguistically sophisticated tone in the under-standing of politics-as-activity and the modes of theorizing about it. We can also detect a Weberian rehabilitation of the value of pol-itics as a contingent activity in Skinner's work, at least as a critique of depoliticizing tendencies in political theory. The pro-political ori-entation serves as a heuristic instrument also in Skinner's seemingly pure historical studies and, consequently, turns them into a mode of political theorizing (cf. Palonen 2002c).

A Political Reading

A perspectivist view of historical understanding and the criterion of novelty also serve as guiding principles for this volume. My 'Quentin Skinner', as a shorthand title for a certain complex of texts, has a definite profile of its own. As opposed to a common tendency to accuse Skinner of one-sidedness, I want to present a perspective that, according to Weber's suggestion (1904, 194), one-sidedly accentuates some aspects of Skinner's work at the cost of others. It is only within such a specific perspective that I can hope to reach an improved understanding of Skinner's work.

A clue to the perspective is contained in my subtitle *History, Politics, Rhetoric*. The words indicate a multidisciplinary profile to Skinner's work. He was trained as a historian, then became a political theorist in his own right, and since around 1990 his 'turn' to ancient and Renaissance rhetoric has given a further profile to his work, both as historian and as political theorist.

To me politics is the crucial word in the title. I am using Skinner's contributions to historiography and rhetoric as contributions to the understanding of politics. This is partly due to my lack of knowledge of his period, the fourteenth to the seventeenth century, as well as the immense number of primary sources from that time which are handled by Skinner. Moreover, my awareness of the specialist debates among the 'ordinary' historians and scholars of rhetoric is insufficient to enter into them myself. Nevertheless, having studied the history of the concept of politics for two decades, I am competent to detect debates on politics in which Skinner's contributions have not been sufficiently considered and from which I can also read a 'surplus meaning' implied in the texts of Skinner (cf. Skinner 1988c, 272).

I will consider Skinner to be a 'theory politician' in contemporary academic culture, which consists of a complex of polities at the level of universities, disciplines, debates, approaches and other kinds of conventional practices. I intend to explicate Skinner's moves of politicking within the existing complex of polities as well as politicizing moves altering the constellations within this complex. As he says in 'A Reply to My Critics': 'the types of utterance I am considering can never be viewed simply as strings of propositions; they must always be viewed at the same time as arguments' (Skinner 1988c, 273).

In Weberian terms I consider politicking as the search for new power shares within an existing polity, while politicization concerns the redistribution of such shares in a polity-complex in a manner that opens new *Spielräume* for politicking (cf. Weber 1919a, 36). Weber regards power-chances as a necessary medium to achieve any political aims or purposes. Analogously, I think that the rhetorical moves and strategies of Skinner are a condition for understanding his theoretical contributions, always related to a situation, constellation and an audience to be 'moved' (cf. Skinner 1974a and b). Theories and interpretations are for Skinner arguments in specific controversies. The historical moment aims at identifying those controversies to which such theories and interpretations intentionally contribute, and explicating the rhetorical tropes and figures he is using. The moves in politicking attempt virtuosity within the range of the acceptable, whereas the politicizing moves provoke the audience or attempt to create new chances to power by opening a new dimension in the debate.

According to Nietzsche's well-known formula, there are 'no facts, only interpretations' (Nietzsche 1981, 904), or in Skinner's words, 'the social and political world is interpreted through and through' (Skinner 2001a, 22). Within a perspectivist view the disputes about the facts, as presented by Skinner, are part of the specialist debates, which are not my concern in this volume.

As a scholar outside the Anglophone academic provinces, I hope that I can provide a detached reading of Skinner. This allows me to take a fresh look at his work and to avoid the usual labels, attributions and classifications. I will, above all, not write a reception study. I will, however, mention some tendencies in reception and occasionally go into a detailed discussion, if it serves my own point on that occasion.

A distance from Skinner's work is also gained by my studies in continental twentieth-century political thought. Presenting both the contrasts and parallels between Skinner and some German and French scholars is a key device in this volume. Skinner himself has on various occasions acknowledged his debt to Weber's historical and methodological views. In my interpretation this link has been further accentuated.

This book is, of course, no apology. Already our different backgrounds, research interests, and lifestyles make discrepancies between Skinner and me obvious. When readers use this volume as a guide to Skinner's own work, they will see that I have presented my critiques mainly as remarks and suggestions, without disturbing the main task of interpretation.

Today, the inclusion of contextual evidence has become a commonplace in the history of political thought. But how to contextualize Skinner's work? I have avoided the temptation to write a political-cum-intellectual history of Europe or Britain from the 1950s to today with a focus on Skinner. I have presented the contextual evidence as far as possible as already known to the readers and complemented it with remarks, notes or explications. I think that my perspective as a continental scholar has helped me to discern where explications are needed.

In rhetorical terms, my reading of Skinner's work both does justice to the internal history of his work and looks for certain recurrent *topoi* in different writings of Skinner. The internal history of the *œuvre* serves as a point of departure for the presentation, analysis and assessment. By means of such *topoi*, I occasionally want to detect in the Skinnerian *œuvre* contributions to political theorizing which he himself has not accentuated (cf. Skinner 2001a, 15). My point is to make use of the 'freedom of the reader' (Sartre 1948, 95–9) to underline some aspects in Skinner at which he merely gestures.

In order better to assess Skinner's contribution, I have selected for each chapter some other works of related interest, mainly those written earlier than Skinner, as a basis of comparison. My point is to accentuate the work of Skinner by referring to that which he has, intentionally or not, left out of his own discussion.

In each of the chapters I will present a single main argument to support my general thesis on the novelty and singularity of Skinner's work for political theorizing. Skinner's intellectual profile is thus constructed through thematic layers, partly historical, partly analytical, which, if considered together, render his *œuvre* inimitable. Although to some extent a 'mythology of coherence' is a necessary condition of the intelligibility of the profile of an *œuvre*, I want to leave the reader tools to discuss parts of Skinner's work without subscribing to my highly personal interpretation.

In the second chapter I have thematized the intellectual and political situation and the Cambridge milieu which shaped Skinner's education, experiences and early work. My interest is neither to present Skinner as a paradigmatic example of 'the Cambridge school' nor to discuss the formation of such a school through his work. Rather, I want to discuss the history of those distinctive moves that have given Skinner's work its individual profile and, at the same time, made it interesting for readers from widely different backgrounds.

When discussing the situation of political theory and intellectual history in the world that Quentin Skinner was entering, I want to illustrate the rise of a historical approach to political thought, especially at Cambridge. My point in this chapter is to analyse the use of 'history' as a normative value in the work of Skinner. The normative usage of history is strongest in Skinner's early studies on Hobbes, but the accentuation of the historical dimension remains a critical tool throughout his work.

One of the instruments through which Skinner, in the late 1960s, began to transcend the argument of a strict historian is the performative perspective of linguistic action, used both as a means of critique of existing scholarship and as a tool of historical analysis. My argument in the third chapter is that Skinner constructs an approach that transforms Wittgensteinian and Austinian philosophy into an instrument in historical analysis. As transformed by Skinner, the reality of action gains a political dimension, dismissed by both the philosophical and sociological approaches of the time.

Politics is explicitly thematized by Skinner when he transcends the discussion of the role of ideas as principles or as merely rationalizations by invoking their significance for the legitimating of action. In the fourth chapter, *The Foundations of Modern Political Thought* is read as exemplary of the mode in which Skinner makes political agents revise their theories to make them more strongly support the legitimacy of their activity. The 'modernity' of political thought consists in attributing a priority to political action, while the 'foundations' refers to those elements of the history of thought which remained unquestioned by contemporaries.

In the fifth chapter, Skinner's studies will be read as recovering 'lost treasures' from the past, as illustrated by the history of the concept of liberty. Since the early 1980s, Skinner has written on republican, later neo-Roman theories of negative liberty, partly in order to illustrate the one-sidedness and 'provinciality' of the distinctions and classifications in the current philosophical debate. He does not advocate a definite view of political liberty, but, rather, warns against contemporary tendencies to depoliticize controversies surrounding the concept.

The history of losers is also key to Skinner's turn to rhetoric as a pluralistic intellectual and political culture that is based on arguing *in utramque partem*, which is analysed in the sixth chapter. An insight into the presence of rhetorical problematics in Renaissance and early modern authors allows him to revise the intellectual history and character of the political controversies of the period. By generalizing the idea of the *paradiastole* of Roman rhetoric to a perspective of the rhetorical redescription of concepts, Skinner interprets conceptual change through rhetorical shifts. Here Skinner offers us a valuable complement to the continental studies of

Begriffsgeschichte. At the same time, he considers rhetoric as a more pluralist, historical and political style of thought, as compared to the ideologies of science and philosophy.

Quentin Skinner is an 'innovating ideologist' (Skinner 1974b) who has contributed to the political and intellectual debates of the twentieth century. In the final chapter I shall treat Skinner's historical studies of Renaissance and early modern political thinking as an indirect mode of political theorizing, making systematic use of a kind of Brechtian *Verfremdungseffekt* (cf. Palonen 2002c). This also leads me to the conclusion that Skinner is also a contemporary thinker in a strong sense, with a priority of present over both the future and the past in his *Weltanschauung.*

* * *

This book has grown out of a larger manuscript in German, *Die Entzauberung der Begriffe*, which compares the approaches of Quentin Skinner and Reinhart Koselleck to conceptual change. After completing the present book, I reread my German manuscript and noticed that I have managed to write two different books largely on the same subject. Not only are the language and the audience different, but also the approach and the narrative, although I have not altered my main theses. Furthermore, the consideration of Skinner's revised versions of his articles in the volumes of *Visions of Politics* and new contributions on the concept of liberty could be included in this volume. The comparison with Koselleck and the focus on conceptual changes lend a profile to *Die Entzauberung der Begriffe*, which, I hope, can alter the rather reluctant reception of Skinner in the German-speaking world.

In this volume I have followed certain practices, or conventions, as Skinner would probably say, of my own, that are perhaps not so evident and thus require explanation.

I have preferably quoted from the first versions of Skinner's publications, using the formulations presented there. I have only referred to later versions if Skinner's formations alter or complement my interpretation, which is rather rare.

For the quotations I have used the author-date system with two modifications. I have referred to the original date of publication in the text and noted any more accessible modern editions only in the references. To refer to *Wirtschaft und Gesellschaft* as Weber 1980 has always sounded anachronistic to me. Secondly, for Skinner's publications I have modified the alphabet in so far as I have introduced a hierarchy between (a) monographs, (b) articles and (c) reviews, prefaces and other minor contributions: referring to *Reason and Rhetoric* as 1996a and the essay 'From Hume's Intentions to Deconstruction and Back' as 1996b. Furthermore, I have chosen not to refer to Skinner's sources, to Hobbes or Machiavelli, but have used only Skinner's quotations. The case is different with authors, such as Berlin or Pettit, whom I have discussed separately as a background for Skinner.

Finally, emphasizing my interpretation of Skinner as a European scholar, I have both referred to the original editions in French and German and quoted short passages from them in the original language. I have done this even in the cases such as Weber or Wittgenstein in which Skinner himself has used the English translations. One reason for this is that, at least in the case of Weber or Sartre, I know that the translations are usually miserable, another is to resist the provincialist self-sufficiency of the Anglophone world.

As my references indicate, Quentin Skinner himself has been extremely helpful to me. He has been ready to discuss his own work in detail on various occasions. With these discussions and answers to my queries he has, in particular, provided me with references to his lesser known writings, clarified the context and the point of his various publications and offered formulations that are not so explicit in his published works. I have profited from Skinner's comments both with new and publicly unknown information as well as with a tacit encouragement to write my own interpretation, without playing down its profile. Finally, he obliged me to check myself the quotations from his work.

Quentin Skinner has been a key subject in my discussions with colleagues in recent years. My debates with Reinhart Koselleck, Tuija Pulkkinen and Melvin Richter deserve a special mention. For a careful reading of and comments on the manuscript I am especially thankful to Jussi Kurunmäki, Suvi Soininen and Tapani Turkka. Finally, Kris Clarke's (University of Tampere) corrections of my English are crucial to the present book.

2

History as an Argument

Quentin Skinner entered Gonville and Caius College at the University of Cambridge as a Scholar in 1959, gaining admission on the basis of an examination system then distinctive to Oxford and Cambridge (Skinner 2002d, 35). At that time, Skinner was already a *homo politicus* who had, in particular, opposed the policy of the Eden government during the Suez crisis, and had quarrelled with his father on British colonial policy (Skinner to KP, September 2001). His years at Bedford school had provided him with a good education, especially in Latin as well as history and English literature.

What was the political and academic world that Skinner entered like? Some aspects of the struggles and debates of the time are worthy of brief recapitulation.

The Cold War was still the dominant divide in the world, but the growing formal independence of the former colonies, accelerating in 1960, soon began to create a new divide. In the academic world, a certain disgust with Cold War thinking was present already in the 1950s; in Britain it could be seen above all in the form of the Committee for Nuclear Disarmament (CND) with Bertrand Russell as the leading figure.

One indicator that Cold War dualism was losing its force could be seen in the rise of a debate on the 'end of ideology'. Made popular by the Milan meeting of the Conference for Cultural Freedom in 1955, the slogan was repeated in numerous books and articles by many famous thinkers, especially by American sociologists, such as Daniel Bell, S. M. Lipset and Edward Shils, but also by continental authors, such as Raymond Aron in France and

Herbert Tingsten in Sweden. The catchword implied both the decline of old political cleavages and the longing for a consensual, expert-based style in governmental politics. The last aspect was strongly opposed in Britain, where a Conservative government had been in power since 1951, by such 'welfare socialists' as the young Quentin Skinner and his friends in Cambridge (Skinner to KP, September 2001).

The Death of Political Philosophy?

Skinner and his friends tended to regard the view of the 'death of political philosophy' as expressed by Peter Laslett as a British variant of the 'end of ideology' thesis. A historian from Cambridge, Laslett edited the first volume of the series *Philosophy, Politics and Society* in 1956 and wrote in the Introduction what became the most quoted sentence of the entire volume: 'For the moment anyway, political philosophy is dead' (Laslett 1956, vii).

In its contemporary context, Laslett's claim had specific references and targets. Within philosophy, certain variants of linguistic philosophy had gained prominence through the claim to dissolve classical questions. 'It was Russell and Wittgenstein, Ayer and Ryle who convinced the philosophers that they must withdraw unto themselves for a time, and re-examine their logical apparatus' (ibid., ix). As Skinner, surely disagreeing with Laslett on Wittgenstein, later noticed, R. M. Hare's *The Language of Morals* (1952) and T. D. Weldon's *The Vocabulary of Politics* (1953), with the definite article, were prominent in the British debate of the 1950s (Skinner 1999c, 61). Weldon's book claimed to dissolve political controversies by an 'appropriate use' of the vocabulary involved.

Laslett's thesis implies a statement of the fact that analytic philosophy, as then practised, marked the 'death' of political philosophy, as a classical genre of providing answers to crucial political questions. At the beginning of the introduction, Laslett writes:

> It is one of the assumptions of intellectual life in our country that there should be amongst us men whom we think of as political philosophers. Philosophers themselves and sensitive to philosophic change, they are to concern themselves with political and social relationships at the widest possible level of generality . . . For three hundred years of our history there have been such men writing in English, from the early seventeenth to the twentieth centuries, from

Hobbes to Bosanquet. To-day, it would seem, we have them no longer. (Laslett 1956, vii)

One reason for the death of political philosophy was the rise of sociological approaches, of both Marxist and academic variants. As for the Marxists, Laslett claims that 'their immensely successful political following in the twentieth century has apparently found little occasion to present them with philosophical problems of the political sort' (ibid., viii). The sociologists have 'taken over' the area of the activity of 'the social and political philosopher', but they 'do not seem to be doing anything with it, or at any rate, anything of philosophic interest' (ibid., viii–ix).

To the contexts mentioned by Laslett, we can add the turn away from philosophy within political science, just beginning its phase of institutionalization in Britain. The programmatic declarations of 'behavioralism' or functionalist 'empirical theory' indicated a scientistic self-consciousness, as a replacement for philosophy, among prominent representatives of the discipline. Against this background, Laslett's thesis describes a widespread lack of interest in political philosophy, if not a questioning of its very legitimacy.

A further level concerns the mode of conducting political philosophy in the 1950s, especially in the Anglophone world, although partly mediated by German *émigrés* (cf. for example, Gunnell 1979). Such prominent books as Leo Strauss's *Natural Right and History* (1952) or Eric Voegelin's *New Science of Politics* (1956) demonstrated a revival of political philosophy that appeared hardly desirable. In other words, political philosophy had at that time a reputation for being an ultra-classicist and anti-democratic current in thinking about politics (cf. Laslett 1956, xiv).

The historian Laslett had good reasons to argue that: 'it may still be the case that we have no political philosophy because politics have become too serious to be left to the philosophers' (ibid., vii). He, however, had noticed signs among philosophers of a willingness 'to take up their responsibilities towards political discussions once more', and 'on these small signs some might wish to base an expectation of a rebirth of traditional political philosophy' (ibid., x). This leaves open the question as to whether Laslett sees this 'rebirth' as something desirable.

In the 1962 Introduction to the second series of *Philosophy, Politics and Society*, Laslett and W. G. Runciman admit that the provocative Introduction from 1956 was written 'at the heyday of Weldonism'. They 'cannot quite' proclaim a resurrection of political philosophy, 'but the mood is very different' (Laslett & Runciman 1962, vii). They see 'signs . . . of a new interest in political theory' (ibid., viii). In the third series, the editors speak of a 'revival of political philosophy' as an accomplished fact (Laslett & Runciman 1968, 1).

The Defence of the Historian: Laslett and Pocock

Laslett thus left it open to invent a 'political philosophy' better than the available ones. In his own work, he presented a historical approach as a kind of post-philosophical alternative for the study of political thought. He contributed to this debate with his 1960 edition of Locke's *Two Treatises on Government* that revolutionized Locke scholarship. Laslett's edition was particularly directed against the conventional interpretation of the role and significance of Locke's *Two Treatises*: 'In the history books and the works on political theory, Locke on the English Revolution is still the supreme example of the way in which political events interplay with political thinking. This belief is far too deeply engrained, far too useful, to be easily abandoned. Nevertheless it is quite untrue' (Laslett 1960, 46).

The revision of interpretation was achieved through the simple means of redating the writing of the main part of the *Two Treatises*, as a reply to the publication of Filmer's *Patriarcha*, to the 'exclusion crisis' of 1680–3. '*Two Treatises* in fact turns out to be a demand for a revolution to be brought about, not the rationalization of a revolution in need of defence' (ibid., 47). In this perspective, Laslett concludes, it is erroneous to consider the work as political philosophy: 'From the point of view of our discussion, the book as a response to political and literary circumstances, its origins belongs to the autumn and winter 1679–80, exactly a decade earlier than it is traditionally supposed to have been written. *Two Treatises* is an Exclusion Tract, not a Revolution Pamphlet' (ibid., 61).

Laslett's Introduction contained a research programme in which 'history' was turned into a critical instance, in implicit opposition to the philosophers' reading of Locke: 'But our first object must be a modest historian's exercise – to establish Locke's text as he wanted it read, to fix it in its historical context, Locke's own context, and to demonstrate this connection of what he thought and wrote with the Locke of historical influence' (Laslett 1960, 4).

Such an appeal to the role of context as a condition for understanding the point of a text was not new. R. G. Collingwood, in particular, had underlined the role of context as a condition of understanding differences in the use of a seemingly identical concept in his *Autobiography* (Collingwood 1939, 113). Laslett's specific point was to contrast context with Locke's 'influence' and, correspondingly, to go back to 'Locke's text as he wanted it read'.

This leads us to the discussion of intention, frequently considered to be irrelevant in post-war literary criticism and philosophy. The role of intention for Laslett consists in the understanding of Locke's self-characterization of his *Treatises* as a contribution to the contemporary debate. The attempt to recover such a self-understanding, by using the knowledge of both the debate in Locke's contexts and the details in the text, offers the historian a way of understanding the work that makes it a political act. Such an understanding thus requires a disregard for its reputation and influence and a concentration on the sources that were available to Locke.

Laslett defended the craftsmanship of the historian against the contempt for the 'mere historian' shown by contemporary British philosophers. Historians can, at least, contribute to a revision of our received view, while philosophers like Weldon are content with the reconstruction of what is already known, as we could perhaps summarize his general point.

However, this point was not a programme for universal application. Quentin Skinner experienced Laslett's edition of Locke, recommended to him by his teacher John Burrow, as a major event that turned out to be decisive for his own studies (Skinner 2002d, 41). To Skinner, however, Laslett claimed that what he had done for Locke could not be done for Hobbes, because the latter's philosophy was more systematic than Locke's. Skinner considered this to be a challenge: 'I had been sufficiently influenced by the method underpinning his work to think that it was *a priori* certain that it could be done for Hobbes and I set out to try to do it' (Skinner 1997c, 70).

Skinner regarded John Pocock's Cambridge dissertation, *The Ancient Constitution and the Feudal Law*, which was first published in 1957, as 'as one of the works I had most enjoyed in my undergraduate course' (Skinner 2002d, 42). In the second series of *Philosophy, Politics and Society*, Pocock, then a political science professor in his native New Zealand, published an article on the methodology of the history of political thought. Skinner was impressed especially by Pocock's discussion 'on the different "levels of abstraction" at which different political thinkers work' (Skinner 2002d, 48).

Pocock's appeal to history as an argument is different from Laslett's. He presents the history of political thought as a tradition of a special kind, a 'tradition of intellectualizing'. From this perspective Pocock then accentuates the dualism inherent in the study: 'Political thought may be regarded as an aspect of social behaviour, of the ways in which men behave towards each other and towards the institutions of their society; or it may be regarded as an aspect of intellectuality, of men's attempt to gain understanding of their experience and environment' (Pocock 1962, 185).

This formula well expresses two possible ways of understanding and studying 'political thought'. Pocock's view is that both modes are legitimate, and the level of abstraction depends on the subject matter. A philosophical history has to 'ask, whether its abstractions correspond to realities actually experienced' (ibid., 186). Against the 'rational reconstructions' of the philosophers the historian 'is interested in men thinking about politics as he is interested in them fighting or farming or doing anything else, namely as individuals behaving in society, whose recorded behaviour can be studied, by the method of historical reconstruction, in order to show what manner of world they lived in and why they behaved in it as they did' (ibid., 190).

In addition to the philosophers, Pocock had a target of criticism among the historians: 'those who deny that there is any significant relation between political activity and political theory' (ibid., 191). He refers to a school of historians around Lewis Namier, who well understood that principles can be used as 'propaganda', but who overstated their case. In Pocock's words: 'To deny that concepts may be isolated and shown to play a determining role in politics is not to deny that they play any role whatsoever' (ibid., 193).

Laslett's interpretation of Locke led him almost to equate the history of political events and practices with that of political thought. Pocock retains 'a rough division of labour' between 'the historian of action to investigate how ideas, beliefs and arguments help us to understand the actions of men in particular situations' and 'the historian of thought, to study the activity of thinking, of conceptualizing, of abstracting ideas from their particular situations and traditions' (ibid., 194–5). He proposes to 'define political thought as the language of political discussions' (ibid., 197), allowing movement to both directions, especially regarding 'the history of political thought through studying the regular employment of relatively stable concepts' (ibid., 195).

A good approximation is to say that Skinner attempts to construct a position that is between and at the same time beyond the views of Laslett and Pocock. He extends the concept of political events to comprise, in some respect, the 'activity of thinking', without committing himself to the Pocockian view of 'languages' and 'stable concepts'.

A model for Skinner in combining historical and philosophical insights was R. G. Collingwood, whom he had read for his entrance examination to Cambridge (Skinner 2002d, 35). Collingwood personified the union of a philosopher with a historian (in his case, an archaeologist). In his *Autobiography*, he declared: 'The chief business of the twentieth century philosophy is to reckon with twentieth century history' (Collingwood 1939, 79). The 'history' he meant was, thus, that of revising the problems, which he had learnt in his archaeological practices, as opposed to what he calls the 'scissors and paste' historiography (ibid.).

Collingwood's model for a unification of history and philosophy lies in his 'logic of question and answer', which takes its point of departure from the historical question: 'To what question did So-and-so intend this proposition for an answer?' (ibid., 39). For Collingwood, 'the history of political theory is not the history of different answers given to one and the same question, but the history of a problem more or less constantly changing, whose solution was changing with it' (ibid., 62).

The 'Historical' as a Criterion

I want to assess Quentin Skinner's training as a historian through his unknown undergraduate writings, dealing mainly with theatre history. During his vacations in Bedford he analysed the life of the Whig politician Samuel Whitbread II in a series of articles. Like many other history students, Skinner here begins with the sources he had encountered himself, in this case a letter collection that was recently made available to the public.

In his first article, published in 1961, Skinner draws a portrait of this once famous politician, who was MP for Bedford from 1790 until his suicide in 1815. This essay is striking in its complete command of the agents and events of the time: it is hard to believe it was written by an undergraduate student. An interest in 'bringing buried intellectual treasure back to the surface', as Skinner was to put it later (for example, Skinner 1998, 112), as well as in the strangeness of the past world is obvious. The collection of Whitbread's papers 'illustrates the elusive and no less fascinating study of what it was like to live in Jane Austen's England' (Skinner 1961, 21), a period Skinner has never dealt with in detail.

The use of the Whitbread family archives and the tone of a local historian also shape Skinner's essay on John Bunyan, which attempts a secular and political portrait. On Bunyan's participation in the Civil War, Skinner writes ironically towards the existing research but illustrates the contestedness of the concept of liberty that later became one of his own main topics: 'We do not even know for sure on which side he fought. Macaulay believed he must have been fighting for liberty – which for him meant fighting for Parliament. Froude also saw him fighting for liberty – but believed this made him a Royalist' (Skinner 1962, 15).

Both the 'history of losers' and a critical attitude towards received views are manifested in Skinner's studies on Whitbread as the manager of the Drury Lane Theatre and his relations with the theatre's founder and fellow MP, Richard Sheridan. Skinner summarizes the revision he undertook: 'First, the problems that faced Whitbread . . . seem to have been greatly underrated. The accounts . . . of Sheridan's relations with Whitbread . . . appear to give only one side of the argument' (Skinner 1962–3, 40, cf. also Skinner 1963). The rhetorical model of arguing *in utramque partem* is present in Skinner's early use of historical sources as an argument against established narratives.

For Quentin Skinner's *œuvre* these undergraduate essays remain a curiosity, and a retrospective judgement in reading them is almost inevitable. These essays, at any rate, illustrate how Skinner learnt the craftsmanship of the historian, including insight into its rhetorical aspect, the insight that studying history always leads to a reinterpretation of history.

After his BA degree in June 1962, Skinner was elected a Fellow of Christ's College with the task of 'giving tutorials to the students in History', and in 1965 he obtained a 'lectureship in the history of political theory'. He started to do research on his own with no expectation of writing a Ph.D. dissertation, following the still common practice in Britain, and the selection of Thomas Hobbes as the focus of interest was mainly a contingent matter, as a part of the canon, because John Locke was already chosen by John Dunn (Skinner 2002d, 41).

One of Skinner's favourite genres is the review article. His first contribution to this genre, 'Hobbes' "Leviathan"', dealing mainly with F. C. Hood's *The Divine Politics of Thomas Hobbes*, is one of his fiercest polemics, and can easily be identified as a work of a youthful scholar. The theological interpretation of Hood is a target through which Skinner can simultaneously polemize against two novel and rather unconventional views on Hobbes, namely Howard Warrender's (1957) deontological and C. B. Macpherson's (1962) Marxist interpretations. Despite their differences, Skinner offers the same accusation against all of them: they 'are all concerned to reduce Hobbes to coherence in virtue of a theory about the "real" assumptions of his thought' (Skinner 1964, 322). In a strictly nominalist fashion, Skinner parodies Hood's mode of argumentation: 'It must be essential first for the reader to be made aware of the type of evidence being discounted in the name of the higher truth. It must be essential also for the commentator to explain the grounds on which evidence is being dismissed as irrelevant to the writer's "real" design' (ibid., 323). His main point is that a purely philosophical textual analysis leads to a neglect of history: 'The investigation proceeds exclusively by rationalization of texts; it is concluded when the "doctrine" is elucidated; it makes no pretence of considering the intellectual relations between Hobbes's work and other political discourse of the age' (ibid., 330).

Questioning Warrender's thesis on the 'priority' of the content of the theory over the question of 'its historical location', Skinner claims: 'It can be shown, that historical and exegetical consistency cannot fairly be regarded as separate issues.' Additionally, in a footnote he favourably refers to Pocock, but charges that he 'still seems to regard them as alternatives' (ibid.).

In the criticism of Hood an appeal to history serves as Skinner's main argument. In his assessment of Hood, Skinner turns the use of *historical* into a normative argument in political theory:

> For if the study of political theory is to be a properly historical investigation, it has to include some account of political theory as social activity, carried on at a number of interacting levels of abstraction at a given time. . . . To add an historical dimension is to add information relevant to any assessment of a classical text. The consequence of neglecting such location, in the case of *Leviathan*, has been that conclusions which are historically absurd are capable of being seriously canvassed. (Skinner 1964, 333)

The review gives us a glimpse of Skinner's own intellectual profile. Identifying himself as a historian, he uses the adjective *historical* as an evaluative-descriptive term, to use his own later vocabulary. In doing so, he blurs the distinction between 'purely' philosophical and 'merely' historical approaches by insisting on the value of a historical argument for the philosophical questions of interpretation.

This practice of using the *historical* in a normative sense is frequent in Skinner's writings of the 1960s. For example, he characterizes W. H. Greenleaf's approach as 'a valuable corrective to all such fashionable but unhistorical theories' (Skinner 1965d, 137). Similarly, a point of departure for the article 'The Ideological Context of Hobbes's Political Thought' can be detected in the formula 'Hobbes's views have tended to get evaluated in a misleading unhistorical way' (Skinner 1966a, 287). Further expressions revaluing history by opposing it to a derogatory counter-concept are the very title of the article 'History and Ideology in the English Revolution', and formulations such as 'It happened that the most ideologically acceptable use of the historical information was also the least historically accurate' (Skinner 1965a, 176; cf. also 1965f).

A normative usage of the adverb *historically* can equally be found on some occasions, such as the passage: 'The conventional methodology is in fact historically misleading' (Skinner 1965a, 170); or in the demand that an interpretation should be 'of historically possible and credible kind' (Skinner 1966a, 313). The simple adjective is sometimes used in a similar way (for example, Skinner 1966b, 213). At the end of 'The Ideological Context', the relationship between philosophical and historical dimensions in textual interpretation is then rethematized:

> It has been intended in this study to emphasize a link, commonly ignored or even denied, between the activities of philosophers and historians. An attempt has been made to elucidate the ideological context of one classic set of texts, and to construct around them the framework of their appropriate intellectual milieu. The implication has been that when such a framework is lacking the classic text itself may be 'understood' by philosophers in ways that are historically absurd. The aim has been to show that the historian's task of understanding climates of opinion is not disconnected from the philosopher's attempts to interpret texts. It is still for the historian to point out that even the philosopher's most plausible interpretation must still be tested, and might even have to be abandoned, in the light of historical evidence. (Skinner 1966a, 317)

Here Skinner appeals to history as a source of criticism against philosophical interpretations, as a corrective to the danger of too much coherence or too much simplicity, for 'the historical study of

Hobbes's intellectual milieu can be used to help assess the philosophers' various interpretations of Hobbes's meaning' (ibid., 313). The understanding of contemporary debates functions for Skinner as a criterion that not only excludes certain interpretations as implausible but also gives clues to interpretative perspectives as historically possible in the situation.

In 'Meaning and Understanding in the History of Ideas', Skinner turns the normative usage of *historical* into a programmatic principle. It allows him to detect some typical 'mythologies' in the conventional study, that he characterizes as 'historical absurdities':

> I do wish, however, both to insist on the various ways in which to study simply what each classic writer *says* is unavoidably to run the perpetual danger of lapsing into various kinds of historical absurdity, and also to anatomize the various ways in which the results may in consequence be classified not as histories at all, but more appropriately as *mythologies*. (Skinner 1969a, 7)

In 'Some Problems in the Analysis of Political Thought and Action', Skinner also defends 'the value of a strictly historical approach to the study of political thought' (Skinner 1974c, 281). Although he continues to characterize his approach as historical, and insists, for example, in 'A Reply to My Critics', that 'the purely historical study of social and political thought may prove to have a further relevance' (Skinner 1988c, 287), such normative epithets and conceptual oppositions are later much more rarely evoked. As a good historian, Skinner is always more than a historian.

Still, in his recent essay on Isaiah Berlin, Skinner once again both analyses Berlin's famous essay on liberty against its historical background and reproaches Berlin for neglecting the historical dimension of concepts and classifications: 'the belief that we can somehow step outside the stream of history and furnish a neutral definition of such words as *libertas*, freedom, autonomy and liberty is an illusion well worth giving up' (Skinner 2002f).

The normative usage of *historical* in Skinner's publications from the 1960s should also be understood as a heuristic instrument of interpretation. Especially in the essay 'History and Ideology', in which Skinner perhaps most radically inveighs against 'Whig' tendencies in historiography, he discusses the political consequences of the questionable use of historical theses. In seventeenth-century debates, the reality of the Norman Conquest was denied and the antiquity of Parliament was asserted by both sides: 'What every Parliamentarian asserted, no Royalist could deny' (Skinner 1965a,

153). The anachronistic Whig historiography had, according to Skinner, after losing its legitimacy among professional historians, none the less retained its ideological power as a mainstream intellectual current in Britain.

> The other casualty of the 'whig' hegemony proved to be nothing less than the submerging of any predominant rationalism in the English political tradition. This process itself, as can be seen, embodied a notable irony, for while Coke's conception of the continuity of right, his reversion to allegedly immemorial ways, was originally the backing for a revolutionary programme, its legacy was to be a sceptical conservatism, a use of history not so much for political debate as to deny that any such debate could be valid. History itself became seen as the embodiment of what was constitutionally proper – not to be quarrelled with or altered, except at grave peril. The attitude has become one of the most influential voices in English political thought. (ibid., 177–8)

Instead of accepting history as a legitimating ideology for a certain style of political thought, Skinner in his studies on Hobbes in the 1960s underlines the heuristic value of the historialization of the thought of this 'rationalistic' thinker. The very title, 'The Ideological Context of Hobbes's Political Thought', illustrates his programme. Hobbes is removed from the series of canonized thinkers and considered as a participant in contemporary political struggles – the Civil War, the Commonwealth – around which new legitimations for the unprecedented situation were sought. The historializing reading of Hobbes, in the form of analysing the contemporary reception, the disciples, the connections to the circles of the Royal Society and the links between the French and English debates of that time, served to accentuate aspects in Hobbes's texts that the canonical or philosophical reading had neglected (cf. Skinner 1966a, 1966c, 1969b, 1972a).

A problem in the normative usage of *historical* lies, of course, in the contested character of what is 'historical' and how a historical inquiry should be conducted. Skinner's first contribution to the contemporary debates on 'historical explanation' leads him to question the vocabulary of influences in history. In 'The Limits of Historical Explanations', Skinner demonstrates the vagueness of such jargon; and in his review of More's *Utopia* he illustrates its practical consequences: 'It is hard to see . . . how any such studies could ever actually tell us anything new about More's work' (Skinner 1967a, 165). Programmatically, Skinner comes to sceptical conclusions about historical explanation in favour of 'a more descriptive, more inclusive, perhaps even much more metaphorical language for the whole business of trying to provide explanations of the past' (Skinner 1966b, 215).

In the 'Meaning and Understanding' essay, Skinner manifests the heuristic value of a historical approach above all in his detailed critique of 'mythologies'. The common background is the real difficulty for all historical studies, the projection of one's expectations on the work of past authors.

> We must classify in order to understand, and we can only classify the unfamiliar in terms of the familiar. The perpetual danger, in our attempts to enlarge our historical understanding, is thus that our expectations about what someone must be saying or doing will themselves determine that we understand the agent to be doing something which he would not – or even could not – himself have accepted as an account of what he *was* doing. (Skinner 1969a, 6)

Skinner's claim is to detect in the 'current historical study' forms that are 'contaminated by the unconscious application of paradigms . . . applicable to the past' (ibid., 7). He presents the four mythologies of doctrine, coherence, prolepsis and parochialism as the distinct contemporary forms of such *ex post* projections. The critiques of doctrine and coherence in particular continue the critique of the shortcomings of 'philosophical' approaches suppressing the variety of history. The mythology of parochialism concerns, above all, 'the apparent reference' (ibid., 25), when 'familiarity' in the past is too easily detected, instead of using the strangeness of the past to make the present appear less familiar. Perhaps the most noteworthy mythology is that of prolepsis, described by Skinner in the following terms: 'The characteristic, in short, of the mythology of prolepsis is the conflation of the necessary asymmetry between the significance an observer may justifiably claim to find in a given statement or other action, and the meaning of that action itself' (ibid., 23).

This critique of judging past writers and texts in terms of their 'retrospective significance' (ibid., 22) is probably the most provocative aspect in Skinner's heuristic usage of an historical approach. He directs this criticism against the programmatic *Wirkungsgeschichte*, so common also in sophisticated attempts to write the history of ideas. It is this aspect that has been crucial in the objections to Skinner, beginning with Margaret Leslie's essay 'In Defence of Anachronism' (1970). Skinner's own view has consequently been directed 'against any teleological form of explanation: the action has to await the future to await its meaning' (Skinner 1969a, 24).

The question Skinner evokes is: which kinds of history should be written? The criticism of the mythology of prolepsis is directed against the alleged self-movement of ideas with different 'bearers' in different contexts, whereas Skinner is interested in the 'activity of thinking' of human beings in order to participate in specific debates (ibid., 30).

The Collingwoodian denial of 'perennial problems' in the classic texts leads Skinner to the claim that 'the classic texts cannot be concerned with our questions and answers, but only with their own' (ibid., 50). In the concluding remarks in the 'Meaning and Understanding' essay, Skinner legitimates the study of classic texts, evoking once more the mythologies of parochialism and prolepsis, through an emphasis on historical distance:

> For it is the very fact that the classic texts are concerned with their quite alien problems, . . . which seems to me to give not the lie but the key to the indispensable value of studying the history of ideas. The classic texts . . . help to reveal – if we let them – not the essential sameness, but rather the essential variety of viable moral assumptions and political commitments. (Skinner 1969a, 52)

These ideas of strangeness and distance have, since then, played a main role in Skinner's justification of the historical character of his approach as well as his own studies. Already in 'Meaning and Understanding', this distance means to him that historians cannot find the questions in the sources, but 'we must learn to do our own thinking for ourselves' (ibid.). In a later essay it becomes clear that the historical approach he advocates by no means legitimates tradition, heritage or continuity, but, on the contrary, 'if we are interested in such issues as the process of ideological formation and change, we cannot avoid involving ourselves in extensive historical enquiries' (Skinner 1974c, 282).

In the 1970s, Skinner also directed his perspectivist criticism against 'total history' in the style of Fernand Braudel. For Skinner, the search for a 'full picture' of the past 'seems to be nothing but the most discredited form of inductivism in smart sociological disguise' (Skinner 1974b, 101, cf. 1974c, 281). Against this view Skinner argues, in a Weberian manner, 'that we must be prepared to make some crucial decisions at the outset about what deserves to be studied and what is best ignored' (Skinner 1974b, 101). He does not think this to be opposed to the critique of 'Whig' history, for the demand to apply the criteria of the time presupposes an improbable degree of consensus, and those persons not appreciated by the contemporaries wouldn't have any chance. 'So the question remains: what role should we ask the past to play, what lines should we make history speak to us' (ibid.). Or, as he put it on another occasion: 'the decisions we have to make about what to study must be our own decisions, arrived at by applying our own criteria for judging what is rational and significant' (Skinner 1974c, 281).

The critique of empiricism and the authority of contemporary sources is accentuated in Skinner's critical tribute to Geoffrey Elton, one of his predecessors as Regius Professor of Modern History at Cambridge. Elton programmatically advocated a craftsmanship model of the historian, according to which the questions asked by historians 'are forced by the material upon the historian' (quoted in Skinner 1997b, 307). Skinner turns Elton's example of a 'house' into a parody: 'The House of Commons is described as a house in all relevant documents, but it is not a house' (ibid.). Even if the concept is not in question, it 'would take a lifetime for the apprentice to accumulate a full description (whatever that may mean) of the house itself' (ibid., 308). It is such a Nietzschean and Weberian uncompromising perspectivism – Skinner here refers to Foucault (ibid., 310), a well-known Nietzschean thinker – that makes the Skinnerian legitimation of a historical approach appear entirely different from the 'cult of fact' of the conventional historians like Elton, as he has put it in the revised version of the Elton essay (Skinner 2002a, ch. 2).

This critique of typical commitments of historians does not prevent Skinner from still believing in the power of history in liberating us from the parochial tendency of absolutizing current beliefs, for example on the concept of liberty. To the question 'how much history do we need?' Skinner answers in a recent essay: 'As much . . . as possible' (Skinner 2002h, 112).

The Politics of History

A remarkable tendency noticed since the 1980s has been the rise of disputes on interpretations of the past serving as instruments in contemporary political struggles. The German debates since the *Historikerstreit* of the 1980s, the reinterpretation of Soviet history in the

Gorbachev era, as well as the entire post-Communist historiography have raised the profile of such disputes. To speak of *Geschichtspolitik* is today a commonplace in the German-speaking world.

In Koselleckian terms (cf. Koselleck 1979) the space of past experience has, as an instrument of the analysis of the present situation, turned out to be at least of equal pertinence as the horizon of expectations. Considered from the viewpoint of the political agent, this is intelligible in more general terms: the contingency of the future is so obvious that expectations of the future, independently of their content, are bound to be disappointed. The very idea of long-term planning has, for good reasons, become dubious. The claim that what has happened is not only irreversible but also something 'given' has been a common assumption difficult to question. Even professional historians hardly face radical consequences from their theoretical insight that the interpretations of the past are continuously subject to revision, and that the distinction between events and their interpretation is inherently controversial. In this sense, every historical revision still serves as a potentially subverting instance that dethrones something of that which we have believed to be 'given', 'hard facts' or 'simply there'. Revisiting our space of experience also challenges our interpretation of what it is possible to do in the present.

In this perspective, the use of history as an argument can be a politically subversive move. This holds true for Skinner's central claim against the 'parochialism' of current commonplaces, namely his sense of strangeness of the past, its resemblance to a foreign country. In 'A Reply to My Critics', Skinner explicitly resorts to an 'anthropological justification for studying intellectual history':

> The investigation of alien systems of belief provides us with an irreplaceable means of standing back from our own prevailing assumptions and structures of thought, and of situating ourselves in relation to other and very different forms of life.... such investigations enable us to question the appropriateness of any strong distinction between matters of 'merely historical' and 'genuine philosophical' interest, since they enable us to recognize that our own descriptions and conceptualizations are in no way uniquely privileged. (Skinner 1988c, 286)

A historical Skinnerian perspective allows us to appreciate both the discontinuity with the past and the contingency of the present. Such an attitude towards the contingency of both history and the present is a precondition for avoiding a history of the winners and a tacit legitimation of facticity as a value. To avoid such a historiography, it is also politically decisive to shake the implicitly monopolistic claims of some successful positions. In such a political judgement we can understand, for example, Skinner's project of rewriting the history of the concept of liberty.

It is in this perspective that we can reassess Skinner's discussion of the relationship between history and philosophy. Besides and beyond the use of imagination, philosophy also has the aspect of a search for coherence, unity and system. The appeal to plurality, complexity and even imperfection in history serves for Skinner as a further subversive instance against the totalizing claims of philosophical system-builders.

Against this background we can now better understand the special opportunities for a consciously historical approach to the study of political thought that were implicitly involved in Laslett's claim about the death of political philosophy. Skinner's own explicit judgement on the topic is expressed by the Introduction to the fourth series of *Politics, Philosophy and Society*, edited by Laslett, Runciman and Skinner (for the authorship Skinner to KP, September 2001). According to him, 'it is arguable that we were never right to think in terms of such pathological metaphors . . . It has by now become a commonplace that both the intellectual movements prevailing at the time of our first introduction, in terms of which it looked plausible for sociologists to speak of the "end of ideology" and even for philosophers to speak of "the death of political theory" were themselves the masks of disputable ideological positions' (Laslett, Runciman & Skinner 1972, 1). What we can learn, according to Skinner, is 'the need for greater self-awareness about the difficulty of giving any uncontentious and value-neutral statements of the "facts" about moral and political issues' (ibid.).

Skinner, furthermore, characterizes the approach of Weldon and Hare on the behaviour of a rational moral or political agent in the following terms: 'His grasp of the relations between the relevant principle and the relevant facts then shows him how to make the appropriate choice – the rational, unideological choice – of the appropriate course of action to adopt. The whole business of inculcating this sense of the proper relationship between principles and action is seen, as Hare put it in *The Language of Morals*, as very like the business of "teaching African soldiers to drive"' (ibid., 2).

As related to Skinner's own approach, the 'lesson' of the Laslett thesis and of the academic practices which made it plausible in the mid-1950s, can be understood as a double challenge. On the one hand, the boring philosophy that tried to dissolve political questions into operations of calculation, gave an opportunity to a historical approach to understand conceptual controversies as a discontinuous series of political moves, without worrying that philosophers would intervene. On the other hand, when even the philosophers were interested in 'an examination of "the fact of the case"' (ibid.), a replacement of the conventional *wie es eigentlich gewesen* historiography with a self-consciously perspectivist view was needed.

In short, Skinner was, at the end of 1960s, in search of an approach in which there was no need to make a dividing line between philosophy and history, but which would allow an interplay between them. A look at the reviews of Skinner's work also makes it clear how delicate his position between and beyond the divide philosophers vs. historians has been. He has been repeatedly criticized for maintaining mere 'antiquarian' interest in the past, whereas professional historians tend to accuse him of neglecting or misunderstanding 'facts'. I take this as a sign of the originality of Skinner's position.

In a recent interview, Skinner characterized his position between 'strict historians' and those who make claims for contemporary significance as 'walking a tightrope' (Skinner 2002d, 55). In this chapter I have characterized some of his rhetorical usages of *the historical* as an argument. In the following chapters I will add the arguments which prevent him from falling from the tightrope on the side of the 'strict historians'.

3

Theories as Moves

Intelligibility of Politics as Activity

I have already quoted Skinner's formulas such as 'political theory as social activity' (Skinner 1964, 333) and 'the activity of thinking' (Skinner 1969a, 30). Thinking of politics as an activity may appear to be a commonplace, but in British discussions of the 1960s such views were rare: Bernard Crick with his *In Defence of Politics* (1962), inspired by Hannah Arendt, and J. D. B. Miller in his *The Nature of Politics* (1962) were exceptional.

The mainstream of behavioralists, functionalists, system theorists, Marxists and 'rationalists' borrowing models from economics formed a great coalition searching for regularities, invariants, structures and similar entities in a 'scientific' study of politics. Their critics doubted the possibility of finding such regularities rather than questioning the explanation of the activity of politics through 'deeper factors'. Even historians dealing with 'high politics' subjects, such as Namier, looked for factors 'explaining' politics by entities beyond politics itself.

Critics such as Miller and Crick were also less interested in the activity of politics than in the 'order' of the polity. They shared a deeply rooted Anglophone assumption according to which the 'public' and the 'political' are practically synonymous, thus delimiting the activity of politics to the 'public sphere', although disputing its 'borderlines'. Even in Miller's inaugural lecture, *Politicians*, the main interest concerns the 'functions' of politicians in the polity (Miller 1958, 1–2, 5) rather than the performance of politicians.

In the wider European intellectual scene, however, there were several modes of reflecting upon politics in terms of activity. On the continent, the activity of politics was explicitly thematized in phenomenologically inspired Arendtian or Sartrean thinking. Max Weber's action theory, although misinterpreted due to poor translations as well as the sociological 'mythology of prolepsis', remained present in the post-war Anglophone debate. Among the British thinkers, Collingwood in his *Autobiography* had specifically thematized action deviating from 'action according to rules' (Collingwood 1939, 102–6).

In post-war Britain, by contrast, a different style of the philosophy of action flourished. The dominant figure was, of course, Ludwig Wittgenstein. In a recent interview Skinner remarked: 'He was our image of philosophical genius' (Skinner 2002d, 46). Among the various attempts to 'apply' the Wittgensteinian philosophy of language to political questions, T. W. Weldon's *The Vocabulary of Politics* (1953) is a rather vulgar 'ordinary language philosophy', while Peter Winch's *The Idea of a Social Science* (1958) contains an 'idealistic' alternative for sociology and anthropology (with a questionable Weber interpretation).

J. L. Austin's posthumously published *How to Do Things with Words* (1962), which introduced the perspective of 'speech acts', was more important to Skinner. He underlined Austin's links to Wittgenstein, and more surprisingly, to Collingwood and his search for questions: 'Now, this use of language to *do* things was what Austin above all highlighted' (Skinner 2002d, 47). The obvious connection to Wittgenstein is, thus, interpreted as follows: 'Wittgenstein had instructed us to think about the use of language, and it appeared to me that Austin in effect picked up this suggestion and ran with it. The outcome was a wonderfully precise anatomy of what might be meant by talking about the enormous range of uses to which language can be put, and hence the range of things that can be done with it' (ibid., 47–8).

To a certain extent, the Austinian vocabulary soon became a jargon that could to be interpreted differently. Miller in *Politicians* speaks of the 'performance' of the government (Miller 1958, 11) without otherwise using the Austinian vocabulary. John Dunn's article 'The Identity of the History of Ideas' (1968) and Skinner's 'Meaning and Understanding' (1969a) appear to have been first to use the speech act theory for the study of political thought.

It is not difficult to imagine why the Wittgensteinian and Austinian vocabulary was not adopted by mainstream political scientists. If their project of self-legitimation was based on a strong distinction between rhetoric and reality, the aim of a scientistic approach was to go beyond the vocabulary and self-understanding of political agents. Hence the very idea of speech acts, of 'doing things with words', was a real provocation to their claims of 'scientific progress'. Both the questioning of the categorical distinction between 'words and deeds' and the indicated possibility of analysing a plurality of different modes of using 'words as deeds', referred to possibilities denied, or at least consciously neglected, by the scientistic approaches. The analysis of speech acts rehabilitates the perspectives of political agents, against tendencies to 'functionalize' them.

The 'application' of speech act theory to politics should not be compared with transferring, say, economic models or physical metaphors to the political sphere. Explicating speech acts can rather be understood as an immediate concern of politics-as-activity, although this may be further accentuated with specific types of actions, such as contested actions. Or, we can turn the tables and claim that all speech acts can refer to definite forms of political activities and situations. For example, the Austinian typology of performances can, accordingly, be interpreted as a preliminary classification of ideal-typical forms of political activities (cf. Austin 1962, 148–64).

The Action Perspective on Political Thought

Quentin Skinner first presents aspects of his constructive alternative to the study of political thought in terms of 'linguistic action' in the 'constructive' part of 'Meaning and Understanding'. Skinner's point of departure is to ask what kind of *doing* is involved either in a text or in the utterances it contains. His critique of what he calls 'textualism' (a term he later abandoned due to the misunderstandings it provoked, cf. Skinner 1988c, 282 and the 2002 version of 'Meaning and Understanding') is that such an approach is content to 'study what each classic writer has to *say* about each given doctrine' and does not pose the question of 'doing' at all: 'the methodology remains incapable in principle of considering or even recognizing some of the most crucial problems which must arise in any attempt to understand the relations between what a given writer may have *said*, and what he may be said to have meant by saying what he said' (Skinner 1969a, 31).

Here Skinner uses for doing-by-writing the ambiguous term 'mean', of which he later distinguished three variants: 'What do the words mean, or what do certain specific words mean, in this work?'; 'What does this work mean to me?'; and 'What does the writer mean by what he says in this work?' (Skinner 1972b, 396–7). Skinner himself is mainly concerned with this third sense, referring to the question, 'what *point* a given expression might have had for the agents who used it' (Skinner 1969a, 38). From this perspective, he also criticizes the examples dear to linguistic philosophers, which literally tend to miss the point: 'It is a striking fact about current discussions of the claim that actions are caused that they tend to be mounted in terms of such excessively simple and routine examples – always things like putting on one's coat, never things like writing the *Iliad* – that the question of the *point* of the action is very easily made to seem wholly transparent, or quite unimportant' (ibid., 44).

Skinner has been able to replace the trivial everyday examples, which Wittgenstein and Austin prefer to use, by historical and political ones. The way he has used the Wittgensteinian and Austinian resources has given him a profile of his own among political theorists and intellectual historians, seldom appreciated by his critics.

From the perspective of speech acts, 'performatives' illustrate the possibility that the point of interest is that 'the same thing' may be said in a number of ways and for a number of purposes. Hence the strict meaning of the words, *what* is said, is not the only and not even the main question that interests, but also *how* and *why* (by which intention) it is said. Skinner has been, above all, interested in this kind of situation. In a wider sense, however, we can also claim that such *how* and *why* questions are a precondition to understanding the *what* question, especially in cases where the same words refer to different concepts (cf. Skinner 1999c) as well as when the problem is to 'understand what strategies have been *voluntarily* adopted to convey their meaning with deliberate obliqueness' (Skinner 1969a, 32). In his critique of the 'history of an idea' as expounded by Arthur Lovejoy, he also repeats Wittgenstein's thesis that the meaning of a concept consists in the ways it is used (cf. Wittgenstein 1953/1958, §43).

> The appropriate, and famous, formula . . . is rather that we should study not the meaning of the words but their use. For the given idea cannot ultimately be said in this sense to *have* any meaning that can take the form of a set of words which can then be excogitated and traced over time. Rather the meaning of the idea must be its uses to refer in various ways. (Skinner 1969a, 37)

My thesis is that Skinner's search for linguistic action (for the
term see Skinner 1970a and 1996a, 8) and its point implies an inherently political reading of the history of thought. It rehabilitates the
doings of the agents, against all variants of devaluation or func-
tionalization by sociological approaches considering the performative moment either as trivial or as something to be superseded.
Through the analysis of speech acts, Skinner is able to direct attention to the numerous politically significant variants of doing, even
when saying the same.

The performative perspective also concerns the politics of language, not only the just presented choice between the different performative modes – politicking in my terminology (cf. Palonen 1993,
2002b) – but, in addition, the possibility of politicizing the attitude
towards language. Skinner with his perspective of linguistic action
refuses to subscribe to the assumption that the main 'function'
of language is to 'inform' us about world, whereas other uses of
language are something extraordinary and in need of a specific
legitimation. The 'locutionary' statement forms just one level of language, and the illocutionary and perlocutionary uses are no less
important.

The primacy of the locutionary use of language is frequently
joined with a 'realist' ontology, assuming that a clear distinction
between the realms of reality and language that describes it can be
undertaken. The point of a performative, for example the naming
of a street, is that it brings into existence something new: only after
being named can it be identified as a separate street on the city map.
Thus, the perspective of linguistic action at least puts a question
mark on 'realist' claims to distinguish between 'language and
reality', and in this respect it restores the perspectives of ancient
rhetoric and Sophistics. In other words, by using a performative
approach to language we already politicize, in the sense of both contingency and contestability, the constative paradigm of language
and the realist ontology it is customarily connected with.

In 'Conventions and the Understanding of Speech Acts', Skinner
argues for a view that we have to supplement Austin's views on the
reception of speech acts: 'Austin himself provided no analysis on
the conditions necessary for such an act of communication to be performed, and so no account of what is involved in A's successful
uptake and understanding of S's statement and its intended illocutionary force' (Skinner 1970a, 118). This aspect adds to the analysis
of speech act the dimension of audience and reception, which has
to be, however, distinguished from the 'perlocutionary effects'.

Skinner extends the Austinian analysis to the role of oblique illocutionary acts through presenting a list of 'verbs for which, while
they name genuine illocutionary acts, there is no *possibility* of
avowal by means of an explicit performative at all' (ibid., 122–3).
With this list he will oppose the restrictive views of Austin and
Strawson and broaden the horizon of intentions to such oblique
forms that even the agents themselves cannot avow being engaged
in.

It is quite obvious that, for example, 'flatter', 'mock/scorn' or
'lure' as well as verbs of allusion are commonplaces in a politician's
repertoire. The situation of persuasion among politically 'literate'
audiences is clearly one in which the plurality of the intentional
levels may be grasped or such a grasp is a condition of doing the
illocutionary act. For Skinner such verbs 'appear to apply to situations in which the speaker intends both that it should be firmly
understood that he feels in a particular relation to his audience and
that this intention itself should also be firmly understood' (ibid.,
126), despite the fact that 'the avowal . . . seems . . . not to underpin,
but actually to undermine . . . the intended act of communication'
(ibid., 128). In one of his examples, Skinner explicitly alludes to the
political role of seemingly meaningless speech acts:

> Children and Members of Parliament, for example, conventionally
> register their objections to unduly evasive or sententious utterances
> by means of a range of locutions the utterance of which is accepted
> as having a quite clear significance or non-natural meaning, even
> though the utterances themselves, while they thereby have a par-
> ticular force, have no meaning as locutions at all. (ibid., 120)

With this formula, Skinner parodies the everyday lamentations of
parliamentarians as speaking only nonsense and acknowledges
instead that even admittedly meaningless utterances may turn into
something politically decisive. In addition, his example also makes
clear that the illocutionary and perlocutionary uses of language
are not only supplementary resources, but, in certain cases, can be
explicitly used in opposition to the locutionary uses.

Regarding a performative view of politics-as-activity, we can
notice parallels between Skinner and Hannah Arendt's conception of
politics in *The Human Condition* (1958), especially her strong distinction between fabrication and action as well as her corresponding
insistence that the modern misconception involved in treating
politics in terms of fabrication. Skinner has formulated an analogous

distinction between doing and achieving something (cf. esp. Skinner 1971, 9). Moreover, the Skinnerian perspective of linguistic action cannot be understood in terms of the purposes or results of the action, but rather by its performative characteristics. Arendt's comparison of politics to the performing arts (esp. 1968, 153–4) thus has a parallel in the Skinnerian view of understanding politics through the performative uses of language. However, the oblique and non-avowable illocutionary act surely points out verbal possibilities beyond the Arendtian horizon of a heroic politician, but can also be included in the repertoire of a competent parliamentarian.

Ideas and Concepts as Moves in Argument

A traditional problem of intellectual history has been how to deal with oblique strategies such as irony when reading classic texts. A number of major thinkers have sometimes been regarded as ironists. To decide upon the value of such interpretations Skinner insists that 'the text in itself is shown to be insufficient as the object of our inquiry and understanding' (1969a, 35). With the performative view on action, we must always ask questions, such as what is the point and what is the rhetorical character of a text, as a necessary condition of an interpretation.

Skinner's rejection of the 'textualist' history of ideas concerns not so much what is said about 'ideas themselves', but the very tendency to regard 'ideas' 'as an appropriate unit of analysis' (ibid., 36). A target of his criticism is 'the Fregean assumption that meanings must somehow be timeless' (ibid., 32) and specifically Lovejoy's 'history of an idea', which presumes a strong degree of continuity between various expressions of the idea (the same is also true of Meinecke's *Idee der Staatsräson*). The 'great mistake' lies, according to Skinner, 'even in thinking any "essential" meaning (to which individual writers contribute) at all' (ibid., 37). His Wittgensteinian objection to Lovejoy's styling of a history of ideas is formulated as follows:

> the project of studying histories of 'ideas', *tout court*, must rest on a fundamental philosophical mistake. The underlying confusion itself may perhaps be most conveniently characterized, by adopting an extension of the basic distinction between meaning and use, as the result of a failure to distinguish between the *occurrence* of the words (phrases or *sentences*) which denote the given idea, and the *use* of the

relevant sentence by a particular agent on a particular occasion with
particular intention (*his* intention) to make a particular *statement*.
(ibid., 37)

Here Skinner interprets Wittgenstein in a nominalist mode. All
tendencies to treat ideas as if they are universally valid or widely
shared appear dubious to him. A history of ideas should instead
consist of the singularization of the use of words (in statements) in
relation to agents, situations and intentions. The historization of the
uses marks a discontinuity between ideas, conceived as moves of
the agents. The singularization politicizes intellectual and conceptual change in so far as in a political situation a plurality of agents
are always competing with each other, and in some respects
striving for specific shares of power.

A failure to understand this situation means 'that statement-
making agents appear more or less only because relevant ideas . . .
can be shown to occur in their works' (ibid., 38). The lack of agency
makes it impossible to understand 'what part, trivial or important,
the given idea may have played in the thought of any individual
thinker who happened to mention it, or what place, characteristic
or unusual, it may have taken in the intellectual climate of any given
period in which it appeared' (ibid.). Further questions neglected by
Lovejoy's approach are: '*what* questions the use or the expression
was thought to answer'; 'what *status* the given idea may have had
at various times'; 'what *point* a given expression might have had for
the agents who used it'; 'what range of uses the expression itself
could sustain; what meanings the given expression must have had'
(ibid.).

This repertoire also indicates that Skinner's agency-oriented
perspective on political thought and intellectual history requires a
clarification of what is studied and introduces a number of new
topics for such a study. Instead of concentrating on the idea-unit,
Skinner claims: 'The only history to be written is thus a history of
the various statements made with the given expression' (ibid., 39).
In other words, he by no means objects to writing histories of intellectual and conceptual change, but requires that this should be done
by treating ideas and concepts from the perspective of linguistic
action. In linguistic action no strict distinction between content and
expression can be made, but the style, vocabulary, and other dimensions of the expression are part of the political content.

It is this action perspective on conceptual change that is, then,
expressed in Skinner's later work. In a comment made at a sympo-

sium on intellectual history, Skinner repeats his criticism of Lovejoy: 'But the main doubt about the method has been that, in focusing on ideas rather than their uses in argument, it has seemed insensitive to the strongly contrasting ways in which a given concept can be put to work by different writers in different historical periods' (Skinner 1985c, 51). 'Argument' should here be understood not in the logical but in the rhetorical sense, as related to a controversy. The formula 'in argument' is later repeated by Skinner in two contexts. First he speaks about a 'move':

> To put it another way, there is a sense in which we need to under-
> stand why a certain proposition has been put forward if we wish
> to understand the proposition itself. We need to see it not simply
> as a proposition, but also as a move in argument. So we need to grasp
> why it seemed worth making that precise move; to recapture the
> presuppositions and purposes that went into the making of it.
> (Skinner 1988c, 274)

'Move', in the sense of chess and other games, is used here to characterize how theories are understood in Skinner's perspective of linguistic action. A move is a contingent measure, which aims less to achieve a definite result than to alter a constellation. Move is an excellent metaphor for the uses of ideas, theories and concepts in which Skinner is interested. It is from such a perspective, then, that Skinner turns the 'in argument' formula into a condition for studying conceptual change:

> I can best restate my objection by observing, in Wittgenstein's phrase,
> that concepts are tools. To understand a concept, it is necessary to
> grasp not merely the meanings of the terms used to express it, but
> also the range of things that can be done with it. This is why, in spite
> of the long continuities that have undoubtedly marked our inherited
> patterns of thought, I remain unrepentant in my belief that there can
> be no histories of concepts as such; there can only be histories of their
> uses in argument. (ibid., 283)

In other words, a condition for conceptual histories, such as Skinner's own work on the concept of the state (Skinner 1989b), is that 'concepts' are not reduced to their meaning, but, on the contrary, the meaning-dimension of a concept is always related to linguistic action. Such an action can be analysed paradigmatically through studying them as moves in controversies. In 'Rhetoric and Conceptual Change', Skinner refers to a tradition which he 'first encountered in the work of Max Weber' (Skinner 1999c, 62). He shares the heuristic character of concepts by Weber in his 'Objektivität' essay and explicates his own view as follows:

> It is characterised by the belief that our concepts not only alter over time, but are incapable of providing us with anything more than a series of changing perspectives on the world in which we live and have our being. Our concepts form part of what we bring to the world in our efforts to understand it. The shifting conceptualisations to which this process gives rise constitute the very stuff of ideological debate, so that it makes no more sense to regret than to deny that such conceptual changes continually take place. (ibid.)

From this formula, also indebted to Skinner's more recent studies on 'ancient theorists of eloquence' (ibid., 67), we can see that he has moved even further away from Lovejoy's style of treating ideas as independent units, towards understanding concepts as key linguistic elements in political struggle. Regarding the acceptance and contestedness of a concept as a condition of its intelligibility, we can hardly see a difference between Skinner's views and Reinhart Koselleck's *Begriffsgeschichte* (cf. Koselleck 1994 and 1996). Whereas Skinner's use of speech act theory in the 1970s still presupposed a 'standard meaning' of concepts, this combination of Weberian and rhetorical insight has led him away from such a presupposition.

Conventions and Intentions

One of the dead ends of political theory has been to construct in advance a set of normative demands, although everyone knows that they are not 'politically realistic' in the current situation. The solutions to this problem have resided in attempts either to 'maximize' the degree of the realization of demands or to minimize them in the name of *Realpolitik*, a term invented by L. A. von Rochau in 1853, and be content with what is surely realizable (cf. Palonen 1985). The criticism of this dichotomy, as presented for example by Max Weber (1917a, 514; 1919a, 88), is taken up by the Skinnerian perspective of linguistic action. To Skinner action contains more than a practice of realization, and the role of principles in politics is different from the demand 'to realize' them.

In 'Meaning and Understanding' Skinner's target of criticism was also the 'contextualist' approach to the history of ideas as practised in the post-war era. While Skinner accepts the role of 'social context' in intellectual history and regards this as a commonplace, he none the less insists that 'the fundamental assumption of the contextual methodology, that the ideas of a given text should be understood *in terms of* its social context, can be shown to be mistaken' (Skinner 1969a, 43). The sociological determinism of such a contextual approach is equally incapable of rendering intelligible the contingency of human actions. 'Even if the study of the social context of texts could serve to *explain* them, this would not amount to the same as providing means to *understand* them' (ibid., 46).

The frequent designation of Skinner's approach as contextualist needs to be redescribed more specifically as a concern 'to trace the relations between the given utterance and this wider *linguistic* context as a means of decoding the actual intention of the given writer' (ibid., 49). In this sense, 'context' is not determining but a horizon for the possible, 'an ultimate framework for helping to decide what conventionally recognizable meanings, in a society of *that* kind, it might in principle have been possible for someone to have intended to communicate' (ibid.).

Although Skinner continues to speak of contexts, he always points out the plurality of contexts and thematizes contexts in relation to the linguistic action and its point in the text. In Skinner's view of linguistic action contexts are, literally, an implicit part of the text rather than opposed to it. In 'A Reply to My Critics' he remarks that his 'upshot' is 'to challenge any categorical distinction between texts and contexts' (Skinner 1988c, 276). What appears as 'text' and 'context' is thus relative to the questions discussed. This is crucial, for example, for the understanding of Skinner's *Reason and Rhetoric in the Philosophy of Hobbes* (cf. below chapter 6).

In order to classify types of relevant contexts in linguistic action, Skinner adopts aspects of the post-Austinian speech act theory. In 'Conventions and the Understanding of Speech Acts' he admits, with Strawson, that all illocutionary acts need not be conventional. In addition, he regards conventions as a condition of understanding the point of non-avowable illocutionary acts that are not rule-governed but presuppose 'the presence some element of convention much stronger than Strawson allows' (Skinner 1970a, 130). In such cases, 'some fairly extensive awareness of social as well as linguistic conventions seems indispensably necessary for the successful uptake of such illocutionary acts' (ibid.). More specifically:

> The point is that any intention capable of being correctly understood by A . . . must always be a socially conventional intention – must fall,

> that is, within a given and established range of acts which can be con-
> ventionally grasped as being cases of that intention. It must follow
> that one of the necessary conditions for understanding in any situa-
> tion what it is that S in uttering utterance x must be doing to A must
> be some understanding of what it is that people in general, when
> behaving in a conventional manner, are usually doing in that society
> and in that situation in uttering such utterances. (ibid., 133)

Here it is clear that conventions form the tacit context which is presupposed if the illocutionary act is to be grasped in its different
levels of intention and can thus have some illocutionary force for
the intended audience. To return to Skinner's example of Members
of Parliament: what distinguishes an experienced and a dilettante
MP is, among other things, that the former is able to grasp the allu-
sions to past debates, to understand that there are certain conventional parliamentary practices and cases in which the Speaker may
reproach an MP for the use of 'unparliamentary' language, and that
there are MPs who can consciously provoke such remarks and turn
them into an advantage in their political career. A modern MP is,
accordingly, also obliged to consider that there are those in Parliament who understand the definite parliamentary conventions and
those who do not. Skinner writes that 'such conventions themselves
may appear to have been modulated rather than followed in the
situation under consideration' (ibid., 135).

Skinner's specific move is to extend the language of intentions
and conventions to non-symmetrical situations to explicate 'the
dilemma, in which any historian or social anthropologist characteristically finds himself when attempting to understand the verbal
behaviour of an alien culture or some utterance uttered in the
past' (ibid.). In such situations, 'an understanding of conventions,
however implicit, must remain a necessary condition for an understanding of all types of speech act' (ibid.).

Perhaps we could characterize Skinner's point to be that we
cannot oppose intentions to conventions. Rather it is characteristic
of illocutionary acts that both dimensions are always present. Even
convention-breaking acts presuppose the existence and knowledge
of conventions:

> If S's speech act is also an act of social and linguistic innovation which
> S nevertheless intends or at least hopes will be understood, the act
> must necessarily, and for that reason, take the form of an extension
> or criticism of some existing attitude or project which is already con-
> vention-governed and understood. It seems a necessary truth that

unless the innovation either takes such a form, or can be reduced to it, it will stand no chance of being understood, and so can hardly count even as an intended act of communication. (ibid.)

This formula contains a linguistic principle with immediate consequences for both the historian and the political agent. In the 'Conventions' essay, Skinner returns to his critique of the 'mythology of parochialism' among historians, as compared with social anthropologists in particular. 'It is the very impression of familiarity, however, which constitutes the added barrier to understanding' (ibid., 136). Or, as Skinner puts it in more technical terms, the dilemma of the historian consists in understanding and mediating the conventions at a temporal distance:

On the one hand such understanding clearly presupposes that A should be so imbued with the concepts and conventions available to S at t1 that he can elucidate not simply the question of how far (or whether) S's utterance makes any sense at t2, but can also explain what exact meaning and force S's utterance of his utterance at t1 must have registered. On the other hand, if it is to be said that S has been understood by A it also seems indispensable that A should be capable of performing some act of translation of the concepts and conventions employed by S at t1 into terms which are familiar at t2 to A himself, not to mention others to whom A at t2 may wish to communicate his understanding. (ibid., 136)

The historian has a double problem, both detecting and explicating past conventions of which she cannot have such direct, albeit tacit, knowledge as, for example, the experienced MP has of current parliamentary conventions. Such conventions are never exhaustively explicated in the sources. Primary sources and historical studies can give clues to the conventions the historian needs to understand as a condition to deal with a specific problem concerning intentional acts and their point in this definite context.

We should note that here Skinner speaks of conventions in the sense of tacit assumptions and practices prevailing (to a certain degree) in a definite past context. His claim has nothing to do with the normative value of conventions, such as the claims of 'conservative' thinkers that without upholding certain conventions 'order' or 'society' breaks down. Neither does he present any claims about the strength of the conventions or about the degree to which they are in fact followed in the context in question. His assumption is simply that, in all situations, there are some conventions which can be used as resources or as targets of criticism, whereas others form implicit assumptions or practices which have not been thematized for apologetic or critical purposes: 'it is open to any writer to indicate that his aim is to extend, to subvert, or in some other way to alter a prevailing set of accepted conventions and attitudes' (Skinner 1974c, 287). In order to understand the revision or suppression of some conventions, we have recourse to some other conventions that are not thematized in this specific context.

The second objective of the historian is, then, the 'translation' of conventions from the past in order to explicate them in a manner intelligible to the present. In this sense Skinner's historian is not an 'antiquarian' addressing herself to the other specialized antiquarians of the past context, but someone who intends to mediate an understanding of past contexts and their conventions as contributions to current debates about other topics. Unlike Winch's anthropologist in *The Idea of a Social Science*, Skinner's historian is not content with the impression of the strangeness of the past context. By the act of translating we can treat past and present contexts and conventions as commensurable, at least to a certain degree: 'it is the limit of our imaginative grasp as well as our lack of information that makes the past a foreign country, just as it is imaginative grasp as well as the control of information that makes the historian' (Skinner 1970a, 137). This does not, however, mean that the conceptual distinctions would be the same in all languages: the ancient Romans and contemporary Britons could disagree even on the notion of 'raining': what would be termed *imber* in Latin could perhaps be 'nothing more than a drizzle' in English (Skinner 1988c, 249–50).

When speaking the jargon of strict linguistic philosophy in the 'Conventions' essay, Skinner rejects the paradigm of (allegedly) immediate and direct communication. He thus analyses particularly the role of historical distance. From this perspective he, once again, insists that philosophers have to admit that they have much to learn from historians:

> This would amount to suggesting that if the social studies in general, and the history of ideas in particular, do raise special issues about the conditions of understanding speech acts, then philosophers interested in these issues might do well to give some attention at least to the sheer amount of relevant information, and of attempts to make sense of it, which these disciplines can supply. (Skinner 1970a, 138)

In 'On Performing and Explaining Linguistic Actions' (1971), Skinner introduces the concept of 'linguistic action' and casts a closer look at the relations between intentions and illocutionary acts from the viewpoint of describing and explaining linguistic actions. He distinguishes between 'intentions to do' and 'intentions in doing' something, and limits his own interest to the latter, as the moment of expressing the point of the action (see also Skinner 1969a, 60–1). Considering the implications of the performative perspective, Skinner, in particular, accentuates the role of the non-causal explanation of action.

> I now wish to illustrate and defend two further theses about such illocutionary redescriptions. First, that when the facts about such an episode are capable of being redescribed in the unique form in which the intended illocutionary force of the utterance is revealed, this provides not merely a redescription but also a mode of explanation of the given episode. And secondly, that although such explanations function by citing reasons, these cannot in this case be construed as causes of which the corresponding actions are effects. (Skinner 1971, 13)

Revising his earlier scepticism about explanations, Skinner has moved to explaining by referring to the point of the action (ibid.), 'focusing primarily on the agent's intentions *in* his acting' (ibid.,14). Referring to intentions has appeared in many contexts as a famous fallacy, but Skinner argues, using John Milton's intentions in writing *Paradise Lost* as his example, 'that it must actually be an exegetical duty and not a fallacy at all, for critics and historians to concentrate on attempting to recover the intentions of speakers and writers *in* the performance of these complex types of (linguistic) action' (ibid., 16).

For Skinner the search for intentions does not mean, as it does for certain literary scholars such as E. D. Hirsch, 'the whole of the interpreter's task'; it is only one 'amongst the interpreter's tasks' (Skinner 1972b, 404–5). Neither does he claim that the writer should be regarded as a 'final authority' on her intentions (ibid., 405), the interpretations of which remain, of course, always hypothetical. Skinner has no difficulty in admitting that 'any text of any complexity will always contain far more meaning – what Ricœur has called surplus meaning – than even the most vigilant and imaginative author could possibly have intended to put to it' (Skinner 1988c, 272). The critics of Skinner's advocacy of intentionality have literally missed the point of his point-searching.

Maybe we could speak here of point-explanations, marking a neglected dimension in non-causal explanations. Indeed, Skinner is one of the few thinkers who has taken seriously the question 'what is your point' in acting in the manner you are actually acting. The point is here to be understood as a key dimension in the horizon of intentions, addressed to the audience, trying to persuade, provoke or otherwise alter the conduct, attitudes, concepts or other dimensions of action within the audience. In this sense, point-explanations focus attention on definite moves adopted in order to alter the constellation.

Such point-explanations, at least when presented to a plural audience, can be regarded as attempts to render the specifically political moment of the linguistic action itself intelligible. Marking a point is an illocutionary act with certain levels of intended illocutionary force, whereas there never exists a guarantee of obtaining definite perlocutionary effects. The distinction is relevant, for example, in cases in which the agent has no control of the effects, these being indifferent and impossible to assess in advance or known in advance to be fatal, independently of how one acts.

In this sense we can compare Maurice Merleau-Ponty's discussion, in his *Humanisme et terreur*, of Bukharin's performative choices in the Moscow trials of 1938, when understanding that he was practically condemned to death already, but still faced the problem of how to face this death sentence. When Bukharin realized that he would be sentenced to death, it was still left to him to nuance, rhetorically attack, to have recourse to irony (Merleau-Ponty 1947, esp. 138). But whereas Merleau-Ponty claimed that historical responsibility transcends the 'liberal categories of intention and act' (ibid., 133), Skinner claims that the illocutionary acts, in such situations in which the outcome is given, are perhaps best understood in terms of their intended point.

The respective roles of conventions and intentions is discussed by Skinner in ' "Social Meaning" and the Explanation of Social Action' in heuristic terms:

> The methodological injunction then becomes: begin not by trying to recover the agent's motives by studying the context of social rules, but rather by trying to decode the agent's intentions by aligning his given social action with a more general awareness of the conventional standards which are generally found to apply to such types of social action within a given social situation. (Skinner 1972c, 154, cf. 1972b, 406)

In other words, the intentional point of action can hardly be detected by an attempt to depart from the text itself, but rather as a move in favour of altering or affirming the conventions available. What is conventional and what is deviant cannot be identified by the formulations used but presupposes an analysis of what others have written in that context. The point of a classic text thus becomes, correspondingly, much less difficult to identify when the surviving text is related to less known contemporary publications. Using one of his favourite examples, Skinner illustrates this with the case of Machiavelli:

> . . . the fact that *The Prince* was in part intended as a deliberate attack on the moral conventions of advice-books to princes cannot be discovered simply by attending to the text, since this is not a fact contained in the text. It is also clear, however, that no one can be said fully to understand Machiavelli's text who does not understand this fact about it. To fail to grasp this fact is to fail to grasp the *point* of Machiavelli's argument in the latter chapters of his book. (Skinner 1972c, 155)

The value of analysing conventions and intentions is not limited to identifying the rhetorical character of a text in relation to its contemporaries. A similar procedure concerns the use of a concept in a text in order to detect the linguistic action: 'to understand what any given writer may have been *doing in* using some particular concept or argument, we need first of all to grasp the nature and the range of things that could recognizably have been done by using that particular concept, in the treatment of that particular theme, at that particular time' (Skinner 1972b, 406).

The conventional and context-bound character of particularly political action does not turn Skinner into a determinist. On the contrary, in his approach it marks a further dimension of the contingency of the situation. Alluding to Weber, he also distinguishes causal explanation from determinism and sees it as complementary to *Verstehen*. For this, Skinner uses Martin Hollis's example of Romeo sending red orchids to Juliet: 'while our explanation needs to start with meanings and motives, it only ends when we have identified the underlying conditions which caused Romeo to come into the possession of the motive which then prompted him (caused him?) to act' (Skinner 1978b, 66; cf. 1972c, 138). As the parentheses indicate, the non-causal point-explanations are what mainly interests Skinner.

Skinner's discussions of the 'rationality' of actions are always conducted in nominalist terms. He parodies Hollis's 'Hegelian image of a society in which we are able to discharge our roles rationally' and search for 'real interests' (Skinner 1978b, 68). 'Rational' should not be confused with 'optimal', and therefore, it can serve as a exclusion criterion for action but not as one to understand its specific and singular point. 'No social agent can normally be expected to be aware of all the possibilities open to him, or of all the possible outcomes of embracing different strategies, in the manner presupposed by the requirement of optimality' (ibid., 60). Such choices are only 'appropriate', one among many possibilities.

This criticism uses the omnipresence of the contingency of actions as a condition of their intelligibility. Against all theories of 'rational choice', in so far as they take the conditions of choice as given, Skinner problematizes the conditions as not being given facticities, but rather consisting of a horizon of possibilities, *Chancen* in Weberian language, which is regularly richer than the agents in the situation tend to assume and which, therefore, is liable to unexpected consequences, characterized by Weber as something that regularly accompanies political action (esp. Weber 1919a, 80–1). From a Weberian perspective it is, however, both the known and the unknown *Chancen* that serve as a horizon for the entire action. Skinner, however, does not enter into the discussion of the singularity of the *Chancen* in the situation.

In Skinner's perspective, a voluntarist declaration of normative principles and their maximal realization can be considered as unpolitical apriorism (cf. the critiques of Rawls in Skinner 1983 and Habermas in Skinner 1982a). This further accentuates the contingency of both conventions and intentions. The conventions refer to mere facticities of the situation, always alterable with singular conditions and specific strategies. What to do with these conventions? What and how are they turned into instruments? Which intentions are attempts to revise or suppress conventions? Are they worth attempting? In which respects are they simply treated as a given that should be accounted for in the assessment of the unintended consequences of attempted changes? All of these are political questions regarding whether conventions should be upheld, altered or given up.

Legitimation of Action

In 'Meaning and Understanding', Skinner refers to two variants of contextual reading, 'its Marxist and Namierite version (they are oddly similar)' (Skinner 1969a, 42), as expressions which claim that ideas and thoughts are only epiphenomena. When simultaneously rejecting the opposing claims, such as by Lovejoy, of ideas as autonomous entities, Skinner appears to fall between the poles of the debate. For the commentators it has been difficult to classify his views, as he states in the beginning of 'A Reply to My Critics': 'I am perplexed to learn that I am at once an idealist, a materialist, a positivist, a relativist, an antiquarian, a historicist, and a mere methodologist with nothing of substance to say at all' (Skinner 1988c, 231).

In three essays, published in 1973–4, Skinner partially accepts the Namierite criticism of the instrumental – rather than guiding – role of ideas for politics, but refuses to treat them as epiphenomena or as *ex post* rationalizations for a course of action already chosen. Characteristically, by this very move, Skinner can criticize both the Namierite and the Lovejoyan position on the same grounds, namely regarding both of them as approaches that devalue political activity itself. In doing so, he uses the Weberian language of legitimation.

Skinner's polemic against the Namier school historians and also against their critics is most explicit in 'The Principles and Practice of Opposition: The Case of Bolingbroke versus Walpole'. Skinner wants 'to argue that the existing facts . . . fit a theory about the behaviour of Bolingbroke and his party which does not seem to have been entertained by any of Bolingbroke's interpreters, but which nevertheless seems to offer the best explanation of his political beliefs and actions' (Skinner 1974a, 94). The more general question in which he is interested is: 'what weight should be placed on the opposition's profession of principle in attempting to explain their actual political actions?' (ibid., 100). Skinner then characterized the Namierite view: 'Bolingbroke and his party were solely motivated "by an insatiable ambition for power"' (ibid.), or more generally: 'The sole aim of the politicians, it is said, "was simply to get into office"' (ibid., 102).

This is a simplified variation on the Weberian view on power as the general medium of politics. It is no wonder that Skinner accepts this view as a point of departure: 'I shall assume, indeed, that the Namierites are right in claiming – and the revisionists naïvely mistaken in denying – that the motives of Bolingbroke and his party were entirely unprincipled and self-interested' (ibid., 108). To put this in a strictly Weberian manner: the motives for striving for power are simply irrelevant, because striving for power (for specified power shares) is a condition of any significant political action. In such terms the appeal to principle does not oppose a striving for power, but rather alludes to a strategic variant of it. The insistence on the sincerity of Bolingbroke's beliefs is, correspondingly, analysed by Skinner as one that 'follows exactly the account of his behaviour which Bolingbroke always insisted upon himself. This is perhaps quite enough in itself to make one suspicious' (ibid., 107).

The clue to Skinner's approach lies in combining an acceptance of Namierite premises without subscribing to their conclusions. 'It is then claimed to follow that their professions of principle . . . ought not to be given any weight at all' (ibid., 100). Even if the principles are regarded only as flapdoodles, 'there is still a decision on the part of Bolingbroke and his party to be explained, the decision to propagate one brand of flapdoodle rather than another, and to propagate one particular brand with such remarkable consistency' (ibid., 103). Skinner's point is to argue that the appeal to principles was a measure of legitimation.

The need for legitimation arose for Bolingbroke from a simple historical convention within the Walpole regime, namely that '"general opposition" was normally regarded as immoral'. Consequently, 'Bolingbroke and his party were engaged in a *prima facie* unjustifiable course of political action' (ibid., 109–10). The point of Bolingbroke's politics – to gain a share in governmental power – was to question and try to alter this very convention:

> It was thus essential for Bolingbroke and his party . . . to try to offer a rival evaluative description of their own behaviour, in terms of which their Whig opponents might in effect be given a reason for believing, and might thus be forced to accept, that despite its *prima facie* appearance of unconstitutionality, their campaign was justifiable in the circumstances. (ibid., 110–11)

We can detect here a difference between Namierite and Weberian views on power in general. The former tend to understand 'power' as a zero-sum concept and identify 'government' as a status of 'possessing' power and opposition as a lack of power, in a manner comparable to Niklas Luhmann's 'political code' (for example, Luhmann 2000, 88–94). One problem with this view is that it does not make any distinction between the lack of power of an opposition and those of disparate common citizens. With a Weberian view we could, on the contrary, claim that already the use of the name opposition grants specific power-shares by the means of a legitimation. Conversely, the *de facto* rule of a government is not enough, but in order to maintain its position, every government is also in need of legitimation.

Furthermore, the convention that opposition was viewed as illegitimate, can be, in Weberian terms, understood as a successful measure of legitimation in a specific context. As such it could be, however, questioned, and this was what, according to Skinner, Bolingbroke did by claiming that opposition, in a certain respect, was already considered as legitimate in the polity of the time: 'it was essential to refer to some already accepted political principle as a means both of characterizing their opposition and their alleged motive for engaging in it, and thus as a means of seeking to legitimate as well as to redescribe their own behaviour' (Skinner 1974a, 111). This was the case in particular with the appeal to the principle of patriotism: 'the claim that their behaviour could properly be described as patriotic would entail the defeat of most of the wilder accusations which had been made against them. . . . the same claim could also be used to override the one major criticism of their campaign which they could not hope to defeat' (ibid., 112).

In order to validate such a claim, Bolingbroke, however, was obliged to renounce his previous (Tory) policy. For Skinner, 'Bolingbroke's great *coup* as a politician' (ibid.) consisted in the move through which he succeeded in doing this by appealing to 'the Whig's own most cherished beliefs about political liberty' (ibid., 113). It was sufficient that he was able to use for his own ends principles previously cherished by the Whigs, who under Walpole were criticized – also by other Whigs – for the neglect of such principles: 'Bolingbroke simply wanted to remind his Whig enemies . . . of the views held by the accredited theories of their own party about the concept of political liberty, in order to be able to make use of the immensely strong resonances of this tradition of thought to further his own wholly cynical and self-interested political ends' (ibid., 126).

If principles can be understood in terms of legitimation, their political role becomes more flexible than when regarded as guidelines to be applied or as delimitations of what is acceptable. When Bolingbroke and his adherents were at risk of being entirely played out from the political scene, they turned 'opposition' from a vice into a virtue, indeed into a 'patriotic' duty, in order to be better accepted as legitimate players in governmental politics.

The legitimation of opposition by Bolingbroke signified a politically remarkable move. Such a move was made possible by persuading the Whigs to believe that opposition, after all, was not so dangerous, and that it could even be combined with the Whig principles of patriotism and liberty. In other words, the legitimacy of opposition was made possible through illustrating that there was something that was shared by government and opposition. The shift towards a legitimacy of opposition was based on a certain further continuity in broader values, and this continuity was also rhetorically used as an instrument of change.

In Weberian terms, we can argue that all politics requires some legitimation. The choices between policy alternatives are contingent in so far as there never exists any sufficient ground for them, but this does not render them purely accidental, rather always connected with other policies, both the agents' own and those of others. In particular, retaining or obtaining some power-shares requires legitimation, and this is especially true of the asymmetrical shares of *Herrschaft*. In this sense, a persuasive dimension is always part of political action and it is in such a rhetorical role that thoughts are an inherent part of politics-as-activity in Skinner's thinking.

A more systematic explication of the relationships between action and legitimation in politics is contained in Skinner's essay 'Some Problems in the Analysis of Political Thought and Action'. The legitimation topic is situated in a wider perspective through the question of 'what precisely ought to be studied in the history of political thought' (Skinner 1974c, 278). Skinner's point of departure is, then:

> We can hardly claim to be concerned with the history of political theory unless we are prepared to write it as real history – that is, as the record of an actual activity, and in particular as the history of ideologies. . . . It would enable us to illuminate the varying roles played by intellectual factors in political life. It would thus enable us to begin to establish the connections between the world of ideology and the world of political action. (ibid., 280)

Here Skinner affirms, with a more explicit emphasis than before, that political thought is to be analysed as a part of political activity, thus committing himself to a *vita activa* perspective on political theorizing, strongly denied by more conventional studies on the history of ideas (cf. Parekh & Berki 1973). What is more ambiguous here is Skinner's expression 'history of ideologies', which, due to the history of this concept, has led to serious misunderstandings.

To some extent, this vocabulary illustrates Skinner's indebtedness to the teaching of political thought in Cambridge, in which the Marxian or Mannheimian heritage was present (Skinner to KP, January 1999) and 'ideology' was treated as 'a distorting perspective' (Skinner 1974c, 280). In more general terms he uses the word, following the conventions of contemporary political science, for the role of 'intellectual factors in political life'. His more specific usage of 'ideology' is, however, related to his interest in the legitimizing role of thoughts in politics.

Independent of the question of whether we think the vocabulary of ideology to be appropriate here, the legitimizing perspective is used by Skinner to sketch an alternative to Namierite epiphenomenalism. His point of departure is 'the situation in which the agent is engaged to form a social or political action that is . . . in some way untoward, and also possesses a strong motive for attempting (in Weberian phrase) to legitimate it' (ibid., 292). For the sake of argument, he accepts the Namierite view on the role of motives, namely 'the situation of an imagined agent who never actually believes in any of the principles he professes, and whose principles never serve in consequence as the main motive of his actions' (ibid., 293). As in his discussion of Bolingbroke, Skinner, however, denies that this premiss leads to an epiphenomenalist view on the role of principles: 'My aim is to show that even in this case it still does not follow . . . that we have no need to refer to this agent's professed principles if we wish to explain his behavior' (ibid.).

The Innovating Ideologist

As an alternative view Skinner constructs the ideal type of an 'innovating ideologist' facing the task of 'legitimating untoward social actions' (ibid.). He reinterprets the situation of the ideologist by recourse to speech act theory, namely by emphasizing the political possibilities contained in 'a group of terms which perform an evaluative as well as a descriptive function in the language' (ibid.). In other words, not only the understanding of the meaning but also a definite normative colour is at least tacitly implied by the use of a concept in the prevailing conventions of a situation. 'They are standardly used, that is, to perform such acts as commending . . . or else of condemning . . . the action or state of affairs which they are also employed to describe' (ibid.). As Skinner put it in his essay on democracy, the use of the concept has become such that 'to describe a political system as democratic is to perform a speech act within the range of endorsing, commending or approving of it' (Skinner 1973, 299).

This dual perspective of assessing politics in terms both of performance and consequences is again evoked by Skinner. Through Austinian vocabulary he expresses this as follows:

> The sorts of perlocutionary effects which an agent may hope to achieve by using these terms are effects such as inciting or persuading his hearers or readers to adopt a particular point of view. . . . The sorts of illocutionary effects, however, which it is open to an agent to achieve in using these terms are effects such as evincing, expressing, and soliciting approval or disapproval of the actions or states of affairs which he uses them to describe. (Skinner 1974c, 294)

As Skinner writes, the first task is 'empirical', namely, its success always remains an open question, whereas the second is linguistic and related to the tactics and strategies of persuasion. It is in this perspective that Skinner describes the situation of the 'innovating ideologist':

> . . . the task of the innovating ideologist is a hard but obvious one. His concern, by definition, is to legitimate a new range of social actions which, in terms of the existing ways of applying the moral vocabulary prevailing in his society, are correctly regarded as in some way untoward or illegitimate. His aim must therefore be to show that a number of existing and favourable evaluative-descriptive terms can somehow be applied to his apparently untoward actions. If he can somehow perform this trick, he can thereby hope to argue that the condemnatory descriptions which are otherwise liable to be applied to his actions can in consequence be discounted. (ibid.)

The point in an innovation is not to attempt to do too much at a time. Skinner follows Weber's distinction between two types of possibilities, those which are 'realizable' and those which are merely 'thinkable' (cf. esp. Weber 1906a). The innovating ideologist is neither a utopian nor a *Realpolitiker*, but someone who deals with 'untoward' claims by using some possibilities as resources which are recognized as being available in the situation but which are not commonly used to alter the situation. To legitimate a change means, thus, to persuade the audience to accept the view that it is really only a question of using some already legitimate possibilities in an unconventional manner. The converse side of such a change is, then, a shift in the vocabulary in favour of 'neutralizing' the prevailing derogatory connotations for the untoward claims. 'Every revolutionary is to this extent obliged to march backward into battle' at least in so far as he has 'to show that at least some of the terms which his ideological opponents use . . . can be applied to include and thus legitimate his own untoward behavior' (Skinner 1974c, 294–5).

Skinner refers to the example of 'those who were concerned in early seventeenth-century England to legitimate their novel commercial and capitalist enterprises' (ibid., 295). This example hints at Weber's *Protestantische Ethik* as a paradigm for the analysis of the situation of the 'innovating ideologist' (used also in Dunn 1969), and at the end of the essay Skinner understands his argument 'as an attempt to reinterpret what I take to have been Weber's real meaning' (ibid., 300). In the 2002 version of the article – renamed 'Moral Principles and Social Change' – Skinner remarks that 'Weber undertook no investigation into the rhetorical strategies' of the ascetic Protestants, thus completing Weber's classical work by means of speech act theory and rhetoric (Skinner 2002a, 151).

His main point is to discuss the strategies and tactics of rendering such political change legitimate by altering the rhetorical dimension in the use of the descriptive-evaluative concepts. The first strategy consists, according to Skinner, 'in effect of manipulating the standard speech act potential of an existing set of descriptive terms' (Skinner 1974c, 296); whereas the second strategy 'consists in effect, of manipulating the criteria for the application of an existing set of favorable evaluative-descriptive terms' (ibid., 298). We could perhaps say that the first strategy concerns the modes of linguistic action available in the use of a descriptive-evaluative concept, while the second deals with the dimension of meaning of the concept, as used in the situation in question.

The point of the first strategy is 'to challenge his opponents to consider the feelings of disapproval or even of mere neutrality which they are standardly expressing when they use these particular terms' (ibid., 296). This strategy concerns the politics of naming, the creation of neologisms, such as *ambition*, and what they connotated for the Protestants: 'He may try to introduce some wholly new and favorable evaluative-descriptive terms into the language' (ibid.).

Skinner regards this renaming of a concept to be 'an extremely crude device' (ibid.) and he is right to the extent that there remains a common linguistic stock in parliamentary and partisan politics in all European languages. You cannot simply replace such concepts as power, politics, citizenship, state or parliament by something else, although the natural languages to some extent differ in this respect from each other. At a tactical level I think that the creation of new slogans or catchwords is a key device for a successful modern politician, because they can provide new topics to the political agenda (for an analysis of West German politics around key slogans contributing to the alteration of the agenda cf. Stötzel & Wengeler 1995).

The other variation of the same tactic 'consists of turning a neutral description into a favorable evaluative-descriptive term (usually by means of a metaphorical extensions of its uses) and then applying it in virtue of this extended meaning to describe some course of action which one wishes to see commended' (Skinner 1974c, 296–7). This 'transformation of ideology' (ibid., 297) through its metaphorization of the 'ordinary' usages is regarded by Skinner as a commonplace.

The second, 'semasiological' tactic (cf. Koselleck 1972a) is connected with linguistic action. It 'consists of varying the range of speech-acts which are standardly performed with an existing set of unfavorable evaluative-descriptive terms' (Skinner 1974c, 297). The point is to get rid of pejorative usages, either 'to apply a term normally used to express disapproval in such a way as to neutralise this speech-act potential' or even 'to reverse the standard speech-act potential of an existing and unfavorable evaluative-descriptive term' (ibid.). In these cases, the availability of a 'standard usage' is taken as a given and then the task is to invent deviating usages with a different colouring. For example, the pejorative slogan *Finnland-isierung*, as it was used by the Bavarian Prime Minister Franz-Josef Strauss and others, was subjected to attempts at rehabilitation in the debates on Finnish foreign policy in the 1970s. After the fall of the Soviet Union, the original pejorative meaning was then reactivated among some Finnish writers in the 1990s.

The analysis of Bolingbroke illustrates Skinner's second strategy of rehabilitating 'apparently untoward social actions' through insisting on their conformity with existing favourable usages. 'The point of this strategy is to challenge his ideological opponents to reconsider whether they may not be making an empirical mistake . . . in failing to see that the ordinary criteria for applying an existing range of favorable evaluative-descriptive terms may be present in the very actions they have been condemning as illegitimate' (ibid., 298).

To speak of 'an empirical mistake' is here, of course, part of the rhetorical move that appeals to the variety of modes in which the same concept is 'ordinarily' used. According to Skinner, 'the attempt to make this move is, of course, ideological in the most pejorative sense, since it depends on the performance of a linguistic sleight-of-hand' (ibid.). The 'ordinary way' to use the term is, in fact, not the statistical normalcy or historical priority, but consists in 'trying . . . to drop some of the criteria for applying it, thereby extending the range of actions which it can properly be used to describe and commend' (ibid.). In Weber's Protestant context, Skinner notes, such concepts as *providence* and *religious* 'soon became stretched and confused' (Skinner 2002a, 153).

In the 2002 version of the article Skinner no longer makes a distinction between ideological and non-ideological uses of the concepts, but accepts that some 'ideological' content will be present in all the usages. After his 'rhetorical turn' in the 1990s, Skinner neither distinguishes between 'ordinary' and 'extended' or 'metaphorical' uses of a concept nor does he speak of a 'standard' meaning of them (cf. Skinner 1999c, 67).

Skinner summarizes his criticism of the Namierite position by claiming that 'even if the agent is not in fact motivated by any of the principles he professes, he will nevertheless be obliged to behave in such a way that his actions remain compatible with the claim that these principles genuinely motivated them' (Skinner 1974c, 299). The principles are decisive in legitimation precisely for the reason that the availability and acceptability of evaluative concepts 'serve as rather specific constraints and directives to the agent about what precise lines of conduct afford him the best means of bringing his untoward action in line with some accepted principle' (ibid., 300). In other words, there are always some historically contingent conventions that limit the practical realization of some principles but which also can be turned into resources in a politics trying to alter these conventions.

In the 1974 'Some Problems' essay, Skinner refers to the obvious possibilities of using converse cases of the same figures. Already in 1973 he published an article on the contemporary discussions on democracy in which he presented the counter-figure to the innovative ideologist, namely the apologist of the existing order. 'Any apologist will need to be able to show that these unfavorable characterizations can in some way be *defeated* or at least *overridden*', but the problem remains, how to do it (Skinner 1973, 302). In the American debates, 'democracy' became a descriptive-evaluative term during the twentieth century, and even the most sophisticated view applying that term to an existing order, namely that of Robert Dahl, is written in the style of an apologist.

> It is no longer open to Dahl to insist that although some empirical theorists may commend what they describe, they could equally well condemn what they describe. . . . because they have described these systems as democratic, and it is a 'non-contingent fact' (as Searle puts it . . .) that to describe a political system as democratic is to perform a speech act within the range of endorsing, commending or approving of it. (ibid., 299)

One of Skinner's legacies in the study of contemporary political thought consists in his insistence on the omnipresence of a normative dimension in the key concepts, such as democracy, freedom and equality. These concepts tend to revalue the phenomenon by their very use, then there are other concepts, for example those of the party or the (professional) politician, which – in spite of the academic and public acknowledgement of their indispensability – have commonly retained even in parliamentary regimes a pejorative tone. The more formal concepts, such as politics, power or the state, are highly disputed in their normative content and, just for this reason, immediately require a specification of their use.

The tendency towards a value-laden usage of the concepts presupposes such a specification. In this respect, Skinner's Dahl essay remains incomplete in so far as he regards the Lincolnian criterion of 'rule by the people' as a necessary condition for speaking about democracy, thus leaving both 'rule' and 'the people' as well as their interconnection without further examination. This is, of course, sufficient for Skinner's purpose, but still gives the impression – especially when Skinner does not consider the dispute about 'changing the meaning of democracy' as essential (ibid., 296) – that even such a concept as democracy does have a 'standard meaning'.

Linguistic Action and its Legitimation

Quentin Skinner's reorientation of the study of political thought can be considered as a continuation of the Weberian view of striving for power as a necessary condition of all politics. Such a political dimension is present in any debate, even though it may appear to the participants to be polite, academic and consensus-seeking. For Skinner this dimension of debate is explicit, it is not formed according to the model of solving a given problem or resolving a common task, but according to the paradigm of a political struggle. In 'A Reply to My Critics' he puts it as follows: 'to argue is always to argue for or against a certain assumption or point of view or course of action. It follows that, if we wish to understand such utterances, we shall have to identify the precise nature of the intervention constituted by the act of uttering them' (Skinner 1988c, 274).

Skinner's discussions of linguistic action thus also explicate 'microscopic' levels of politics-as-activity. Austin's distinctions between locutions, illocutions and perlocutions or between illocutionary act and illocutionary force as well as his list of performatives can be given a political interpretation, and it is largely thanks to the work of Skinner that we now better understand this. Although he has never been interested in constructing context-independent typologies, his discussions give us clues to the rich and strange world of *doing* things with words, through naming different activities, by shifting their range of reference and also by discussing their combinations, as in the tactics and strategies of legitimation. When Skinner is mainly interested in contested uses of speech acts in controversial situations, this renders his view *per se* politically significant.

The Skinnerian style of 'micro-politics' differs, however, from the classical contractarian style. He does not construct abstract norms or limit-situations, such as the 'state of nature', but his approach accentuates the situatedness of all human action. He acknowledges the conventions as omnipresent facticities of the situations, which have no value in themselves. At the same time, the conventions, although serving as delimitations of the horizon of action and indicating some constraints, do not dictate anything for the agent. She has to choose how to respond to the facticities of the situations, how to 'play' in them. In this sense, Skinner's view has parallels not only to Weber but also to other theorists of action, such as Arendt, Oakeshott or Sartre (cf. Palonen 1998). Through the perspective of legitimation, Skinner continues Weber's work by the means of linguistic actions.

Among Skinner's critics it is not uncommon to encounter the view that his discussion of language is 'structuralist' or even an expression of 'metaphysical determinism' (Minogue 1981, 192). Skinner thus sees a need to affirm that for him 'language constitutes a resource as well as a constraint' (Skinner 1988c, 276). The entire perspective of linguistic action, indeed, signifies a rich usage of linguistic resources, and this is also the point that Skinner attributes

to the views of Austin and Wittgenstein on language: 'Their
achievement is better described as that of finding a way of describing, and thereby of calling to our attention, a dimension and hence
a resource of language that every speaker and writer exploits all the
time, and which we need to identify whenever we wish to understand any serious utterance' (ibid., 262).

Analysed from the perspective of legitimation, speech acts are
intrinsically constituted power-shares in a controversy. In other
words, a nuanced, imaginative and multidimensional use of 'doing
things with words' offers political resources in a power struggle,
especially to those lacking other sources of power – such as physical
force or the power of numbers (cf. Weber 1919a) – or as additional
resources for competing politicians disposing over those sources.

The value of such resources can be further accentuated by the
mode in which Skinner has reformulated the Weberian view that
every *Herrschaft*, as an asymmetric form of power, is in need of legitimation. Linguistic sources of power are not only linguistic, they are
– as the debates on illocutionary force and perlocutionary effects
indicate – connected with other sources. In other words, there
cannot be any politically crucial action that would not have a linguistic dimension. That this was also the case with physical force
was, indeed, already understood by Carl von Clausewitz. One
variant on his famous thesis of war as a continuation of politics
through other means is explicitly connected to linguistics. According to Clausewitz, war has 'seine eigene Grammatik, aber nicht
seine eigene Logik' (Clausewitz 1832, 675).

Skinner has, in his critique of the Namierites, made it clear that
the legitimizing role of the use of theories and concepts should not
be mixed with *ex post* rationalizations of existing forms of rule or of
attempts to overcome them. Neither can the perspective of legitimation be limited to serve as theoretical supports or ornaments to
other sources of power and rule, but it should, rather, be understood
as an indispensable part of them. All linguistic action has a political potential also constituting new shares of power and altering the
existing distribution of power-shares.

As opposed to perlocutionary effects and illocutionary force, illocutionary acts are, as I quoted Skinner above, purely a 'linguistic'
matter. The use of them as power-shares may not be effective in its
results – as in the case of Bukharin – but the choice of the performative mode may be still important as a response to the situation.
The chance of selecting the speech acts or specific styles, tactics and
strategies of acting with them, can serve as a political resource, disposing over certain linguistic and literary competences.

With the essays on legitimation in 1973–4, Skinner applies the resources of linguistic action to an explicit dimension of politics and revises the task of the study of political theorizing to concern the legitimizing role of theories. At the same time, these articles actualize the political dimension in the Wittgensteinian and Austinian perspectives on linguistic action.

Skinner rejects the search for a 'substantial and objective conception of reason' (1988c, 243) and regards the 'truth' of the beliefs that past agents hold as an irrelevant question. He admits that anyone with such views 'is certain sooner or later to find themselves denounced (or commended) as a relativist' (ibid., 255). He defends himself against this accusation:

> But at no point have I endorsed the thesis of conceptual relativism. I have never asserted that it was true that at one time there were witches in league with the devil, even though such a belief nowadays strikes us as false. To put the point generally, I have merely observed that the question of what it may be rational to hold true can vary with the totality of one's beliefs. I have never put forward the reckless and completely different thesis that truth itself can vary in the same way. (ibid., 255–6)

Here Skinner defends himself mainly with the thesis of the interdependence of one's beliefs, in the sense of 'semantic holism'. For him 'a term such as *virtù* gains its "meaning" from its place within an extensive network of beliefs' (ibid., 253). The questions remain, how intense such a relationship can be, and when the tight interdependence of beliefs would lead to something analogous to the mythology of coherence.

Certain variants of perspectivism can clearly be called relativism, if the perspective used is just a reflection of a given social or ideological position, as advocated in the Mannheimian 'relationalist' sociology of knowledge or in certain 'standpoint' doctrines of today. Skinner's perspectivist approach has nothing in common with such a view. The very concept of 'move' illustrates that his point is not to elucidate already fixed positions but to shift the current constellation of debate so that everyone has to alter previously held positions.

Besides rejecting the search for objective reason and considering truth as an irrelevant question in historical studies, Skinner also denies a third pillar of the narrowly rationalist scheme, namely progress, at least in the history of ideas. For the journal *Cogito*, he responds with a metaphor: 'I think of the image of flowing and ebbing of tides. There are things we gain and there are things we lose', and he then argues that we should 'take very seriously some of the losses we have suffered as our history has developed in the way that it has' (Skinner 1997c, 74).

This should not, of course, be taken in the sense of a cyclical philosophy of history. Rather, we could speak of an analogy to alternation in government, in which the parties do not represent 'progress' and 'reaction' but rather two current tendencies, both of which have their strengths and weaknesses. With a perspectivist model of change in our understanding, the alternation presupposes that there are not the same parties throughout a longer period of elections, but, rather, that every electoral defeat of a governing party enables the party to renew itself, indeed to turn into something like a new party, namely, to revise its principles and to reorientate towards the electorate. Only such a party system being continuously in movement would form a political analogy to the Weberian ideal on the eternal youth of the historical disciplines (Weber 1904, 206).

Perhaps we can summarize Skinner's view, as it was presented before his 'rhetorical turn', as follows: it is always possible to argue against even well-established theories or conceptions, and similarly it is always possible to question the legitimacy of even the best established forms of rule. The main point is that, within the Skinnerian perspective, these two themes are both variations on the same political topic of legitimation.

4

The Foundations: *A History of Theory Politics*

Quentin Skinner's international reputation is due above all to his two-volume book *The Foundations of Modern Political Thought*: the first volume deals with *The Renaissance*, the second with *The Age of Reformation*. Originally, Skinner had planned 'to write a synoptic survey of early modern political thought' for the Penguin Press (Skinner 1978a I, xvii). This book was intended 'to have covered the whole period from the sixteenth to the early nineteenth century'. Skinner, however, then 'found the undertaking to be far beyond my powers' (ibid.). Perhaps we can speculate on whether such a 'survey' is compatible with his vision of the entire project as a 'study of political thought'. At any rate, *The Foundations* is doubtless more original and thought-provoking than the 'synoptic survey' would have been.

The Foundations was Quentin Skinner's first proper book. What was he doing when writing it? What is its genre, or which generic conventions did Skinner intend to blur in writing the book? Why is the book called simply *The Foundations of the Modern Political Thought*? What kind of 'foundations' is he speaking of? Or, is this just idly raising an anachronistic question in the light of the critique of 'foundationalism' made prominent by Richard Rorty in his *Philosophy and the Mirror of Nature*, published just one year after Skinner's *Foundations*?

Genres of Studying Political Thought

The shift from the previously intended volume to *The Foundations* was a shift in genre. The remarks in the Preface as well as the very breadth of the original period intended to be dealt with, give us a clue to the character of the unwritten book: it would have been a subversion of the genre of 'textbooks'.

In Anglophone academic culture, introductory textbooks play a prominent role. As no professor can be assumed to have firsthand knowledge of all relevant political thought, textbooks on the history of political thought are indispensable. However, good textbooks are subversions of the genre, made possible by the author's own studies. Janet Coleman's recent two-volume narrative on political thought from Antiquity to the Renaissance is an excellent example of such an anti-textbook (Coleman 2000). She has clearly combined both detailed studies and profiled interpretations of thinkers or topics with the necessary presentation characteristic to a textbook.

Still, even such an anti-textbook would have been hard to write for Skinner, if we remember his special indebtedness to Collingwood, who notes:

> . . . text-books always describe not what is now being thought by real live historians, but what was thought by real live historians at some time in the past when the raw material was being created out of which the text-book has been put together. And it is not only the results of historical thought which are out of date by the time they get into the text-book. It is also the principles of historical thought: that is, the ideas as to nature, object, method and value of historical thinking. . . . there is a peculiar illusion incidental to all knowledge acquired in the way of education: the illusion of finality. When a student is *in statu pupillari* with respect to any subject whatever, he has to believe that things are settled because the text-books and his teachers regard them as settled. When he emerges from that state and goes on studying the subject for himself he finds that nothing is settled. . . . On the other hand, if he emerges from the status of pupil without continuing to pursue the subject he never rids himself of this dogmatic attitude. (Collingwood 1946, 7–8)

This Collingwoodian critique of textbooks was a crucial aspect of the Cambridge criticism of the conventional history of political thought, as presented by Laslett, Pocock and Skinner himself in 'Meaning and Understanding'. One of Skinner's favourite targets was John Plamenatz's two-volume textbook, *Man and Society*, with its principle of 'reading the text "over and over again"' (Skinner 1969a, 32).

Relieved from the requirements of a textbook, Skinner shifted the genre. In his Preface, Skinner presents as his first main aim 'to offer an outline account of the principal texts of late medieval and early modern political thought' as well as to 'survey the transition from medieval to modern political thought' (Skinner 1978a I, ix). 'Outline' and 'survey' still seem to imply a textbook-like genre, but they are superseded by higher aims. Skinner gives a paradigmatic example of such a 'survey': Pierre Mesnard's *L'essor de la philosophie politique au XVIe siècle*, published in 1936. For Skinner, 'it has seemed worthwhile to try to furnish a more up-to-date survey of the same period, taking account as far as possible of the more significant findings of recent research' (ibid.).

To understand the genre to which Skinner intends to contribute through *The Foundations*, a look at Mesnard's book is required. I have also compared *The Foundations* with an older Cambridge contribution to the history of political thought of the same period, J. N. Figgis's lecture-based *Studies of Political Thought from Gerson to Grotius 1414–1615*, first published in 1907, which obviously inspired the structure of Skinner's second volume. As a more contemporary object of comparison I have selected John Pocock's *The Machiavellian Moment* (1975), to which many reviewers of *The Foundations* – including Pocock himself (cf. Pocock 1979) – have compared Skinner's work.

All of these books deal roughly with the same period and with political thought on a broad European scale, as opposed to the plentiful national studies. They are interested in specifying the 'modernity' of political thought. The books by Figgis and Pocock are, however, more thematically concentrated. In this respect, Skinner's self-understanding of using the same genre as Mesnard is appropriate. An obvious difference though lies in the period, with Skinner exploring the 'renaissance' of political thought from the thirteenth century onwards.

Figgis was originally a theologian. When he characterizes his book as an 'embryology of modern politics' (Figgis 1907, 30), this points to the fact that he was highly indebted to organic thinking, especially to the corporate pluralism of Otto Gierke's *Deutsche Genossenschaftsrecht* (cf. Runciman 1997). He attributes the origins of political liberty to 'the result of the struggle of religious organisms to live' (Figgis 1907, 5). His political reading of church controversies, especially of Conciliarist reformism within the Catholic Church in the fifteenth century, doubtless caught Skinner's attention. Figgis practised a type of historical study in which minor figures could play decisive roles.

More importantly, Figgis acknowledges the slow formation of the modern state as the main topic of the Reformation controversies, realizing that for the church-dominated medieval polity 'there is no sovereign' (ibid., 10) and even that 'the very term State is an anachronism' (ibid., 14). The specificity of the 'modern' consists in the identification of 'the post-Reformation State' that is 'unitary, omnipotent and irresistible' (ibid., 13) and 'is found in perfection . . . in France' (ibid.). Despite his warnings against anachronism and the history of losers in analyses of the Council of Constance, the term embryology illustrates that Figgis's approach largely remains a *Wirkungsgeschichte*, invoking contemporary examples and speaking, for example, of 'the conservative liberalism of Gerson and Halifax' (ibid., 32).

Mesnard's book is still readable. The author's primary interest is philosophical, although he acknowledges that politics is precisely the *domaine* that philosophers have the greatest difficulty in facing. He regards this problem mainly in sociological terms, considering that a political philosophy should understand that a 'transformation constante du fait en droit, de la société en norme idéale' takes place in its subject matter (Mesnard 1936, 1). Although of Durkheimian background, Mesnard accepts that a strict sociological determinism would prevent 'la politique rationnelle'. He is therefore content with the statement that in order to understand politics, we must admit that 'En politique plus qu'ailleurs, les faits passent avant livres' (ibid., 3). In other words, an analysis of the classical texts is not enough, we have to relate them to the events and the social conditions of theories. It is in this perspective that he also regards the sixteenth century as an age of rupture that requires new thinking in response to the factual changes that already had taken place.

The most impressive aspect of Mesnard's book is the broad international orientation. Due to the Latin language and culture of Christianity, the intellectual life of the sixteenth century is regarded by Mesnard as still (*encore*) to a large extent international (ibid., 13). It is in this respect that Skinner's book can be regarded as an 'updating' of Mesnard's, although the latter's long discussion of Polish thinking, for example, remains absent from *The Foundations*.

Mesnard's design is traditional in so far as he presents the work of major thinkers, such as Machiavelli, Luther, Bodin and Althusius, as a totality. Correspondingly, historical variation as a response to events is generally played down. Hence the response to historical events or the variety of intentions is subsumed in an assumption of the core of thinking, for example, by assessing Machiavelli as advocating a *république autoritaire* (ibid., 60).

Mesnard uses anachronistic expressions, such as *communisme* and *extrême gauche* for the Anabaptists and related movements, as well as *la société civile* in the post-eighteenth-century sense (ibid., 286). In the introduction he speaks of the relations between church and state as the main topic of the study (ibid., 3) and attributes the creation of the first *Église d'État* in Zürich to Zwingli (ibid., 296), but on another occasion he regards Théodore de Bèze as the first in France who in 1575 'définit . . . la structure idéale de ce corps complexe que nous appelons l'État' (ibid., 325). Sensitivity to the historical character of concepts and their political point is thus, despite the anachronisms mentioned, present also in Mesnard's work.

John Pocock's *The Machiavellian Moment* originated from a publisher's wish 'to write a study on European constitutional thought in the sixteenth and seventeenth centuries' (Pocock 1975, ix). What remains is a concern with the form and order of the polity as a framework of discussion in three contexts considered analogical, namely the Florentine and Venetian Renaissance, the English seventeenth and eighteenth centuries, especially the work of James Harrington and his followers, and the formation of the constitution of the United States. Within this framework Pocock's study is, however, a highly selective thematized history of the variations on the republican language of *virtù*, as opposed to *fortuna* and later to corruption.

Where Pocock differs from both Figgis and Mesnard is, above all, in his insistence on the republican heritage of the Florentine and Venetian Renaissance. This allows him both to locate Machiavelli among the republicans and to analyse a number of his contemporaries who shared this language even in the face of overwhelming opposing forces. Pocock's main point lies in the claim that although republican language was a lost cause in sixteenth-century Italian politics, it played an obvious political role in two contexts, both of which shared the problematics of the 'Machiavellian moment'. Pocock constructs a structural analogy between the situations in Italy, England and the United States, which allows him recourse to the republican language developed in Italy. The idea that 'moment' is not momentary, but characterizes a type of political situation, has been borrowed by others (cf. Rosanvallon 1985, Palonen 1998).

For Pocock the republican language of the Machiavellian moment is a response to a definite type of situation. At the same time, it attempts to do justice to the inherent temporality that republics were opening up and to control this temporal contingency of *fortuna* by *virtù* (cf. Pocock 1975, esp. 49–54). The republican language deals with this temporal problematic, and forms a *langue* to master, which affirms a stable but still temporal polity, an order of *virtù* as opposed to the erosive forces of *fortuna* and corruption. To detect such 'islands' of republicanism within the mainly monarchist order of European states has been Pocock's legacy to the history of political thought.

Perhaps we can interpret Skinner's term 'outline' in *The Foundations* as an attempt to do something between an overview of the thought of a period, such as Mesnard's, and a strongly thematic monograph, such as Pocock's. What advantages and disadvantages does such an 'outline' of the political thought of a period or, rather, of the two thematic complexes of Renaissance and Reformation offer, especially in relation to writing a proper monograph?

It is obvious that such an outline can gain something in the breadth but lose more in the depth of the analysis. Such a study is always liable to be opposed from two directions, to be accused of neglecting something crucial and of insufficiency in detail. These are the two most common objections among the reviewers of *The Foundations*. Max Weber saw the problem of being accused both of the *Stoffhuber* of neglecting some sources and of the *Sinnhuber* of not going into a discussion of the 'deeper significance' of the analysis (cf. Weber 1904, 214).

Some reviewers of *The Foundations* also accuse Skinner of not following his own programme. Massingham even writes: 'If Skinner had not written this book but was reviewing it, he would probably have dismissed it as yet another example of a work in the history of ideas written in a well-defined but methodologically incorrect tradition' (Massingham 1981, 128). I think Skinner could have disputed his examples, but taking, for the sake of the argument, this critique as valid, I think it is by no means fatal to Skinner. Methodological principles have to be considered as heuristic tools and not as legislative prohibitions, and in this sense there may always be good reason sometimes to disregard them to avoid deviation from the main narrative or over-extension of the analysis. This is true particularly of such outlines as *The Foundations*, in which the possibility of saying something original and new about the details is highly limited.

Besides the obvious advantage of offering an overview to non-specialists, the main strength of such a broad outline is the ability to study the connections between the different thinkers, topics and controversies of the period. It is in this respect that *The Foundations* offers us both a broad view of the multiplicity of the 'local' contexts in which the main topics of the period were discussed and clues to the intellectual resources available for the authors, which could, if a controversial political situation arose, be turned into a political argument in a new context. In this sense, Roman Law, Canon Law and the medieval 'ancient constitutions' could all be used by the Protestants in defence of their political positions. *The Foundations* thus contains as much context-transferring as context-bound analysis. Such context-transfers are also used by Skinner as tools of criticism against widely shared views, such as Michael Walzer's thesis on the 'Calvinist theory of revolution' (cf. also Skinner 1980a).

In his review of *The Foundations*, John Pocock compares it with *The Machiavellian Moment*. For him Skinner's 'is a very "Cambridge" book in its determination to operate from phenomena, not from models'. Pocock further speaks of 'Skinner's decision to use microscope first and telescope second' (Pocock 1979, 101). Indeed, here we can detect a characteristic difference: in linguistic terms, Pocock is interested in *langue*, Skinner in *parole*. Or, to formulate it with political vocabulary: Pocock's main interest lies in the polity, whereas Skinner focuses on the activity of politicking. Pocock's telescopic and Skinner's microscopic approach is partly a difference of the genres, the Skinnerian approach being better suited to broad comparisons without submitting the agents and their languages to a given model.

One of the main objections to *The Foundations* concerns the brief presentation of the content of the ideas discussed. This is, of course, intended by Skinner. Unlike Mesnard, Skinner assumes that the main ideas of Machiavelli, Luther or Bodin are well known and not in need of presentation, when mainly writing a broad outline for generalists. Presentation is thus necessary only so far as it enables the reader to understand Skinner's argument.

Here, I think, Skinner skilfully manages to do what he promises, namely 'to practise my own precepts' (Skinner 1978a I, x). The precepts should not be understood as methodological rules, but follow from his perspective of linguistic action. The theories of Renaissance and Reformation authors are analysed by Skinner, not in their own right but as 'moves in argument', and as speech acts in political controversies. Thus, he would rather discuss the relations of Machiavelli's *Il Principe* to the genre of the princely advice-books than the content of its specific paragraphs (although in his *Machiavelli*, a more comprehensive view of this author is presented). It is in this shifting emphasis from the content to the argument, from thoughts about politics to thinking politically, that the 'Skinnerian revolution' in the study of political thought is explicitly manifested. At least for the contemporary readers of *The Foundations*, this shift in the entire subject matter of political thought remained largely invisible.

My proposal for the genre of *The Foundations* is history of 'theory politics'. I mean by theory politics a political action that deals with striving for shares of power based on theorizing, as opposed, for example, to those based on the sheer number of the adherents. Theories, concepts, interpretations of situations, normative judgements about the strengths of certain positions, strategies of argumentation and so on also can serve as shares of power for political action. Theory politics in this sense is directly concerned not with what is done or what should be done, but with what *can* be done or *could* have been done in a situation. To a certain extent, such shares of power are indispensable, and a political agent can always attempt to create new power-shares by revising existing theories or by contesting hitherto unproblematic ones. Studies of legitimizing political decisions also deal with questions of choice among the available possibilities, with their advantages and faults, sometimes even legitimizing or delegitimizing a definite policy, but it is not the theorists who take the responsibility for the decision.

In *The Foundations*, Skinner practises theory politics on several levels. He criticizes contemporary interpretations about the past, such as Walzer's on 'the Calvinist Revolution'. But the main dimension consists in a revision of the contemporary understanding of the study of political thought. Both classical and contemporary theorists are analysed as politicians working with theories and concepts. Some commentators have wondered why Skinner has not moved on to the level of the writings of political agents? Indeed, he has focused on the theorists evoked in the political controversies of the age or intervening by their own initiative. I think this is the proper level to deal with theory politics, as opposed to the 'reality' of the politics of decisions, events and processes.

It is at this level that we should understand, for example, Skinner's analysis of the debates between theologians and princely advisers among the German Lutherans who faced the crisis of the entire Lutheran 'movement' after 1530. When accepting Luther's doctrine condemning all resistance towards worldly authorities, the question remained of whether this acceptance left any room for manoeuvring in such extreme and exceptional situations as the continued existence of the Lutheran 'movement'. Legal specialists found clear arguments, both in the 'constitutional law' of the

German Empire and in civil law, which could be used as legitimations of such resistance as a 'duty' on specific occasions (cf. Skinner 1978a II, esp. 191–206). However, it was not their task to decide whether these arguments, ultimately, were acceptable for the case at hand, but they served Luther and the other leaders with arguments that extended the horizon of what was regarded as politically possible while remaining Lutheran. In other cases, theory politicians can, of course, act contrarily and argue against the possibility or necessity of something that political agents would otherwise be likely to attempt doing.

Skinner's central principle that 'political life itself' sets the problems for political theorizing (Skinner 1978a I, xi) can thus be interpreted as a move contributing to the revision of the genre which can be used to analyse modes of thinking politically. In Skinner's theory politics, it is not 'systems of thought' but political dilemmas that challenge the rethinking and reopening of controversies regarding the legitimacy of certain standpoints, policies and programmes that are the focus of discussion. It is not past thoughts in themselves, their content or validity that interests us, but rather their political role in the struggles of the era and the possibility of transferring them to new contexts as politically valuable instruments. A broad comparative approach as used in *The Foundations* is most useful for a study on attempts to resolve dilemmas and change the horizons of the possible or legitimate. The depth of the description or analysis of a definite theory or the clear use of a concept in an author's work should be considered as related to their political point.

The actual transfer of theories and conceptions from one context to another signifies, then, that the political role of theories should not be understood too narrowly. The role of theories cannot be reduced to the intended level, but the surplus meaning, not visible to anyone in the actual context, may be activated for entirely different purposes. In this sense, theories serve not only as instruments for the analysis of the actual situation but also as resources, as a repertoire of arguments, rhetorically as 'common places' (*topoi, loci communes*) for moves in theory politics.

Why 'Foundations'?

Some of my students who have read *The Foundations of Modern Political Thought* for their examinations have been suspicious of a book with 'foundations' in the title. Indeed, it is worth asking, what is Skinner's illocutionary act in entitling the book? We cannot detect any explication of the title in the text. In fact, it is only at the last lines of the final chapter of the second volume that Skinner speaks of 'foundations' at all: 'With this analysis of the state as an omnipotent yet impersonal power, we may have said to enter the modern world: the modern theory of the State remains to be constructed, but its foundations are now complete' (Skinner 1978a II, 358).

What does Skinner mean by 'foundations' in this passage? He later wrote that the state had become 'a master noun of political argument' (Skinner 1989b, 123). When Skinner, once again, alludes to 'argument in controversy', it is clear that the concept of the state clearly lacks a secure basis for political reasoning in the 'modern' era. Skinner's *Foundations* have nothing to do with 'foundationalism', as presented in Rorty's *Philosophy and the Mirror of Nature*, a book to which Skinner gave an enthusiastic review. The 'foundations' refer, rather, to a kind of indispensable *topos* of modern political debate, which every participant has to consider.

A few of the reviewers of *The Foundations* seem to have realized the point of Skinner's title. Alan Ryan describes it as follows: 'What Skinner reckons himself to be uncovering here is just what he says – the foundations of modern political thinking. That is, what he is after is the process by which the ways in which we now think about politics came to be available to us' (Ryan 1979, 568). Thus 'foundations' refers to a historical process, not to any ground, basis or fundament, on which we can base our thinking. For James Tully, 'the foundations of modern political thought are the unintended and mostly unrecognized product of 400 years of political thought and action' (Tully 1981, 18). Consequently, he argues that such foundations 'lack rational foundations' (ibid., 21). In other words, the 'foundations' are contingent, both in their origin and in their role as unquestioned assumptions for political argument.

There was a clear model for the title. Skinner was impressed by Donald R. Kelley's book *Foundations of Modern Historical Scholarship*, and borrowed the metaphor. Kelley too fails to explain why he speaks of *Foundations*, but one of his points is to insist on the role of unexpected consequences in political philosophy: 'many of the important insights and breakthroughs in the interpretation of history were made not by the grand figures of historical narrative or political philosophy but by pioneers labouring in relatively obscure and technical fields of scholarship and concerned more with the texture than with the structure of history' (Kelley 1970, 13). He also refers to the famous philosopher A. N. Whitehead, who had spoken of 'some fundamental assumptions' that are so obvious to the users 'that people do not know what they are assuming because no other way of putting things has ever occurred to them' (ibid.).

Skinner's title should, I think, be understood in exactly that sense. It is an analysis of a historical process, which unintentionally leads to such 'fundamental assumptions' that both differed from those of the previous era and which have continued to remain unquestioned. Skinner's object of study is, rather, the history of the 'foundationalization' of a style of political thought. Skinner's guiding idea about this process is the turning of the state into a 'master noun of the political argument'. When a conceptual history of the state is added to the Conclusion of *The Foundations*, this also corresponds to Pocock's understanding that Skinner first uses the microscope and then the telescope in the final instance.

In a recent interview, for the first time Skinner himself publicly discussed the title:

> I was trying to identify the most basic concepts out of which we in the modern west constructed the legitimising theories we continue to deploy in talking about the duties of citizens and the rights of states. The first volume of my book focused on theories of civic virtue and self-government; my second focused on the rise of absolutism and the emergence of rival theories of natural rights. These, I tried to show, were the conceptual foundations on which we in the modern west went to build the theory of the state. (Skinner 2002d, 52–3)

Skinner affirms that 'I have always been an anti-foundationalist, although it is true . . . that this particular piece of jargon was not yet current in the 1960s' (ibid., 52). More interestingly, he now admits that there was something wrong with the metaphor. His Italian translators had already remarked on this and the book is entitled *Origini* in Italian and not *Fundamenti* (Skinner to KP, January 1999), although the 2001 French translation is called *Fondements*. Skinner now writes self-critically, of both himself and of Kelley's more cautious formula without the definite article:

> Where I think we were both wrong was in using a metaphor that virtually commits one to writing teleologically. My own book is far too much concerned with the origins of our present world when I ought to have been trying to represent the world I was examining in its own terms so far as possible. But the trouble with writing early-modern European history is that, although their world and our world are vastly different from each other, our world nevertheless somehow emerged out of theirs, so that there's a very natural temptation to

> write about origins, foundations, evolutions, developments. But it's not a temptation to which I would ever think of yielding in these post-modern days. (Skinner 2002d, 53)

Skinner refers here to an ambiguity that many reviewers already noted when the book came out. The metaphor of foundations in the sense of a contingent and unintended process was used to enable a translation from the language of past agents to the language of the readers. Skinner now thinks that the translation in *The Foundations* did not sufficiently underline how strange and different from the contemporary world was the world which he analysed. One consequence of this aim was, according to his current view, that the title gave the misleading impression of a teleological form of writing, as a kind of mythology of prolepsis. (Minogue's accusation of this, 1981, 184, does not catch Skinner's specific use of 'foundations'.)

The point is, however, that Skinner now almost regrets the title. In the text he occasionally uses teleological formulations, for example comparing the Thomist contract theory with John Locke's views, which are outside the scope of the book (cf. Skinner 1978a II, 156–9). This usage is more an instrument of translation for contemporary readers than an inherent part of Skinner's analysis of 'foundationalization'. But, with his *Reason and Rhetoric in the Philosophy of Hobbes* in the background, Skinner can now point out that such occasional teleological formulae in *The Foundations* suggested all too ready-made translations. The perspective of the 'modern' also tended to contribute to a misunderstanding of the conceptual horizon of the political thinkers of the Renaissance and Reformation era.

Skinner's formula of 'examining in its own terms so far as possible' requires, of course, a qualification with regard to his critique of Elton and others who deny the historian the right to pose such questions. I think we have to distinguish between a conscious analytical usage of such heuristic tools as the speech act theory and the implicit projection of some commonplaces of the political vocabulary of the time, such as speaking of 'the society', in the political 'moves' of pre-eighteenth-century agents. The problem of anachronism appears, as Skinner now more clearly than ever underlines, in the second type of vocabulary, while in the heuristic use of analytic tools it is obvious for any reader that such a usage is only an instrument of explication and elucidation. Such tools are no 'excess theoretical baggage', as Minogue claims (1981, 190), at least not for the kind of history of theory politics Skinner himself is engaged in.

Perhaps a further qualification is also needed concerning the 'political' in Skinner's title. He refers to it as 'that the sphere of politics should be envisaged as a distinct branch of moral philosophy, a branch concerned with the art of government', a view he attributed to Aristotle's *Politics* (Skinner 1978a II, 349). However, Skinner understands that at that time politics was a discipline-concept, not a phenomenon of its own. Using the spatial metaphors of 'sphere' or 'branch' for politics largely follows a nineteenth-century vocabulary.

One main project of *The Foundations* is, however, to question the distinction between political and religious spheres as inapplicable to the Reformation thinkers. In this sense a sphere-independent, qualitative interpretation of the 'political' is appropriate to Skinner's analysis. To return to the example of the Lutherans in the face of an imminent defeat after 1530, it seems to me that the crux of their argument consists in their being unwilling to compromise the fate of the entire Lutheran confession in the name of Luther's doctrine of non-resistance to worldly authorities. Thus, we see clearly that even among so-called 'orthodox' adherents of a theological doctrine, this doctrine could not be regarded as a question of 'faith' alone, at least not in the case when the conditions for adhering to such a faith were themselves threatened. When the Lutherans had already become a 'power' on the religious scene, they could not simply surrender or rely on the intervention of superhuman 'power' alone, but were obliged to treat their own doctrines in a political manner. Compared with the medieval Christian universe, such a political use of doctrine can already be understood as a mark of 'modernity' in the sense of Skinner's book title.

The Matrix of Questions

One of the disparities of *The Foundations* from a traditional history of political thought is the principle that Skinner has 'focused instead on the more general social and intellectual matrix out of which their works arose' (Skinner 1978a I, x). This mathematical metaphor, readily evoked by structuralist authors, refers to a synchronic similarity of certain topics and ideologies present in the Renaissance and Reformation context. Still, I think it ought to be interpreted differently from its structuralist usages in the work of Skinner, namely in the Collingwoodian perspective of the primacy of questions over answers. Once again, Skinner denies that perennial questions matter in the history of political thought. He asks of classical texts 'what their authors were *doing* in writing them'. More specifically 'what questions they were addressing and trying to answer, and how far they were accepting and endorsing, or questioning or repudiating, or perhaps even polemically ignoring, the prevailing assumptions and conventions of political debate' (ibid., xiii).

The Collingwoodian priority of questions over answers can thus be regarded as one of the main keys to understanding *The Foundations.* 'Each question has to "arise",' wrote Collingwood in his *Autobiography* (1939, 27), and what Skinner is doing in *The Foundations* is analysing how new types of questions arose, how they were partly added on to the old ones, thereby altering them, or in certain cases even made the old questions entirely obsolete. A famous case of the latter is Luther's vision of the Church, which at once dissolved the main political controversy between *regnum* and *sacerdotium.* 'For Luther, this means that the tremendous theoretical battle waged throughout the Middle Ages by the protagonists of the *regnum* and the *sacerdotium* is suddenly brought to an end' (Skinner 1978a II, 15).

The two volumes make it clear how, at least since the rise of the Italian city-republics in the thirteenth century, the common agenda of medieval Christian culture dissolved and new questions arose. The controversies of city-republic vs. monarchy, secular vs. ecclesiastical polity, absolute or constitutional monarchy are complemented by discussing such topics as the role of princes and their advisers, non-resistance, the duty and right to resist. Skinner's main point is, rather, to discuss more specific questions, partly of ancient heritage, such as the relation of popular government to wealth and poverty, the opposing interpretations of such concepts as *nobilitas* and the rerun of the twelfth-century Azo vs. Lothair debate on relations between the *imperium* and inferior magistrates. Such questions were seldom entirely new, but they received novel political significance in the context of unprecedented political struggles.

The narrative of *The Foundations*, then, consists in the dissolution and diversification of the agenda, without dissolving old intellectual resources, traditions, ideologies or languages, but using the possibility to 'recycle' them into new political purposes and ideological projects. The 'matrix' consists of a complex that thematizes the interconnections between the changing and multiplying political agenda of questions with the old intellectual resources, such as Roman and Canon Law, or with theorizing surrounding republican experiences in more or less autonomous Italian cities or around local princely courts.

Intellectual innovations and revisions are thus by no means politically irrelevant. The Lutheran Reformation was in its origins a strictly theological matter, which, however, had political implications that vastly exceeded Luther's intentions and expectations. Skinner writes, for example, of the interpretation of chapter 13 of St Paul's Epistle to the Romans that 'Luther's influence helped to make this the most cited of all texts on the foundations of political life throughout the age of the Reformation' (ibid.). An analogous role was played by legal and constitutional interpretations, in which the struggle between different juridical schools is analysed by Skinner in terms of their political implications rather than as direct responses to the controversies of the day. For example, he analyses Claude de Seyssel's *freins* upon the king's authority, '*la police, la religion* and *la justice*', presented in 1515 (ibid., 260). Skinner takes it as a point of departure for subsequent debates between centralizers and decentralizers and between the adherents of Catholic and Protestant confessional parties, a struggle of interpretations that could not have been intended by the pre-Reformation writing of Seyssel.

The diversification of the agenda of questions allows us to reconsider such moves as invention, differentiation, interconnection and dissolution – and here I am using this twentieth-century concept in a purely analytical sense – as a politicization of the world in the contexts of the Renaissance and Reformation. I mean by politicization both an increase of contingency through the opening up of new questions and an increase of controversiality in the horizon of potential answers to them. Of equal importance is, of course, what was not politicized and thematized in controversies. For both the limits and resources of political controversies 'the nature and limits of the normative vocabulary available at any given time will also help to determine the ways in which particular questions come to be singled out and discussed' (Skinner 1978a I, xi).

Once politicized, questions cannot be simply reversed, but they can be placed at the margin of the agenda. The main aspects of the book could, consequently, be called a 'foundationalization' of the terms of theory politics, regarding both the topics and vocabulary used. Such a relative unification of the agenda, as an exhaustion of the politicizing potential of the controversies between republic and monarchy, Protestantism and Catholicism, on the level of the formation of regionally distinct and centralized states, is the reverse side of the politicization of questions.

In other words, there is a tension in *The Foundations* between politicization and 'foundationalization', between the moments of the subversive revision of old doctrines which open up new questions and the unintended stagnation, normalization and tamping down of these new politicizing moments to unquestioned presuppositions. Skinner's project is, in a sense, to present a balanced view of both moments, now once again affirmed in the volumes *Renaissance Virtues* and *Hobbes and Civil Science* (2002b and c), without hiding a *Wertbezug* in favour of the former perspective. Maybe we can interpret the moment of foundationalization now, in the light of Skinner's self-criticism of the title and his later works on liberty and rhetoric, as a study of how certain political chances and intellectual resources were lost. What came to serve as 'foundations of modern political thought' was not only a contingent product of the Renaissance and Reformation struggles but also something that was for a long time accepted uncritically by later political theorists. It is in this perspective that we need to understand Skinner's analysis of the formation of the modern concept of the state.

In more formal terms, the priority of questions over answers also means a certain priority of interest in breaks and discontinuities over the continuities, a priority later explicitly affirmed by Skinner (1998, 111). In other words, the questions open up new and contingent horizons for action, but in order to respond to them we must turn to old intellectual resources, which, even when recontextualized for new political purposes, retain something of the old and establish a continuity with past debates.

The dualism between moments of discontinuity and continuity is also present in the titles of the two volumes, *The Renaissance* and *The Age of Reformation*. Both refer to something old to which we appear to 'return', while precisely such an attempt to return is impossible in the strict sense, but can play a role as a rhetorical strategy to alter the existing order. A key aspect of Skinner's analysis of the Renaissance is his attention to the insight that there is an irreparable abyss between the ancients and the world of thirteenth-century humanists: 'A new sense of historical distance was achieved, as a result of which the civilization of ancient Rome began to appear a wholly separate culture, one which deserved – and indeed required – to be reconstructed and appreciated as far as possible in its own distinctive terms' (Skinner 1978a I, 86).

The situation of the humanists was that of innovating ideologists. They had to face the novelty of their situation but made use of it by appealing to the ancient world as something that was more easily acceptable in their context than openly declaring that they were entering into a new world, for which there were as yet no conceptual tools.

The combination of a discontinuous set of questions as well as continuity in answers renders intelligible how the accentuation of older political languages, vocabularies and traditions helped Skinner write a history of lost possibilities and strange modes of thought in *The Foundations*. For example, his critique of Hans Baron's thesis on the origins of Renaissance humanist republicanism is only seemingly a question of dating the origin of this strain of thought. The main point for Skinner in predating the origins of this thought to the thirteenth century is to mark the presence of Roman elements, both Stoic and rhetorical, in a humanism that originated before the rise of scholasticism (cf. ibid., 27, 71–2). This defence leads him to revise earlier views about where to search for the modes of theorizing about politics, and here Skinner clearly moves closer to political practice, for example towards advice-books in the style of *ars dictaminis*.

A certain 'deconstruction' of the presentation of the intellectual world of a thinker is one of the main aspects of Skinner's *Foundations* that is frequently criticized by more traditional intellectual historians. Machiavelli's *Il Principe* and *Discorsi*, for example, are treated in different chapters, without asking the classical question concerning the compatibility of the two works (which is, then, done in the *Machiavelli* volume of 1981). Luther, in particular, is first presented as a strict advocate of obedience to worldly authorities, but then, some 100 pages later, this thesis is relativized, as a response to the changing situation. To understand this response, its presentation, content, point and illocutionary force, as complexes of a 'move in argument' is the main point.

Another consequence of Skinner's 'decentring' approach is, of course, a certain devaluation of the 'great names' in favour of the revival of forgotten authors and controversial pamphlets. One of his aims is 'to construct a general framework within which the writings of the more prominent theorists can be situated' (Skinner 1978a I, xi). This work is partly a history of losers at the cost of the 'mythology of prolepsis' of posterior interpretations. Yet, at the same time, it is connected with politically interpreting what counts in the history of ideologies. 'Systemic' works frequently tend towards the search for an eternal order, but they become interesting to Skinner when they are brought into the context of contemporary political controversies. Unlike Mesnard, he never presents the 'system' contained in Bodin's *Six livres de la république*. Rather he links Bodin's discussions on sovereignty with the crisis of French politics after the St Bartholomew massacre and analyses the structure of the work as an expression of the 'anti-Aristotelian canons of Ramist logic' (ibid., 291). Thus, the attempted systems themselves are historicized and considered from the perspective of the political point.

When Skinner speaks of a social and intellectual matrix, this should not be understood in a sense that renders the political agents as bearers of largely given roles or masks. On the contrary, the matrix is constituted through agency, through the opening up of new questions, through an activation of various layers of intellectual resources and through the unexpected consequences of the responses. It is the urgency of the political struggles that keeps the situation in motion, requiring innovation and inspiration from theory politicians, partly in search of a new stable order.

Ideologies and Legitimation

One of the main commitments of Skinner's *Foundations* is 'to write a history centred less on the classic texts and more on the history of ideologies' (Skinner 1978a I, xi). Compared with his programmatic views, especially in the 'Some Problems' essay of 1974, what is new here is that Skinner speaks of ideologies in the plural. By this he does not mean the nineteenth-century isms, or any morphological complexes around a given core like Michael Freeden (1996), or 'distorted' views. Skinner's main problem remains the relation between 'political theory and practice', which has been difficult to understand when remaining on the level of the classic texts. His advice to the historians of political thought is, then: 'But if they were instead to think themselves essentially as students of ideologies, it might become possible to illustrate one crucial way in which the explanation of political behaviour depends upon the study of political ideas and principles, and cannot meaningfully be constructed without reference to them' (Skinner 1978a I, xii).

Thus, ideologies refer mainly to what I have termed theory politics, and Skinner is above all interested in their legitimizing role. Indeed, it seems to me unnecessary to distinguish ideologies from languages or traditions, as these concepts are used in *The Foundations*. Skinner does not seem to make a systematic distinction when speaking of monarchism and republicanism, Lutheranism and Calvinism, Roman and Canon law, rhetoric and scholasticism as traditions, languages or ideologies. In all of these cases, the core consists of 'a vocabulary already normative within his society, a vocabulary which is capable of legitimating at the same time as describing' (ibid.). The main aspect of such vocabularies lay in their legitimizing potential.

Skinner's focus 'on the study of ideologies' also accentuates their role as resources to understand authors' points. In other words, 'to equip ourselves . . . with a way of gaining a greater insight into its author's meaning than we can ever hope to achieve simply from reading the text itself "over and over again"' (ibid., xiii). Here we can detect a further reason why he has not described 'thought systems' in detail. The wider intellectual horizon of each of the authors can rather be understood as a contextual element that facilitates our understanding of the different aspects of their current moves. Correspondingly, the writers are dealt with less as concrete persons than as agents who intervene in debates on contemporary theory politics. Or, to put it in another way, individuals are only interesting in so far as they facilitate the understanding of what they are doing when intervening in acute controversies.

Pocock's mode of treating languages and traditions as quasi-independent entities is not shared by Skinner, and this is perhaps one of the reasons he prefers to use the openly political concept of ideologies. Despite this, he treats rhetoric and scholasticism not only as different answers to the same problems, but as intellectual complexes, within which different questions appear problematic. Such ideologies are reservoirs of old controversies, bearing both their heuristic value and their inability to see the novelty over the contextual borderlines.

What Skinner is doing in *The Foundations* is to insist on the political flexibility of combining the resources of different ideologies. In other words, the historialization of the ideologies consists in their mixing with each other, combination, selective usage, transformation or even dissolution as separate intellectual currents. All this is, of course, due to their character as a response, which makes them, in the Skinnerian perspective, dependent on the shifting questions.

Combining a new problematic with old ideological resources is perhaps best manifested in Skinner's analysis of the Huguenot responses to the St Bartholomew massacre in France in 1572. Their first response preferred recourse to positive law within the domestic constitutional traditions and they evoked them against the centralizing tendencies in the contemporary French monarchy. Such attempts, most explicitly Hotman's *Francogallia* (1574), were criticized as historically deficient in the political debate of the time. Here Skinner analyses how the Huguenot leaders then shifted to another type of defence that could not be criticized as easily on seemingly 'factual' historical grounds. To find such a response, the author of the most famous Huguenot pamphlet, *Vindiciae contra tyrannos* (1579), was ready to make use of the intellectual resources of his Catholic adversaries, and indeed uses the conciliarist variant of natural law contractarianism (Skinner 1978a II, esp. 309–38).

The flexibility in the use of ideologies is another consequence of Skinner's principle of the primacy of political life over theorizing about it. But, as he has emphasized previously, he does not subscribe to the thesis of conventional 'political historians' that the connection 'between ideology and political action is a purely instrumental one' (Skinner 1978a I, xii). In other words, there must be limits to the legitimating capacity of different ideological tools, depending on how far they can be made acceptable in the prevailing context. This leads him to reformulate the problem of legitimacy in the following terms: 'Thus the problem facing an agent who wishes to legitimate what he is doing at the same time as gaining what he wants cannot simply be the instrumental problem of tailoring his normative language in order to fit his projects. It must in part be the problem of tailoring his projects in order to fit the available normative language' (ibid., xii–xiii).

More clearly than in 'Some Problems', Skinner claims that a political project must be adapted to use linguistic resources. By doing so he gives a more active role to 'theory politicians' in constructing and modifying political projects. Such a role can equally be that of legitimating a traditional *Realpolitik* which adapts to the certainly possible and acceptable within the audience or, on the contrary, claiming like Weber that without an attempt to transcend what is now possible we cannot attain the best possible results (for what is possible appears different within such a transcendence project than outside it) (cf. Weber 1917a, 514).

In comparison with the unilinear office-seeking perspective that Skinner adopted in the Bolingbroke essay, we can, of course, claim that the project to be 'tailored' may be regarded as aiming beyond the search for office. A more interesting interpretation could, however, be one in which the search for power is retained as the inherently ultimate aim of all politics, but in which the role of theory politics would consist of the specification of definite but partial shares of power.

The most interesting struggles for power, discussed in *The Foundations*, seem, indeed, to be of this kind. The struggle of Italian cities against the Empire, in particular the struggle of republican cities against princely forms of government, as well as the struggles of largely Protestant religious minorities in Germany, France, the Netherlands and Scotland, are struggles for some limited shares of power. The chances, duties and rights of resistance form a paradigm for these kinds of fragile shares of power which are always in need of legitimation. The papal, imperial and etatist claims of a unitary authority are treated as responses to such attempts to create power 'from below'. In this sense, we can clearly detect the Weberian tacit asymmetry of politics in *The Foundations*: the striving for power, precisely to change the existing distribution of power-shares, is the constitutive moment of politics-as-activity, whereas the defence of the status quo turns to politics only in response to such attempts to change.

The Formation of the Concept of the State

One of the main aims of Skinner's *Foundations* was a conceptual history of the formation of the modern concept of the state. In his Preface, Skinner legitimates his decision to close the book at the end of the sixteenth century by the argument that 'it was during this period . . . that the main elements of a recognizably modern concept of the State were gradually acquired' (Skinner 1978a I, ix). This concept is explicitly Weberian: 'One effect of this transformation was that the power of the State, not that of the ruler, came to be envisaged as the basis of government. And this in turn enabled the State to be conceptualized in distinctively modern terms – as the sole source of law and legitimate force within its own territory, and the sole appropriate object of its citizens' allegiances' (ibid., x).

It is from this admittedly teleological perspective that Skinner then turns 'from history to historical semantics – from the concept of the state into the word "State"' (ibid., x) with the following specific legitimation: 'The clearest sign that a society has entered into self-conscious possession of a new concept is, I take it, that a new vocabulary comes to be generated, in terms of which the concept is then articulated and discussed' (ibid.).

Before entering into a discussion of Skinner's version of the conceptual history of the state, it is worth making some remarks on previous, related enterprises. It was in the Germany of the early twentieth century that the question of whether we can speak of a 'state' in the Middle Ages (Georg Below, Heinrich Mitteis) was fiercely debated, especially among jurists and historians. Figgis's oft-quoted position is clearly indebted to this debate, in his case to the anti-etatist views of Gierke, as opposed to the centralist and ahistorical views of the dominant variant of legal positivism (Paul Laband etc.) in the constitutional law of the German Empire.

Max Weber's famous 'definition' in *Wirtschaft und Gesellschaft* (Weber 1922, 29) to which Skinner refers is only the tip of the iceberg. The Weberian state is a variant of *politischer Verband*, as such 'durchaus modern' (ibid., 30, cf. Weber 1919a, 35–6), a product of a specific and contingent history. In German jurisprudence, Weber's view of the state as a means (*Mittel*) was original: it was opposed to the German tradition that continued until Georg Jellinek's *Allgemeine Staatslehre* (1900), in which the state was characterized by its ends (*Zwecke*). Weber's political point is, of course: as a means or instrument the state can be used for a variety of ends, and the choice between them is a central subject of political struggle.

This demarcation of his concept of the state is already sufficient to distinguish Weber from the normative idealization of the state, as expressed in Heinrich Treitschke's state-worship in his lectures on *Politik* (published 1896) as well as in numerous academic pamphlets during World War I. The Treitschkean idea of a separate 'state morality' is entirely alien to Weber (cf. esp. his parody of 'organische Sozialethik' in Weber 1915, 220). Weber was no admirer of the formation of the modern 'patrimonial-bureaucratic' state, when the monopolization of violence and the centralization it required were realized at the cost of the autonomy of the medieval cities (esp. Weber 1922, 794–5). The state-bound character of modern politics, emphasized by Weber in *Politik als Beruf* (Weber 1919a, 35–6), is also for Weber a contingent condition, not a value.

Weber gives clues in the different chapters of *Wirtschaft und Gesellschaft* to the formation of a patrimonial-bureaucratic *Anstaltsverband*, as *Staat*, or *moderner Staat*. He manages in his late work largely to avoid the projection of the concept to ancient and medieval times, speaking in particular on 'Ständestaat' in quotation marks (cf. Anter 1995, 163–72). On the medieval Empire he writes: 'Ein Staatsbegriff unabhängig von der Privatperson des Kaisers existiert nicht' (Weber 1922, 437).

The most militant critique of the projection of nineteenth-century constitutional concepts, especially of the state, to the Middle Ages was presented in Otto Brunner's *Land und Herrschaft*. The book of the Austrian historian has notorious origins: the first edition was published after the *Anschluss* in 1939. His point is directed against the projection of the opposition between *Staat* and *Gesellschaft*, and in particular the criterion of definite borders, to medieval times (esp. Brunner 1939/1942, 126–7). Despite this, Brunner's work is still readable as an illustration of the possibilities of a non-territorial conception of *Land* and the non-monopolized violence of *Fehde*. It has obviously played no role in Skinner's work (Skinner to KP, January 1999).

The same can be said of the work of Carl Schmitt and his attempt to conceptualize the formation and gradual dissolution of the European state system, the *ius publicum Europaeum*, in terms of international law. At any rate, Schmitt's remarks on 'die neue Flächenordnung Staat' are in certain respects parallel to Skinner, although he is more interested in the territorial dimension of the concept. In particular, Schmitt emphasizes the role of France as 'der erste mit juristischem Bewußtsein souveräne Staat' (Schmitt 1950, 97). Furthermore, he stresses the role that it was in France that the religious civil war was first ended 'durch den Begriff der Souveränität des Königs', and remarks that in Bodin's *Six livres de la république* 'muss man das Wort Respublica bereits mit Staat übersetzen' (ibid.). Schmitt's views, especially that of the unification of the domestic policy of the state (ibid., 99), also shaped Reinhart Koselleck's dissertation *Kritik und Krise* (1959).

In the Anglophone debates no similar strongly historicizing debates on the concept of the state were conducted. Rather, the concept of the state was devalued in post-war political science and sociology in favour of the 'political system'. In the 1970s the situation began to change, and two major books on the history of the state were published: Perry Anderson's Marxist interpretation in *Lineages of the Absolutist State* (1974) and Michael Oakeshott's *On Human Conduct* (1975). Although they have little in common with Skinner's *Foundations*, they merit some discussion here.

Perry Anderson's approach gives no place to autonomous city-republics and their struggles with the Empire, and nor does the Reformation seem to play any constitutive role. Anderson does not offer us any textual analysis of the contemporary usage of the state-vocabulary. The counter-concept of the absolutist state is 'feudalism', and aside from class and economic relations, it is solely military organization that is used as key topic for the formation of the state. Anderson's perspective is, strangely enough, strongly 'national', meaning that the main states and empires are considered separately. It is this perspective that makes the opposition to Skinner obvious.

Michael Oakeshott's *On Human Conduct* is a very personal book with a terminology of its own. The more analytical discussions in the two first parts then culminate in the discussion 'On the Character of the Modern European State'. In terms of dating the formation of the state, of its contingent character as a mixed product of diverse intentions, Oakeshott's views well correspond to the Weberian (and Skinnerian) perspective. The difference is made by his claim that the state is a mixture of two definite but opposed types of human associations, for which he uses the Roman private law terms *societas* and *universitas*, the first referring to the common condition of its subjects, the second to their joint enterprise (Oakeshott 1975, esp. 198–206). Weber could share Oakeshott's critique of the *universitas*-type claim that the state is based on a common purpose, but the latter's contractarian opposition of the status of civilization to the status of nature plays no role for Weber. The concrete questions regarding the monopoly on violence and inter-state relationships are largely lacking from the Oakeshottian conceptualization of the state through modes of association.

Although they were personally on good terms, Skinner's few remarks on Oakeshott are critical (cf. Skinner 1965a, 2002d). Their interpretations of Hobbes especially move on different levels, as Oakeshott was not interested in the links to contemporary British politics that Skinner had sought during his early studies. Thus, it seems no wonder that Skinner had not noticed the remarkable change in Oakeshott's views that resulted in *On Human Conduct* (Skinner to KP, April 1999). In Oakeshott's review of *The Foundations* there was no confrontation with his own interpretation, but the main emphasis was placed on doubts concerning the applicability of the concept of the state in the English case (cf. Oakeshott 1980).

Compared with these more recent views, Skinner is much closer to the Weberian conception. With Weber he largely shares both a nominalist methodology – although Skinner does not seem to emphasize the *Chance* character of the concept of the state, as Weber explicitly does (Weber 1922, 13) – and a similar perspective on the formation of the state as well as a *Wertbezug* of the value of political action of the citizens. Weber's historical remarks on the

formation of the concept of the state are explicated and system-
atized by Skinner, as a specialist on the period who ties the perspective on linguistic action to the history of the conceptualization
of the state.

Some of Skinner's remarks on the conceptualization of the state
clearly have a teleological tone that he now regrets having used in
the book. Among the examples are the comments on the use of the
sibi princeps thesis against the Empire by Bartolus and Baldus.
According to Skinner, when they transferred this doctrine to civil
law, they were 'making the first decisive move towards articulating
the modern legal concept of the State' (Skinner 1978a I, 11). I think
we have no difficulty in understanding that a regional republic or
monarchy was possible, even as a player in 'international politics',
without necessarily turning into a state.

In the Conclusion, Skinner presents four different 'preconditions'
for speaking of a state:

> that the sphere of politics should be envisaged as a distinct branch
> of moral philosophy, a branch concerned with the art of government.
> (Skinner 1978a II, 349)

> that the independence of each *regnum* or *civitas* from any external and
> superior power should be vindicated and assured. (ibid., 351)

> that the supreme authority within each independent *regnum* should
> be recognised as having no rivals within its own territories as
> law-making power and an object of allegiance. (ibid.)

> that political society is held to exist solely for political purposes.
> (ibid., 352)

In other words, he sees in autonomy, sovereignty, monopoly and
secularity, four indispensable requirements that should be fulfilled
when we are speaking of a political unit as a state. In 'The State' he
adds the independence of the state from the rulers and the ruled to
this list: 'Rather the state must be acknowledged to be an entity with
a life of its own; an entity which is at once distinct from both rulers
and ruled and is able in consequence to call upon the allegiance of
both parties' (Skinner 1989b, 112).

For his analysis of the question of how far such conditions have
been fulfilled, Skinner uses a double approach: he undertakes both
an onomasiological analysis of the state-vocabulary and a semasiological analysis of the meanings in the use of this vocabulary. The
Conclusion of *The Foundations* can, thus, be regarded as Skinner's
first explicit exercise in conceptual history, and his double approach

corresponds to that of Koselleck's programme (cf. already Koselleck 1967b).

In *The Foundations*, Skinner's onomasiological analysis remains brief and the semasiological part is also limited to a few main steps. These two analyses are not presented in separate chapters, as in the 1989 article. Skinner's point of departure is the analysis of the Latin term *status*, and he concludes: 'Before the sixteenth century, the term *status* was only used by political writers to refer to one of two things: either the state or condition in which a ruler finds himself (the *status principis*) or else the general 'state of the nation' or condition of the realm as a whole (the *status regni*)' (Skinner 1978a II, 353). A step from the ruler's 'maintaining his state' to maintaining the state 'as an independent political apparatus' was, according to Skinner, mentioned by Patrizi in the late fifteenth century, but the most famous of the early users of the concept is, of course, Machiavelli, to whom the older textbooks in political science tended to attribute the coining of the concept. For Skinner, Machiavelli's usage is in most cases rather traditional, but he already speaks of 'the majesty of the state' (*la maestà dello stato*) (ibid., 353–4).

It is in France that the more abstract concept of the state was probably first used. Skinner insists on the connection of this usage with a centralized authority, bureaucratic apparatus and national boundaries. The first candidate for using a modern concept is the legal humanist Guillaume Budé in the early sixteenth century. In addition to traditional usages he also had more abstract ones, such as speaking of *les espèces d'éstat politique*, on some occasions also distinguishing between the state and the power of the prince (ibid., 354–5). As emphasized by Carl Schmitt, Skinner also regards the full shift to the modern usage to have been completed in the work of Jean Bodin, who, besides *république* also uses the term *état*, and who 'arrives at a conceptualization of the State as a locus of power which can be institutionalized in a variety of ways, and which remains distinct from and superior to both its citizens and their magistrates' (ibid., 356). Skinner then analyses analogous steps in England, the first user of the word 'state' probably being Thomas Starkey in 1535, whereas a conscious use of the concept, corresponding to that of Bodin, is presented by Walter Raleigh in his *Maxims of State* around 1600 (ibid., 356–7).

On the final page of *The Foundations*, Skinner then draws the conclusion: 'the acquisition of the concept of the State may be said to be the precipitate of the historical process which this book has attempted to trace', for this also meant a beginning of the analysis 'the rights and powers of the State' (ibid., 358). This characterization can be regarded as Skinner's definitive empirical answer to the Namierite or Marxist style of analysis, in which theories and concepts were regarded only as epiphenomena. For Skinner the formation of a new concept is not only a sign of change but a part of the process of change itself. In this sense, what Skinner writes on the role of the sixteenth-century formation of the concept of the state corresponds to Koselleck's programmatic view that concepts are, at least since the *Sattelzeit* around 1800, not only indicators but also factors of history (cf. e.g. Koselleck 1972a).

Skinner's discussion on the conceptual history of the state in the Conclusion of *The Foundations* is a first step. In a review article on Clifford Geertz's *Negara*, he refers to Geertz's anthropological studies on the political order in Bali, according to which 'the holding of supreme political power need not in the least be connected with the capability to employ coercive force or with the ability to make people to act contrary to their interests' (Skinner 1981d, 36). Skinner concludes that this may also challenge our view of the role of rituals: 'Perhaps our own rituals are far more than drapery; perhaps they too play an altogether different and more substantial role in political affairs' (ibid., 37). Pomp, ceremonies and rituals may be interpreted as a source of power, and the Balinese polity that Geertz analysed is, of course, not a state in the Weberian sense. Still, Skinner's point that rituals may be an inherent part of the modern state as well clearly indicates a dimension not thematized by Weber.

In 'The State', Skinner engages in a detailed manner in the variants of the vocabulary in the transition period from Latin to the vernacular languages (Skinner 1989b, 95). He extensively presents the pre-modern variants of the concept, especially of *lo stato* among Italian Renaissance writers, particularly in Machiavelli's usage, and leaves the less abstract usages as legitimate, not merely as steps towards 'the modern concept' (ibid., 95–102). Skinner attributes a role in the conceptualization to the republican writers who distinguished between the state and its rivals as a 'source of coercive power' (ibid., 107) as well as between 'the idea of governmental authority' and 'the powers of particular rulers of magistrates' (ibid., 108). A second, impersonating abstraction of the state is, however, due to the anti-republican writers, 'as a by-product of their arguments' (ibid., 116), which makes the state a unit independent of the people that constitute it. This was finally affirmed in the Hobbesian view 'that the duties of subjects are owed to the state, rather than to the person of a ruler' (ibid., 90). In addition, Skinner amplifies his remarks in the Geertz review by emphasizing the role of majesty: 'One outcome of distinguishing the authority of the state from that of its agents was thus to sever a time-honoured connection between the presence of majesty and the exercise of majestic powers' (ibid., 125–6).

In a more recent article, Skinner studies Hobbes's usage of theatrical metaphors for the constitution of a 'purely artificial person of the state' (Skinner 1999b). This analysis of the state as an artificial person is then taken into consideration in the revised version of 'The State', to which Skinner has also added an extensive discussion of natural law contractarian theories (*Vindiciae contra tyrannos*, Althusius, Pufendorf) as well as some counter-revolutionary thinkers (Barclay, Blackwood). The role of Hobbes's view appears even more decisive than before: 'The sovereign is an actor who plays the role of the state and thereby acts in its name' (Skinner 2002c, 403), and 'it is Hobbes who first speaks systematically and unapologetically in the abstract and unmodulated tones of the modern theorist of the sovereign state' (ibid., 419).

The clear difference between the 1989 and 2002 versions of 'The State' lies in the consistent attempt to purge teleological formulations from conceptual history. The self-criticism of teleological tendencies in *The Foundations* appears to correspond to the textual changes Skinner undertook when revising the article.

From the History of Ideas Towards a History of Concepts

One of the main points of Skinner's conceptual history of the state is his insistence on its revisionary, even revolutionary role for political vocabulary. It is thus with regard to this role that Skinner uses the formula that the state has become a 'master noun of political argument':

> The immediate outcome of this conceptual revolution was to set up a series of reverberations in the wider political vocabularies of the western European states. Once 'state' came to be accepted as the master noun of political argument, a number of other concepts and assumptions bearing on the analysis of sovereignty had to be reorganized or in some cases rejected. (Skinner 1989b, 123)

Perhaps it can be interpreted that, beginning with *The Foundations*, we can detect a shift in Skinner's genre of historical studies. His early works on Hobbes and others remained within the province of intellectual history, but he at least partially replaced this with conceptual history. He does not consider concepts as independent entities, but analyses them from the perspective of the theory politics of linguistic action. Still, compared to his work in the 1960s and early 1970s, the Skinner of *The Foundations* already gives strategic significance to the concepts in the study of political thought, and this shift is even more prominent in his later work.

This move towards a history of concepts is explicit in the essay 'The Idea of a Cultural Lexicon', commenting on Raymond Williams's *Keywords*, and proceeded towards an independent discussion of questions neglected by Williams, such as 'what exactly we can hope to learn about culture and society through studying the changing meaning of words' (Skinner 1979a, 205). What is remarkable, in retrospect, is that when asking such questions, Skinner had no knowledge of the *Geschichtliche Grundbegriffe* or *Historisches Wörterbuch der Philosophie*, although several volumes of both lexica had been already published (cf. Skinner 1999c).

A noteworthy point in Skinner's essay is the critique of Williams's view that 'equates "the word and the concept"' (Skinner 1979a, 206). He undertakes a thought experiment which allows him to imagine limit-situations when either a concept exists without a word or vice versa (ibid., 207), coming to the opinion that 'the surest sign that a group or society has entered into the self-conscious possession of a new concept is that a corresponding vocabulary will be developed, a vocabulary which can then be used to pick out and discuss the concept with consistency' (ibid., 207, for a parallel formulation Skinner 1978a II, 352).

How a concept can be 'possessed' is a formula that sounds strange for a nominalist such as Skinner, but perhaps he uses it precisely to refer to a linguistic resource at the disposal of the agents. Skinner's main point is to understand the conceptual controversies and changes in broader terms than those of meaning. Once again, the question regards the perspective of linguistic action, in which he 'decentralizes' the conceptual disagreements to three levels. Skinner summarizes his discussion as follows:

> ... we might be disagreeing about one of at least three different things, not all of which are self-evidently disagreements about meaning: we might be arguing about the criteria for applying the word; or about whether the agreed criteria are present in a given set of circumstances; or about what range of speech-acts the word can be used to perform. (ibid., 210–11)

The criteria 'in virtue of which the word or expression is standardly employed' (ibid., 209) refers to the legitimacy of a certain usage in the audience, the range of reference concerns the demarcation of the concept (ibid.) and the range of attitudes indicates what Skinner previously has formulated as the double descriptive-evaluative use of language. Formulae such as the 'proper' and 'correct' use of certain theories should, of course, be interpreted in the legitimating perspective, that is, as dependent on their acceptability to the audience. Still, such formulae indicate that in the late 1970s Skinner considered the audiences in question as relatively homogeneous, and for this reason assumed that there would be a 'standard' use for concepts, and to deviate from this standard would require a special legitimation, whereas that particular use was itself unproblematic.

Another point in the essay was to insist that conceptual controversies are not merely linguistic quarrels, but intertwined with 'kinds of knowledge and awareness we can hope to acquire about our social world through studying the vocabulary' (ibid., 219). In other words, Skinner emphasizes that the 'social' and 'linguistic' levels cannot be strictly separated from one another, in particular that conceptual commitments have wider consequences:

> . . . there are three main types of insight we can hope to gain: insights into changing social beliefs and theories; into changing social perceptions and awareness; and into changing social values and attitudes. I have thus attempted to supply at least a sketch of what seems to me most seriously lacking in Williams's book: an account of the sort of methodology we need to develop in order to use the evidence of our social vocabulary as a clue to the improved understanding of our social world. (ibid., 219–20)

These three levels of insight roughly correspond to the three modes of conceptual disagreement. From my perspective, the 'social' in Skinner's usage here is a euphemism for a view that conflicts about beliefs and theories, perceptions and awareness, values and attitudes always have a political dimension. In this sense, the formula corresponds both to his prioritization of the political life over theorizing about it and to the constitutive role of theories in the very 'reality' of political life itself.

The Skinnerian Revolution

In 1995 the *Times Literary Supplement* published a list of 'The hundred most influential books since the war'. A committee led by

Ralf Dahrendorf with members such as François Furet and Timothy Garton Ash had selected a list of mainly non-fiction works in the humanities. It is no wonder that *The Foundations of Modern Political Thought* was included among the fifteen books of the 1970s together with John Rawls's *A Theory of Justice*, Albert Hirschman's *Exit, Voice and Loyalty* as well as Clifford Geertz's *The Interpretation of Cultures*. The last two were Skinner's colleagues in Princeton, as was Richard Rorty, whose *Philosophy and the Mirror of Nature* for some reason was located to the 1980s. Otherwise the list of '1980s and beyond' is dominated by rather conventional authors, such as Raymond Aron, Norberto Bobbio or Ernest Gellner.

What is absent from the political literature is at least equally interesting. No feminist thinkers, not even Carole Pateman's *The Sexual Contract*, or post-modernist works such as Jean-François Lyotard's *Le différend* are included, nor Michael Oakeshott's *On Human Conduct*. Jürgen Habermas and Ulrich Beck may have been excluded as rivals to Dahrendorf. Without John Pocock's *Machiavellian Moment*, such French studies as Claude Nicolet's *L'idée républicaine en France* (1982) or Pierre Rosanvallon's *Le moment Guizot* (1985), and Reinhart Koselleck's essays published in *Vergangene Zukunft* (1979), Skinner's *Foundations* appears in a rather strange company. I wonder whether the selectors understood its character both as a part of a genre (which they would have missed otherwise) and as an attempt to reach beyond its confines.

Among the contemporary classics, Quentin Skinner's *The Foundations* should undoubtedly be included. Like all of the works I just mentioned, it is a thesis book, highly polemical and with a profiled perspective of its own. To a certain extent, it shares the main 'fault' of all thesis books, namely not going into details in the empirical analysis: they must always be complemented with the patient work of *Stoffhubers* – and their works reassessed by still others with a *Sinnhuber* leaning. Even when compared with the work of the historians Pocock or Nicolet, Skinner's *The Foundations* clearly shows more patience towards the plurality of conceptions among the past agents, as a corollary to his perspective on linguistic action which queries the agent's own problematics, vocabulary and intentions. In this sense, his perspective consciously avoids an over-simplification of the past and does not give ready-made suggestions for the analysis of the present.

For the period between 1978 and 1982 I have found some thirty-five reviews of *The Foundations*. The sheer number already indicates that the book could not easily be neglected, at least within the

Anglophone province of political thought and intellectual history –
remarkable authors, some of them surely Skinner's friends, such
as John Pocock (1979), John Dunn (1979), Judith Shklar (1979) and
Donald R. Kelley (1979), others representing opposing views, such
as Michael Oakeshott (1980), Nathan Tarcov (1982) or Kenneth
Minogue (1981). Also other notable scholars, such as Richard
Ashcraft (1981), G. E. Aylmer (1979), David Beetham (1980), Janet
Coleman (1980) and Keith Thomas (1979), have expressed their
opinions on *The Foundations*.

By reading the reviews one could, however, hardly imagine what
Skinner was dealing with in *The Foundations*. Particularly in comparison with the early comments on Skinner's methodological
writings, the reviewers, almost without exception, deal with *The
Foundations* in a respectful tone. Skinner, who was named Professor
of Political Science at Cambridge the year *The Foundations* was published, has clearly shifted away from the role of the 'angry young
methodologist' to that of the respected colleague, whose achievement could not be denied.

The impression remains, however, that contemporary reviewers
did not detect the singularity of Skinner's book. Of course, this has
been the case with many other pivotal books: Max Weber's *Politik
als Beruf* was not understood as a conceptual rethinking of Weimar
Germany, Hannah Arendt's *Human Condition* received no better
treatment in the United States of the late 1950s (or in West Germany
in the early 1960s), and the reviewers of Jean-Paul Sartre's *Critique
de la raison dialectique* in France of the early 1960s only touched on
the most obvious layers of the narrative in that highly idiosyncratic
book.

Independent of reviews or commentaries, Skinner's *The
Foundations* has become a reference to which scholars of political
thought, not only the specialists of the period, can locate themselves. An explicit reference is most obvious among Skinner's
former students, although they, as critical students always do, try
to transcend the work of their teacher. Almost curious is the
combination of critique and deference in Richard Tuck's Preface to
his *Philosophy and Government*:

> I therefore decided that my volume would in a sense be a very unfair
> project: it would take for granted (to some extent) Skinner's work on
> the character of sixteenth-century constitutionalism, and would pay
> less attention to the heirs of that movement than to their modern
> rivals. In particular, a proper understanding of *raison d'état* theory

became the first priority, and the search for that led me to a reconsideration of the earlier Renaissance. (Tuck 1993, xii)

Thus, Skinner's work has partly been turned into an always available reference volume, in which we can check on theories, interpretations and debates, and which can then be revised or complemented with studies of topics neglected or demarcated outside the time-span discussed. In such a treatment, I am afraid, Skinner's revision of the genre of studying political thought as a part of political life will easily be left in the background if not entirely misunderstood.

I have discussed above the substantial revisions in the interpretation of political thought included in *The Foundations* in some respects. To them we could add further ones. Highly relevant both for Skinner's later work and even for the more general discussion is, for example, the emphasis on the role of rhetoric in the Italian city-republics and the first stage of humanism, an emphasis that is almost entirely neglected even in Pocock's *Machiavellian Moment*, insisting on the links to Aristotle and Polybius in the Florentine 'civic humanism'. This emphasis on rhetoric is partly due to Skinner's revision of the type of commentary literature he considers to be noteworthy: instead of the philosophers he has, rather, stressed the political dimensions in the work of literary scholars, such as P. O. Kristeller, and even found less known but important studies in that field.

In retrospect we can also find that Skinner's entire research programme for the oncoming twenty years was already, to a considerable extent, indicated in *The Foundations*. We can always take *The Foundations* as point of reference in Skinner's own work, particularly with regard to the discussions of his studies on Machiavelli, republicanism and rhetorical culture as well as the key political concepts of state and liberty, and along with them, the relative transition from intellectual to conceptual history in the study of political thought. Thus, the introduction of a new genre of style of dealing with political thought has, at the same time, opened up new horizons of research on which Skinner has more or less exclusively concentrated in his more recent work.

After almost twenty-five years there is still no volume comparable to Skinner's *The Foundations*, either concerning the period of his own interests or for any other period of European political thought. Certainly, it is hard to imagine that someone could imitate what Skinner has done in *The Foundations*. His methodological programme may be shared to a large extent, but neither the specialist competence (including the mastering of languages) nor the vision of the book can be shared, and therefore a simply methodological form of imitation would be rather mechanical.

More specifically, Skinner's reversal of relations between political thought and 'political life' in *The Foundations* gives us a model of how to study political thought by giving a priority to politics over thought. As compared with conventional historical studies on political philosophy, Skinner alters the perspective from the *vita contemplativa* to the *vita activa*. He gives us a model of how to study politics by studying theories, concepts and their role in the shifting horizons of the possible, using the well-known facts and more disputed narratives of the events precisely as auxiliary contextual instruments.

The perspective of linguistic action helps Skinner to give the seemingly harmless everyday activity of politics qualities of its own, inherently connected to theorizing through the perspective of legitimation. The study of theory politics is no mere preliminary phase to be replaced or at least complemented by the history of events or by the 'comparative politics' of facts. It is a specific, though surely one-sided, but exactly for this reason highly interesting form of making politics-as-activity intelligible. Even if I consider speaking about politics-as-activity at the time of the Renaissance and Reformation as anachronistic, because the vocabulary of the activity-concept was created only during the nineteenth and early twentieth century, I can gladly accept that Skinner's studies on the theory politics of these distant times helps us to understand the microscopic dimensions of the politics of the time.

In summary, I think that Skinner's *The Foundations* is not only a modern classic but also a revolutionary work in political theorizing. It has given us a paradigm – in the Wittgensteinian sense of an exemplary model – according to which we can use the perspective of studying thought, the horizon of the possible, as an indispensable perspective on studying politics-as-activity in general.

5

Rethinking Political Liberty

Liberty as the Contested Concept *Par Excellence*

Liberty is probably the most controversial concept in twentieth-century politics. Almost everyone defends it in the Western world, but this only moves the debate further, to concern conceptions of liberty. In order to understand the controversies surrounding liberty, histories of the concept are necessary but rarely written.

Quentin Skinner was among the first to undertake such a project in the Anglophone world. I first relate his views to a broader continental debate in order to consider Skinner's politics-related variant of negative liberty beyond the narrow confines of the Anglophone debate. Once again, I will take Max Weber, who advocates both a 'modern' and a 'negative' concept of liberty and understands this liberty as inherently political, as the starting point for the discussion (cf. also Palonen 1999a).

Max Weber clearly shares Benjamin Constant's rejection of 'ancient liberty', claiming that the freedom of personal life-conduct (*Lebensführung*) was absent in the ancient *polis*: Weber characterized the *polis* as a military camp (*Heerlager*) or guild of warriors (*Kriegerzunft*) (Weber 1909, 124; 1922, 809). Weber also rejected the quasi-natural criteria of citizenship in the *polis* and preferred to them the voluntary criteria of the *homines oeconomici* of the autonomous medieval cities (Weber 1909, 262; 1922, 805). A 'republican' element is present in Weber's admiration of the medieval cities as units of counter-rule based on voluntary *coniuratio* against the patrimonial rule of the Empire. Weber's legitimation of the autonomy of cities was based on the chances of personal life-conduct (Weber 1922, 742, 809) and not on the value of the common participation or of the autonomy of the city as such.

That liberty for Weber is negative, individual and even private, does not make it unpolitical, as in the contractarian legitimation of human rights in terms of natural law. Weber regards it as an empirical question, whether contracts increase individual liberty or decrease it (ibid., 439) and analyses subjective rights as sources of power (*Machtquellen*) (ibid., 398–9). He considers them as counter-powers to autocratic or bureaucratic rule (Weber 1906b, 98–9; 1918, 222). Similarly, Weber also defends democracy as an expression of the possibility of alternation in government (cf. Weber's letter to Michels, 31 December 1910, *Briefe 1909–1910* (1994), 761).

Due to his pessimistic analysis of the trend towards universal bureaucratization, Weber searches for counterweights that could allow at least some parcels of 'individualistic' freedom of movement. As such he advocates parliamentary government and democratization, with the formation of competent professional politicians, who could break down the 'rule of officialdom' (*Beamtenherrschaft*), so characteristic to Wilhelmine Germany (Weber 1917b and 1918). In this sense, he regards the politics of representative democracy as a expression of freedom.

An existential moment of freedom is further implied in Weber's concept of *Lebensführung*, when speaking of the necessity of choosing the *Sinn* of his own life (Weber 1919b, 20). Analogously, the politician has to choose not only between policies but also between incompatible but indispensable criteria of judgement, such as the requirements of the ethics of conviction and the ethics of responsibility (Weber 1919a, 88). The link between individual and political freedom lies in his understanding of citizens as 'occasional politicians' (*Gelegenheitspolitiker*) (ibid., 41).

The common idea in Weber's multiple faces of freedom can perhaps be formulated as the insight into freedom-as-contingency, not in terms of hazard, but in terms of the omnipresence of *Chancen*. The 'Weberian moment' in political thought consists of turning the analysis of *Chancen* into a means of rendering intelligible human actions.

In the Weberian view, human beings are equally 'condemned to freedom' as they are to Sartre and, in so far as they are political agents, that is, as they dispose of any shares of power, they cannot dispense with acting politically. In other words, human actions are free, as there cannot be 'sufficient grounds' for any of the alternative courses, but one has to choose to act, as the activity cannot be controlled in advance. Or, to put it in Sartrean terms, the individuals are always 'sovereign' agents: 'la souveraineté, c'est l'homme lui-même en tant que l'acte' (Sartre 1960, 696). It is an expression of freedom that in the plural and conflictual world of politics the results of action regularly deviate from the projects of all agents (cf. Weber 1919a, 80–1) and lead to counter-finalities, as Sartre would say. This, however, can also be considered as an enrichment of the situation and as an alternation of the horizon of chances (cf. for example Sartre 1960, 882).

The dimension of contingency connecting freedom and politics can also be expressed in Arendtian (1958) terms: politics is free because it is action and not fabrication. Freedom is the 'principle' of politics, 'to be free and to act is the same', and the virtuosity of performance is the freedom expressed in politics-as-performing-art (Arendt 1968, 152–4).

Revising the Conceptual History of Liberty

Quentin Skinner's interest in the concept of liberty is, above all, historical. His first question concerns the proper understanding of definite conceptions of liberty, especially early Renaissance conceptions, those of Machiavelli, and of Hobbes and his adversaries around the time of the English Civil War. A second question concerns the conceptual history of a neglected line of political liberty, which Skinner first calls 'republican' and then alters to 'neo-Roman'. This historical criticism is directed against that specific mythology of prolepsis that results from a tendency to monopolize the concept to a certain 'liberal' or narrowly interpreted 'negative' concept of liberty, aiming to show both the presence of historical alternatives in the past and how the monopolization tendency has been successful due to a gross misrepresentation of alternatives.

With this historical revision Skinner also contributes to contemporary debates on political liberty. But he does not advocate any definite view as applicable today. 'I'm not really interested in taking sides,' he says in the *Cogito* interview (Skinner 1997c, 76): 'I'm not asking you to say "Machiavelli looks a better theorist than Ronald Dworkin." I'm asking you to think about a theory that might have a very different structure and to ruminate about it' (ibid., 75).

Thus, his search through the past for alternatives does not make him 'illiberal', an expression used on Skinner's interpretation of

Machiavelli by Rahe (2000, 278). In reply to a query among historians in the *Times Literary Supplement*, Skinner perhaps best formulates his programme for the study of the history of the concept of liberty, promised for discussion in a forthcoming book:

> Among the moral and political writers of the Renaissance, it was widely agreed that the only way to maximize the liberty of the individual must be to ensure that everyone plays an active role in political affairs. Only by such participation, it was argued, can we hope to prevent the business of government from falling into hands of a governing class. Since the seventeenth century, however, the leading Western democracies have repudiated this view in favour of a strongly contrasting one. It has become an axiom of liberal theories about the relationship between government and the governed that the only way to maximize freedom must be to minimize the extent to which public demands can legitimately be made upon our private lives.
>
> When and why did we come to change our beliefs in this way about the most fundamental concept in our political vocabulary? By answering these questions, a great work of history could I think be written of a kind that no one has hitherto attempted. Such a history would embody the kind of irony that the greatest historians have always particularly relished. For it is surely ironic that the development of the Western democracies should have been accompanied by the atrophying of the ideal that the government of the people should be conducted by the people. Such a history might also prompt us, as the great historians have always done, to think anew about our present predicament. We might find ourselves reflecting in particular on whether the distinction we have inherited between the public and the private is one that we ought to be upholding or seeking to revise. (Skinner 1989c)

As we can see, Skinner has so far only partially carried out this programme. But it gives a guide to reading the fragments, including *Liberty before Liberalism*, in a more detailed way. Above all, Skinner attributes to certain past positions a necessary relationship between the maximization of individual liberty and intervention in politics. His interest is to study those rhetorical moves which contributed to the fact that such a once evident possibility was lost to sight. The remembrance of lost possibilities also serves as an instrument of critique towards present-day Anglophone debate on liberty, especially with regard to the identification of views on liberty as the private–public distinction, and the desirability to uphold such a distinction as quasi-natural.

Liberty of the City-republics

The significance of independent non-monarchical cities throughout Europe, especially in the *regnum italicum*, is well known. In *The Foundations*, Skinner revises the received view in two respects: predating the Renaissance to the thirteenth-century formation of theoretical defences of these republics, and underlining the role of Roman, legal, Stoic and rhetorical legitimation of liberty for the liberty of the cities. He regards these city-republics as a rare expression of the political liberty of that time, and, against the common view of historians, explicitly argues that an ideology of liberty was also constructed among the early defenders of the city-republics:

> It is apparent from a number of official proclamations that the city propagandists usually had two quite clear and distinct ideas in mind when defending their 'liberty' against the Empire: one was the idea of their right to be free from any outside control of their political life . . . ; the other was the idea of their corresponding right to govern themselves as they thought fit – a defence of their existing Republican constitutions. (Skinner 1978a I, 6–7)

The last aspect is discussed by Skinner on various occasions particularly with regard to the work of Latini and other thirteenth-century 'rhetorical' thinkers, by some *glossatores* (Azo) and especially *post-glossatores* jurists (Bartolus, Baldus), by Marsilius and the conciliarists indebted to Aristotelianism, by Bruni, Salutati and other fifteenth-century humanists, again making the connection to the rhetorical tradition. The *topoi* of citizen participation in government and the delimitation of the powers of rulers and officials were the key elements of this defence of liberty, whereas the specific legitimations could differ considerably (cf. esp. Skinner 1988b, 1990a, 1992a).

The most detailed of Skinner's studies on the early modern Renaissance are two long contributions to the Siena frescoes of Ambrogio Lorenzetti. He practises a history of political concepts through the means of the wall-paintings of Lorenzetti from the 1330s. Skinner criticizes the received opinion, affirmed by contemporary scholars such as Nicolai Rubinstein, according to which the world view involved in the paintings is Aristotelian. Instead, he connects Lorenzetti's work to the Roman moralists and to the rhetorical political theory proposed by Brunetto Latini and others during the thirteenth century. According to Skinner's thesis, 'Lorenzetti's cycle is best interpreted as an expression of the pre-humanist rhetorical culture' (Skinner 1987a, 3). He illustrates not only the distinct preference for a republic and elected government but also how both in the conception of peace through contest and in the rejection of the Aristotelian natural sociability of human beings, the rhetorical humanists represented a particular legitimation of republican liberty, regarded as a means to *grandezza*. With this interpretation Skinner can obtain a more complete and at key points revised interpretation of Lorenzetti's frescoes (ibid., cf. also Skinner 1999a).

On another occasion Skinner insists more explicitly on the potential opposition between the ideals of peace and liberty among the Renaissance humanists. He refers to Poggio Bracciolini's views: 'If freedom and self-government are to be upheld against the encroachments of tyranny, it may sometimes be necessary to fight for liberty instead of insisting on peace at any price' (Skinner 1990a, 128). The pre-humanist writers specifically connect equality and liberty through election:

> . . . they treat it as a distinctive virtue of elective systems that they guarantee the equality of all citizens before the law. No one's interests are excluded, no one is unfairly subordinated to anyone else. But this, they point out, is in effect to advance a thesis about political liberty. It is to say that only under elective regimes are individuals able to live a free way of life, unconstrained by any unjust dependence or servitude. (ibid., 133–4)

More clearly than in *The Foundations*, here Skinner makes liberty a counter-concept to dependency or servitude. As in Weber, by quoting the 'city air renders free' principle, liberty here not only marks an opposition towards monarchical or hereditary regimes, but also to the type of feudal relations predominant outside the free cities, as opposed to 'a free way of life'. The city was a *locus* of such a free way of life and deserved to be defended as such.

Perhaps even more crucial is the role given to elections as a manifestation of liberty. Studies on 'electoral behaviour' or 'rational voting' tend to hide both the elementary condition of holding elections and the contingency of the outcome. Elections do not make sense if voters do not have a significant choice to make. The plurality of candidates and the absence of an imperative mandate appear as a condition of speaking of elections in the political sense. Of course, Skinner makes clear that in the medieval cities the 'vote was restricted to male householders', with the additional criteria of taxation or residence (Skinner 1992a, 60). The criterion that votes would be counted and not weighted may not have always been upheld either. Still, elections appear to have been a key event in the polity of the city-republics, and the contingency of their outcome was remarkable.

The electoral regime also signified the temporary nature of rule: 'all political offices . . . should only be held for strictly limited periods of time' (ibid.). The central point of this short electoral term, as used in the ancient *poleis* as well as in the Italian city-republics, was to hold governing officials in check: 'to ensure that their holders acquire a status no higher than that of the salaried representatives of the people who elect them' (ibid., 62). The charismatic moment of modern elective regimes, the possibility of re-election as the key instance of controlling the performance, to some extent also existed in the Renaissance city-republics, but the amateur ideal of politicians was prominent in the republican ideology. As Skinner writes, their contemporaries soon began to consider the city-republics and their self-government as 'simply a recipe for chaos' (ibid., 59) and the republican ideals were tossed to the margins of political theorizing.

There are other objections, such as the applicability of the electoral model solely to small political units, which were considered to be militarily inferior to the new national monarchies. The *homo oeconomicus* character, stressed by Weber, was valuable in so far as it made citizenship at least formally voluntary, as opposed to the quasi-natural and obligatory citizenship of the ancient *poleis* and of the new national monarchies. An appropriate principle of representation was also lacking, for it was the privileges that were represented (cf. Weber 1922, 784).

Still, Skinner's discussion of the self-governing republic cannot simply be reduced to a defence of municipal autonomy. As an expression of political liberty 'self-government is no mere utopian fantasy, but is capable of being turned into political reality' (Skinner 1992a, 60). If the self-governing cities are regarded in terms of legitimating liberty, their practical consequences appeared to be fatal in connection with a situation in which the dominant trend was that of replacing empires by national monarchies or states. For Skinner the point, however, lies particularly in the role of political participation as a necessary condition for individual liberty: 'It follows that a willingness to participate in the political process, to seek one's own highest goals within the public sphere, must in turn be a necessary condition of securing one's own liberty' (ibid., 68).

This thesis, corresponding to Weber's view of self-government as an instrument for the *homines oeconomici*, leads Skinner to Machiavelli. For Skinner, the *Discorsi* of Machiavelli is the very paradigm of a discussion of the inherent connections between political and individual liberty.

Machiavelli as a Philosopher of Liberty

In Quentin Skinner's *Machiavelli* (1981a) the chapter on *Discorsi* is entitled 'The philosopher of liberty'. For historians of political thought this aspect of Machiavelli's thought is by no means the most obvious one, and even in republican interpretations of Machiavelli, such as Pocock's, the dimension of liberty is subordinated to stability and the fight against *fortuna* and corruption. Thus, Skinner's invocation of Machiavelli as a main theorist of political liberty is provocatively directed against both the historians who specialize in Machiavelli and his time and the contemporary theorists of liberty.

Skinner's reply to the compatibility between the 'advice-book' *Il Principe* and the openly republican writings of Machiavelli, especially that of *Discorsi sopra la prima deca di Tito Livio*, is strictly historical. It is only after the disappointment with his courtesy to the Medicis that Machiavelli began to participate in the meetings of *Orti Oricellari*, and it was as a result of these debates that he decided to write his *Discorsi* (Skinner 1981a, 48–50).

In *Machiavelli* Skinner deals with the origins of Machiavelli's views on liberty through his political experiences in the Florentine diplomacy and militia. In the *Discorsi* the connections to Roman authors, Livy as well as Cicero and Sallust, play a prominent role. The classical dimension in the Machiavellian defence of republican liberty, and probably the one which is the most difficult to understand today, concerns the role of liberty as a means to greatness, the main problem of the *Discorsi* being 'why the city of Rome in particular managed to attain "supreme greatness" and to produce such "great results"' (ibid., 51). According to Skinner, such greatness is only achieved if *virtù* 'should be possessed by the citizen body as a whole' (ibid., 54) and it is corruption that 'is invariably fatal to liberty' (ibid., 55). In the republics, corruption more or less takes the role of a malign *fortuna* that has to be fought through the *virtù* of all citizens.

More detailed discussions about the conceptual potential and the political implications of Machiavelli's concept of political liberty have been presented by Skinner in a number of articles since 1983. In these articles the emphasis is less strictly historical, and Skinner has been criticized for constructing interpretations that do not correspond to the views of the historical Machiavelli (Ivison 1997, 71–8). Admittedly, Skinner aims at criticizing contemporary assumptions by constructing a liberty that is negative, individual and political at the same time. Machiavelli serves as an example of a historical ideal type, through which we can reject conventional classifications: 'it is apt to seem much less convincing to suggest that a concept *might* be coherently used in an unfamiliar way than to show that it *has* been put to unfamiliar but coherent uses' (Skinner 1984, 198).

The point of such a procedure is certainly a one-sided accentuation. Skinner's main thesis concerning Machiavelli's conception of liberty remains, however, historical, more of a radical return to Roman thought than the previous humanist thinkers: 'My historical thesis . . . is that . . . perhaps his most central concern is to address that view of *libertas* which had laid at the heart of Roman republican political thought, but had subsequently been obliterated by the very different understanding of the concept characteristic of the middle ages' (ibid., 204).

In criticizing contemporary authors, Skinner argues that Machiavelli defines liberty in a way closely connected with contemporary views on negative liberty, as an 'absence of constraint' (ibid., 206). Thus, to 'speak of liberty as a matter of being independent of other social agents, and in consequence able to pursue one's own ends, is to echo one of the most familiar formulae employed by contemporary theorists of negative liberty' (ibid.). The 'existential' choice of one's ends is thus not at all problematized. Skinner is not deceived into regarding Machiavelli's 'patriotism' as an expression of a 'positive' conception of liberty. This becomes clear from the following paraphrase of Machiavelli's conception:

> He agrees that the overwhelming majority of citizens in any polity can safely be assumed to have it as their fundamental desire to lead a life of personal liberty. A few men, it is true, will always want instead to dominate others . . . But most men 'simply want not to be ruled', they want to be able 'to live as free men' (*vivere liberi*), pursuing their own ends as far as possible without insecurity or unnecessary interference. They want, in particular, to be free (*liberi*) to marry as they choose; to bring up their families without having to fear for their honour or their own welfare; and to be in the position 'freely' (*liberamente*) to possess their own property.

> This is what it means 'to enjoy personal liberty' (*la libertà*); and this
> is what enables people to recognise and rejoice in the fact that
> 'they have been born as free men (*liberi*) and not as slaves'. (Skinner
> 1983, 4)

These examples illustrate dimensions that were considered essential to freedom in Machiavelli's time. Conceptually, this quotation shows that liberty is, above all, a counter-concept of slavery: men are either free or slaves, no intermediate stages between them are acknowledged. Freedom from 'insecurity' and from 'interference' are, as compared with the freedom/slavery pairing, questions of expediency, in which you have to avoid 'unnecessary' restrictions of liberty. Thus, in principle, already here we can see that some interference may be considered necessary by Machiavelli, if it is understood as an instrument of freedom against falling into the state of slavery.

The condition of freedom is related to the ways of living that prevail or legitimate the polity, and here Machiavelli follows the tradition of city-republics in so far as he considers conquest and tyranny as parallel threats to the free way of life.

> While these are the ends that most of us desire above all, there is no
> possibility of our being able to attain them, according to Machiavelli,
> unless we live in a community of which it can be already said that it
> enjoys *uno vivere libero*, a free way of life. It must be kept free from
> subjection to the will of any particular individual or faction; free from
> any *dependenza* or *servitù*, whether imposed by a conqueror in the
> form of 'external servitude' or by a tyrant who arises from within the
> community's own political system. (ibid., 4)

The expressions *dependenza* or *servitù* can specify the freedom–slavery opposition, as applied to the practices of the contemporary era in so far as it is differentiated from the conditions of antiquity. It is in this perspective that the liberty of the polity appears to Machiavelli as a necessary condition of the possibility of individuals to live freely. This assumption of a necessary relation between public and individual liberty, then, allows Machiavelli to speak of common good or public interest. This is legitimated by the dangers of corruption and tyranny. For Skinner it is, indeed, irrelevant, whether such a link can 'really' be upheld – for Machiavelli's time or our own. The point is, rather, that if such a necessary connection has been established as a part of Machiavelli's intellectual horizon, the presence of such a connection, then, renders intelligible how it has been possible for Machiavelli to argue for something that today appears to be oxymoronic, namely an interdependence of liberty and service. 'If we wish to maximise our freedom to control our private affairs without anxiety or interference, the moral is that we must first turn ourselves into wholehearted servants of the public good' (ibid.).

All this means that the conditions of individual liberty appear to Machiavelli in terms that today seem strange. Freedom requires above all a delimitation of the human tendency to self-deception:

> For Machiavelli, accordingly, the fundamental threat to liberty is not simply posed by the fact of human selfishness; it is rather that, in pursuing their self-interested desires, men are at the same time self-deceived. . . . whenever we corruptly permit or pursue such policies hostile to the common good, we begin to subvert the free institutions of our community, and hence our own personal liberty at the same time. (ibid.)

Skinner's point here is that the insight into a necessary condition between a free form of polity and individual liberty allows us to cast attention on the possibility of self-deception. He paraphrases what he considers to be Machiavelli's most precise statement: 'it is only those who live under republican forms of government who can hope to retain any element of personal liberty to pursue their chosen ends' (Skinner 1984, 207). In this respect, Machiavelli's view closely follows those of the pre-humanist republicans on elective government.

Thus, unlike many other theorists of freedom, Machiavelli does not share the assumption that every person is always the best judge of their own interests. Such an assumption would easily lead to self-destructive consequences for liberty. According to Skinner's thesis, Machiavelli manages to transcend the most immediate aims 'without having recourse, even implicitly, to the idea of objective reasons or higher selves' (Skinner 1983, 5) (cf. in this respect also Skinner's discussion of Habermas in 1982a).

Machiavelli discusses various measures to overcome the dangers of self-deception. As compared with the less effective measures, such as education, Machiavelli relies, in the tradition of Rome and early Renaissance republicanism, on the force of law:

> The indispensable role of the law is thus to deter us from *corruzione* and impose on us the 'artificial necessity' of behaving as *virtuosi* citizens by making it 'less eligible'. . . to follow our natural tendency

to pursue our own interests at the expense of the common good. . . .
In a strikingly Rousseauvian phrase, he adds that all citizens ought
ideally to be 'chained by the laws' as a means to coerce them into
respecting the ideal of liberty and behaving 'in a well-ordered way'.
(Skinner 1983, 9)

Once again, Machiavelli uses expressions that appear oxymoronic
to many theorists of liberty, namely the claim that liberty and law,
and even more radically, liberty and coercion, are not logically
opposed, but in an empirical relationship with each other. From his
perspective, the role of law and coercion is instrumentally related
to the opposition between freedom and slavery.

In the passage Skinner refers, however, to another conceptual
opposition of equal significance to Machiavelli, that between
'natural' and 'artificial', as a further dimension of liberty, namely
that of a reflected choice. For Machiavelli, liberty is something
artificial, a product of human activities, and not a natural criterion of the status of all human beings. That which appears as
'natural' is regarded as something unreflected, a tendency that is
followed most easily, if other modes of conduct are not made
explicit or given a fair chance as an unconventional alternative. To
follow one's 'natural tendency' is not forbidden, but it should be
based on a reflected choice – in which case the tendency in question would no longer be natural. For to be free it is not enough to
do just anything possible, but also to choose between the available
possibilities.

Law and coercion cannot, in the Machiavellian conceptual
horizon, be regarded exclusively as restrictions on freedom. They
can also be used as instruments for making choices between real
alternatives and not just a quasi-natural question of tendencies or
inclinations. As presented by Skinner, there is nothing patronizing,
no appeal to 'objective grounds' for doing something, in this Machiavellian usage of law and coercion. The coercive force of law serves
as an instrument of the 'empowerment' of agents themselves to
detect a horizon of alternatives and to face in a reflected manner the
choice between them. It is in this sense that the Rousseauvian
phrase of forcing human beings to be free has a clear political point:
'the law is rather to be seen as a liberating agency, one that serves
to constrain us – if our legislators have been wise – in just such
a way that we are released from the bondage which our natural
selfishness would otherwise impose on us, and are granted our
freedom by means of being coerced' (ibid., 13).

Here two further points are worth noticing. First of all, the 'bondage' of 'our natural selfishness' alludes to Machiavelli's view that what is merely 'natural' is analogous to the state of slavery. In other words, slavery is not only a juridical status of certain human beings, but, at least metaphorically, it expresses a tendency in all human beings to neglect the chances of liberty and to always follow a line of conduct that appears as natural or the least demanding way to act.

Skinner then refers to the degrees of wisdom of 'our legislators' which contains an important specification of the necessary link between public and individual freedom. When moving from the conceptual level to instruments that make human beings realize the presence of such a link, we at the same time move from the necessary to contingent political conditions of individual freedom. In particular, we can, in principle, admit that legislation can serve as instrument of freedom, but whether it does in an actual case depends, according to Skinner's above quoted formula, upon the wisdom of legislators.

Thus, we can consider the Machiavellian conception of liberty as 'interventionist' only concerning principles, whereas the actual measures can be regarded according to their expediency. The Machiavellian view is compatible with what is now called 'affirmative action', but it always remains to be decided separately, whether such an action has to be taken, and if so, whether the measures proposed serve the purpose of enlarging the freedom of choice for the agents.

Machiavelli's ideology of service, his well-known defence of the militia system and critique of mercenary armies allude to tendencies that may be relevant today. Skinner refers to this with the formula 'that liberty presupposes service – in this case (to cite a further phrase we have inherited from this tradition) in civil as well as on military service' (Skinner 1993b, 415, note the distancing expression in the parentheses). Such an argument for 'manhood suffrage' was a commonplace among conservative parties around 1900. But it does not follow that Machiavelli would have unreservedly supported a modern conscript army or denounced 'conscientious objectors' as enemies of liberty. The oft-quoted claim about service is 'not in the least being offered as a conceptual claim about the meaning of the term "liberty": it is merely a causal claim about how liberty is best preserved' (ibid.). Thus, it can equally well be argued, from the Machiavellian premises of negative and individual liberty, that a modern conscript army is analogous to tyranny and slavery and as such *per definitionem* opposed to liberty. The effects of such a 'school of dependence and obedience' may be considered to be politically fatal.

For Machiavelli an obvious threat to liberty was the *ambizione* of governing 'politicians' and of competing powers. Here again, liberty is connected with restrictions: 'there must above all be laws and institutions capable of serving as a *temperamento* – a means of tempering, a curb – to control the selfish *ambizione* of the rich and the nobility' (Skinner 1984, 211). This and other analogous measures refer to Machiavelli's view that freedom cannot mean an 'untempered' cultivation of just anything, but the conceptual link between individual freedom and freedom as a qualification of the polity legitimates restrictions to those variations of individual freedom that may be fatal to a free polity, approach tyranny or dissolve an elective polity by corruption. But, as indicated, which measures can rightly be legitimated in order to avoid such fatal variations is an empirical question.

Maybe we could detect in Machiavelli's critique of *ambizione* and in his preference of republican and elective government not only a restriction of freedom but also a manifestation of freedom-as-resistance. Unlike the self-defensive legitimation of freedom in the city-republics and in pre-humanist and early Renaissance theories (cf. also Viroli 1992), this dimension is mostly present in Machiavelli's provocative apology of dissensus. The Aristotelian or scholastic assumption of common goals is rejected in favour of the emphasis 'that different classes of people will always have varying disposition, and will in consequence value their liberty as means to attain various ends' (Skinner 1986, 240). In addition, Machiavelli praised the role of factions, and the laws for liberty as an expression of dissensus. In Rome, 'each faction was able to keep watch over the other and prevent it from legislating purely in its own interests' (Skinner 1988b, 440).

Even if Machiavelli's words remain cautious and balancing, I think a crucial dimension in Skinner's portrait of him lies in the link between individual freedom and freedom in the polity which consists in freedom-as-enjoyment-of-conflict. Liberty is not an absence of others, but the presence of others, as challenges to oneself, as invitations to competition and at the same time as a limit to hubris, that is, to the potential tyrannizing forms of self-creation. It is in this sense that Machiavelli's views, as presented by Skinner, are opposed to contractarian modes and are closer to the 'agonistic' views of antiquity, as presented by Hannah Arendt (1958) for example. I think this is also Skinner's point in the egalitarian formula 'everyone plays an active role in political affairs' in the reply in *TLS* quoted above (Skinner 1989c).

However, we can ask whether this dimension of individual-cum-political freedom is strictly compatible with Machiavelli's view of the conceptually necessary link between the two levels of freedom, as expressed by the metaphor of *body politic* (esp. Skinner 1986, 239–40). The agonistic dimension of freedom remains negative, perhaps an indication of an 'exercise concept' of liberty (ibid., 233), in the sense that the conflictual character of political activity forms an essential element of negativity itself.

Quentin Skinner with his reading of Machiavelli as a philosopher of liberty manages to illustrate how the Anglophone debate on liberty is conducted in terms that imply mythologies of prolepsis and parochialism. The alternatives have been narrowed to a dichotomy through an extreme simplification of their terms, neglecting not only logical possibilities and combinations but also historically remarkable conceptions, such as Machiavelli's.

Against 'liberals' or contractarians, in his discussions on Machiavelli Skinner emphasizes that historically it has been possible to combine a negative conception of liberty conceptually with a 'republican' polity and with a participatory and interventionist view of public activity, even making use of such figures as service and duty. Against the Neo-Aristotelians or 'communitarians' Skinner holds that Machiavelli is an example of defending the polity, participation and intervention without hypostasing 'community' or 'society' or upholding the 'common good' only as a necessary condition for the negative and individual liberty. Against both the contractarians and the communitarians, Skinner points out that by revaluing dissensus and struggle Machiavelli rejects consensualist assumptions on the polity, so characteristic to both.

Hobbes on Natural Liberty and the Liberty of Subjects

The third context in which Skinner has discussed the conceptual history of liberty is that of seventeenth-century debates surrounding the English Civil War. More clearly than in the 1960s, Skinner presents the struggles between Hobbes and his opponents as a struggle of competing views of liberty and constructs parallels to contemporary debates. In his most recent essays he offers two specific historical reasons why Hobbes's views on liberty are worthy of special attention. The first is that other apologists of the Stuart monarchy still spoke about freedom in terms of a privilege (cf. Skinner 2002e), in relation to which Hobbes as a contractarian shares the views of his 'neo-Roman' opponents. In his Isaiah Berlin Lecture, Skinner claims that, with regard to freedom as non-interference, 'it is very hard to find an explicit statement of such a theory any earlier than Hobbes's in *Leviathan*' (Skinner 2002f).

Already in the first of his essays on liberty, Skinner refers to James Harrington's distinction between 'the era of "ancient prudence" as an era in which the concept of political authority was analysed in terms of civic liberty and equality' and 'the age of "modern prudence" as an age inaugurated by Julius Caesar when the overthrow of "the liberty of Rome" thereby "opened up a pathway to the barbarians"' (Skinner 1983, 3). More specifically, Harrington opposes the two figures of Hobbes and Machiavelli to each other, to whom Skinner himself has in the first instance dedicated his studies:

> The leader of this destructive movement has been Hobbes, whose *Leviathan* Harrington treats as the greatest monument to gothic barbarism in the literature of the art of government. Fortunately, however, there has been one modern commentator on politics who has shown himself a 'learned disciple' of the Roman theorists, and has managed to uphold the fabric of ancient prudence in the face of modern vandalism. This heroic figure is Machiavelli, 'the only politician of later ages'. (ibid.)

Skinner presents the dangers of the current situation as analogous to those described by Harrington. He speaks of the neglect of 'losing touch with one fruitful way of thinking about the ideal of political liberty' (ibid.) as exemplified by Machiavelli, as well as of a hegemonic position of the gothic concept of liberty:

> ... in the writings of such leading contemporary theorists as John Rawls, Robert Nozick and their numerous disciples, we encounter a self-conscious attempt to revive and extend precisely the same 'gothic' vision of liberty as a natural right, of coercion as the antonym of liberty, and of the duty to maximise individual liberty as the chief (perhaps the sole) duty of enlightened governments. (ibid.)

Now, as quoted above, Skinner objects mainly to the monopolizing tendency of a certain conception of liberty. His initial description of the natural right-style conception of 'gothic' liberty has also been revised, both as far as the views on Hobbes are concerned (the unnuanced view is still defended in Skinner 1989a, esp. 83–5) and regarding the possibility of combining a 'neo-Roman' view with the idea of natural liberty.

Skinner's most comprehensive discussion of the Hobbesian concept of liberty is presented in the essay 'Hobbes on the Proper Significance of Liberty' (Skinner 1990c), slightly modified in two shorter versions (Skinner 1992c and 1996c). The title of the 1990 essay refers to Hobbes's anti-rhetorical view of *scientia civilis*, claiming to be able to define the 'constant Signification of words' (quoted from *Leviathan* in Skinner 1990c, 121). Skinner refers to Hobbes's point of departure as 'the liberty of each man to use his power as he will himself for the preservation of his own nature' (ibid., 123). According to Skinner this is negative liberty. 'The presence of liberty is always marked, that is, by the absence of something else. Specifically, it is marked by "the absence of externall Impediments". And by "impediments" Hobbes means anything that can hinder a man from using his powers "according as his judgment and reason shall dictate to him" ' (ibid., 123).

In discussing the hindrances to freedom Skinner emphasizes Hobbes's distinction between 'cases in which the agent is impeded from doing something' and acting freely, where the agent may refuse to do something 'if he will'. The first case concerns physical obstacles, the second concerns slavery, including Hobbes's thesis that 'all religious believers "are God's slaves" ' (ibid., 124–6). Skinner concludes: 'An agent forfeits his liberty if an external force renders him either powerless to act or powerless not to act in some particular way' (ibid., 126). Or, 'while the sick man merely lacks ability, the prisoner lacks freedom' (ibid., 127).

Hobbes's conception of liberty can be contrasted with another view insisting that human beings are always free, neatly encapsulated in Jean-Paul Sartre's well-known thesis that human beings are 'condemned to freedom' (Sartre 1943, 541). Indeed, Sartre's political philosophy has sometimes been compared with Hobbes's. However, their points of departure are different: whereas Hobbes is a determinist, for Sartre freedom is 'la condition première de l'action' (ibid., 487). In their existential condition neither the sick nor the prisoner lacks freedom, they only encounter 'coëfficients d'adversité', which always exist, but which do not 'limit' the liberty, because liberty is always a liberty-in-situation (ibid., 538). In other words, unlike Hobbes, success is no criterion of freedom for Sartre.

A remarkable point for Skinner is that Hobbes does not represent a 'pure negative theory of liberty' (Skinner 1990c, 127). Such an interpretation 'overlooks the possibility that a man's lack of freedom may derive . . . from being unable to act freely' (ibid., 128). For Hobbes freedom is bound by 'ties' such as promises, laws and contracts. In this respect, Hobbes is no less interventionist than Machiavelli, at least in situations when he judges the danger of falling back to the state of nature as imminent.

An equally crucial point is the fact that the 'laws of nature' are to Hobbes ' "dictates of Reason", or "habits of the mind," which "reason suggesteth" are "conducive to peace" '. And Hobbes's point is, according to Skinner: 'Such bonds . . . cannot genuinely restrict our liberty' (ibid., 130). In other words, if the 'laws' are transferred from the state of nature to the contracted state of civilization (of 'society') they should be treated as obstacles beyond human powers in the sense that breaking them is, of course, possible, but liable to lead to fatal consequences.

The contrast to Sartre is again illuminating: whereas to Sartre each individual has in each situation to 'choose herself', to Hobbes there is no choice: 'peace' is the given aim of human activities, dictated by 'reason'. The choice of action is free, but the criteria of judging the choices are given. You can break promises, laws or contracts, but only at the cost of falling back into the state of nature. In this sense, Hobbes has clear similarities with 'communitarian' writers whose conception of liberty is connected to definite 'positive' commitments.

Such a view becomes more understandable when Hobbes's distinction between natural liberty and the liberty of subjects is taken into account. The state of nature is at the same time a state of lawlessness and perfect liberty. Hobbes's transition to civilization through a contract is described by Skinner as follows: 'There is . . . a sense in which, in agreeing to give up our natural condition, we must be deciding to give up a form of liberty. By covenanting to become subjects of a Commonwealth, we agree to regulate our behaviour according to its civil laws. "But Civil Law is an Obligation and takes from us the Liberty which the Law of Nature gave us" ' (ibid., 133).

Hobbes's view, thus, explicitly admits that by contracting out of the state of nature we freely give up our natural liberty. The act of contracting is free and voluntary, but at the same time a dictate of reason, that is, something that cannot be meaningfully resisted within the Hobbesian conceptual horizon. As William Connolly puts it: 'When Hobbes discusses the state of nature he is talking to people already in civil society' (Connolly 1988, 21). The very act of transition from the state of nature to the state of civilization is judged anachronistically, in terms not available to the agents themselves.

For Skinner the interesting question of Hobbes concerns the liberty of a subject, identified by Hobbes as 'the silence of the Law' (Skinner 1990c, 134). But something of natural liberty is also shared by the subjects, although in the sense of 'a better protection for precisely those rights than I could ever have hoped to achieve by my own unaided efforts in the free but warlike condition of mere nature' (ibid.). For Hobbes, the contract 'does nothing to limit our liberty in the proper significance of the word' (ibid.). Even fear does not limit natural liberty (ibid., 136). But, unlike Machiavelli, the use of force to Hobbes always limits the freedom of subjects, and it cannot be used as an instrument of 'affirmative action' to make human beings conscious of their freedom. In the Hobbesian perspective 'liberty belongs to the sphere of nature', whereas 'civil law belongs to the sphere of artifice' (ibid., 138), whereas to Machiavelli liberty is an artificial, political matter.

Skinner specifies Hobbes's problematics: 'Why should Hobbes have been so anxious to insist on such a restricted analysis of the circumstance in which we can legitimately claim that our liberty has been infringed?' (ibid., 139). According to Skinner this is a philosophical question:

> On the one hand, a major concern of *Leviathan* is to explore the relationship between liberty and political obligation. Hobbes accordingly stands in need of a firm criterion for distinguishing between free and unfree actions. But on the other hand, Hobbes is a determinist. He cannot allow that anyone is ever free to will or not to will. To be free is to be unimpeded from moving according to one's desire. (ibid.)

Such a combination of freedom and necessity was unconventional in Hobbes's time. The reasons why Hobbes wanted to 'draw the boundaries of unfreedom in a restricted way' were political. According to Skinner, Hobbes 'felt an urgent need to respond to the dangers he had come to associate with the classical republican theory of liberty' (ibid., 140). In relation to his previous works, this anti-republican tendency is evident in *Leviathan*, namely in the claim that 'the classical republican theory of liberty may be said to embody two false and seditious elements' (ibid., 141). Correspondingly, Hobbes rejects the connection between democracy and liberty and unpopular governments and tyranny. When the liberty of subjects consists in the silence of law, 'all commonwealths have laws, and no subject is free of them', whereas 'natural liberty is obviously common to all states that are "not dependent on one another"' (ibid., 141–2).

A link to Skinner's previous studies concerns Hobbes's interest in pledging allegiance to the government in 1649 (cf. Skinner 1972a). Skinner now distinguishes between the *de facto* theorists' (Ascham, Nedham) and Hobbes's reason for accepting the government as legitimate. Along with many of the regime's republican enemies Hobbes shares the contractarian point of departure, but claims that 'those who believe the government to be imposing a new form of bondage have simply failed to understand the proper significance of liberty' (Skinner 1990c, 146). Even a conquest dissolving the commonwealth would leave a man free. He 'is not merely free to submit, he will also be acting freely', and the act of submission is one of 'a free man voluntarily consenting to a new sovereign power' (ibid., 148). The act is free, because such a man, 'unlike the slave, is offered a condition of submission, and is thus at liberty to accept or refuse that condition "if he will"' (ibid., 148–9). In other words, Hobbes's point to the critics of allegiance is that if such a man would refuse to submit, he would become a slave (ibid., 150).

This Hobbesian thesis on the freedom of subjects to submit refers to a limit-situation, in Skinner's words to 'those who submit to a conqueror to avoid the present stroke of death' (Skinner 1996c, 164). When this is done 'freely', it is a political act, an instrument that at least leaves the natural liberty intact. The heroic act of resistance at the cost of endangering one's own life cannot be required from everyone, and those who opt for life at the cost of submission cannot *per se* be considered as unpolitical agents.

According to Skinner, 'Hobbes's underlying purpose is to defuse the allegedly radical implications of theories both about natural rights and government by consent' (ibid.). Maybe we can call this a relative depoliticization, delimiting the political act to the act of consent (or dissent) itself, but making it independent of the qualifications of the polity beyond the minimal criterion of offering successful protection to life. The state of civilization is *per definitionem* constructed to be better than the state of nature, order is always regarded as better than disorder.

The Hobbesian view thus locates freedom in nature and considers struggles on the form of the polity insignificant and even 'favouring tumults' (Skinner 1990c, 140). 'Free commonwealths' do not exist, because all commonwealths have laws (Skinner 1992c, 247). Such a view is, however, almost a mirror image of those apologies for 'positive freedom', in which the insistence on popular participation is presented as a means of integration and upholding order. Both the Hobbesian and 'communitarian' views on polities without a struggle for alternative modes of life may thus, from a Skinnerian perspective, be considered as similarly depoliticized.

The Neo-Roman Theorists: Liberty vs. Dependence

Following the example of some other British scholars, in *Liberty before Liberalism* Skinner analyses a 'number of supporters of the parliamentary cause', who responded to the royalists, such as Filmer or Hobbes, in England after 1649. They did so by 'giving renewed prominence to what is perhaps best described as the neo-Roman element in early-modern political thought' (Skinner 1998, 11). With this title Skinner now introduces a point of departure different from Machiavelli and other Italian republicans. Neo-Roman thinkers were not strict adversaries of monarchy, but placed emphasis on the liberty of the polity as a condition of individual liberty.

The study can partly be regarded as a continuation of the political possibilities of contractarian theory as developed among Protestant radicals in the late sixteenth century. His starting point is the legitimation of the 'proclamation of England as "a Commonwealth and Free State"' (ibid., 13). What is interesting in this group of thinkers – John Milton, Henry Neville, Marchamont Nedham, Algernon Sidney, George Wither, John Hall, Francis Osborne and John Streater, with the exception of James Harrington – is that they shared with Hobbes the contractarian language of natural liberty and 'rights', whereas their idea of a 'free state' was to Hobbes a contradiction in terms. The Roman allegiances of this group were limited so that their point of departure for the discussion of liberty was different:

> The notion of a state of nature, and the claim that this condition is one of perfect freedom, were assumptions wholly foreign to the Roman and Renaissance texts. Among the seventeenth-century writers, however, they gave rise to the contention that these primitive liberties must be recognised as a God-given birthright, and hence as a set of natural rights which, in Milton's phrase, it becomes 'one main end of government to protect and uphold.' (ibid., 19)

In a footnote, Skinner admits that the assumption of natural liberty, as emphasized by some of his critics, has led him to change his own views on the political role of contractarians. 'One cannot . . . distinguish neo-roman from contractarian accounts of civil liberty by reference to their supposedly contrasting treatment of rights' (ibid.). The contractarian assumptions by no means prevented the above-mentioned authors connecting individual and political liberty in terms widely corresponding to those of Machiavelli and diametrically opposed to those of Hobbes: 'any understanding of what it means for an individual citizen to possess or lose their liberty must be embedded within an account of what it means for a civil association to be free' (ibid., 23).

Among this group the metaphor of 'body politic' was prominently used (ibid., 26). Unlike authors such as Isaiah Berlin, Skinner insists that the metaphor, as used by the 'neo-Romans' of the seventeenth century, can be understood in strictly nominalistic terms: 'But the neo-roman theorists are at pains to insist that they have nothing at all mysterious in mind. When they speak about the will of the people, they mean nothing more than the sum of the wills of each individual citizen' (ibid., 28–9).

As in the case of Machiavelli, the link between individual liberty and 'free state' is to be understood as a conceptual one, as one of necessary condition: 'it is only possible to be free in a free state' (ibid., 60). Unlike for Hobbes, individual liberty remains 'natural' both in the contract and in the state of civilization. The contract is viewed as a *Herrschaftsvertrag*, not an *Unterwerfungsvertrag*. In other words, it is conditional on the acceptability of the form of the polity to the participants in the contract.

Such a construction presupposes a 'state of nature' that is not understood in strict Hobbesian terms as a *bellum omnium contra omnes*, but as one which gives to those living in it a certain veto power, if the terms of contract are not acceptable. The Hobbesian claim that any contract is better than no contract and freedom is limited to the question 'submit or not', seems not to have been tackled by neo-Roman theorists. The mechanism of transferring freedom is understood by the neo-Roman thinkers as that of representation – the form of which is then subject to disagreements between them – which Skinner summarizes as follows: 'The right solution, they generally agree, is for the mass of the people to be represented by a national assembly of the more virtuous and considering, an assembly chosen by the people to legislate on their behalf' (ibid., 32).

The opposite of the 'free state', in which liberty is retained, is for the neo-Roman thinkers 'a condition of enslavement or servitude' (ibid., 37). Unlike Machiavelli, it is not tyranny but an analogy to the condition of the individual in Roman private law that is understood as the state of lost liberty. Here we can clearly detect the contractarian ideology, but also, as Skinner emphasizes, the language of the *Digest* of Roman law. 'The concept of liberty is always defined in the *Digest* by contrast with the condition of slavery, while the predicament of the slave is defined as that of "someone who, contrary to nature, is made into the property of someone else"' (ibid., 39).

The paradigm of slavery as an antonym to liberty does not oppose coercion to freedom of movement, but the states of being *sui juris* and being *in potestate domini*. Skinner summarizes the discussion: 'The essence of what it means to be slave, and hence to lack personal liberty, is thus to be *in potestate*, within the power of someone' (ibid., 41). For the neo-Roman authors it is not only strict tyranny or even colonization and conquest which threaten the public liberty of a free state, but also the situation 'when the internal constitution of a state allows for the exercise of any discretionary or prerogative powers on the part of those governing it' (ibid., 50–1). The political controversies surrounding the English republic are thus directly linked to the neo-Roman conception of liberty, and were later used to transfer the name of slavery even to the *ancien régime* in France and the rule of the British in North America (ibid., 59).

The point of Skinner's exposition of the response of the neo-Roman theorists to Hobbes consists in establishing a hierarchy in the threats to liberty. They do not consider coercion and dependence as opposing concepts (cf. ibid., 83, esp. n. 54) nor do they deny the danger of coercion. They claim, rather, that the chances of coercion will systematically increase with a slavery-like dependence on the discretionary powers of government, for 'to live in a condition of dependence is itself a source and a form of constraint' (ibid., 84).

For the neo-Roman writers it is never necessary to suffer this kind of overt coercion in order to forfeit your civil liberty. You will also be rendered unfree if you merely fall into a condition of political subjection or dependency, thereby leaving yourself open to the danger of being forcibly or coercively deprived by your government of your life, liberty or estate. That is to say that, if you live under any form of government that allows for the exercise of prerogative or discretionary powers outside the law, you will already be living as a slave (ibid., 69–70).

Perhaps the difference with Hobbes could be formulated in terms of differentiating between 'laws' and 'discretionary acts'. Unlike

Hobbes, both Machiavelli and the neo-Roman writers insist that 'law', although a coercive power, is *per se* no threat to liberty. They underline the distinction between the liberty-compatible control through laws enacted by the representatives of the people and the arbitrary control of citizens based on discretionary powers, such as royal prerogatives (ibid., 74). In a footnote, Skinner then distances the neo-Roman writers from the 'positive' concept of liberty as participation:

> This is not to say that individual freedom according to these writers can in some sense be equated with virtue or the right of political participation, and thus that liberty consists in membership of a self-governing state. . . . The writers I am discussing merely argue that participation (at least by way of representation) constitutes a necessary condition of maintaining individual liberty. (ibid., 74–5)

Hobbes and his latter-day followers regard the degree of coercion as the only measure for unfreedom. To Hobbes 'what matters for individual liberty is not the source of the law but its extent' (ibid., 85), which may be greater for the ordinary citizen 'under the sultan in Constantinople' than in 'the self-governing republic of Lucca' (ibid.). As Harrington replied to Hobbes: 'your freedom in Constantinople, however great in extent, will remain wholly dependent on the sultan's goodwill' (ibid., 86). Here we can see in detail how the neo-Roman theorists set tighter criteria for what counts as liberty than Hobbes does, when they insist on the freedom in the polity as a condition for individual freedom. One implication of this is the critique on courtly advisers of monarchs as persons who are particularly unfree. Skinner refers to Algernon Sidney's 'puritanical contempt for the corruption' (ibid., 90) and for 'the slavish behaviour typical of . . . counsellors' (ibid., 93).

Harrington constructed a definite opposition to dependence and arbitrary rule, the 'figure of the independent country gentleman as the leading repository of moral dignity and worth in modern society' (ibid., 95). It was this 'social assumption underlying the theory' that contributed to the fact that 'the theory began to appear as outdated and even absurd' (ibid., 96–7). The theory of liberty itself was, already in the second half of the eighteenth century, judged by Blackstone, Paley, Bentham and others to be 'simply confused' (ibid., 97).

The vocabulary Skinner uses retains an ironic distance towards the country gentleman, referring to the empirical conditions for the neo-Roman theory of liberty. At the same time, he indicates that critics from the eighteenth century on who speak of confusion were not necessarily unwilling, as Hobbes was, but rather unable to understand the key assumptions of the theory itself. Both the proponents and later opponents of the Harringtonian ideal did not understand the neo-Roman view of the necessary condition between public and individual liberty as a condition that could be empirically applied in a variety of contexts. A change in the context altered the empirical conditions of liberty, but did not *per se* render such a conception anachronistic.

More recently Skinner has continued the historiography of the neo-Roman conception of liberty at the time of the English Civil War. He particularly questions the thesis that common law arguments played a decisive role in the legitimation of Parliament's decision 'in favour of taking up arms against Charles I in 1642' (Skinner 2002b, 288). Skinner claims that 'this interpretation overlooks the presence in the Parliamentary debates of what I have characterized as a classical vision, more specifically a neo-Roman vision, of fundamental liberties' (ibid.). This was the case with Henry Parker's suggestion 'that the very existence of the prerogative leaves everyone enslaved' (ibid., 293), whereas John Milton claims that 'no deeds of glory can ever be expected from the enslaved subject of tyrannical governments' (ibid., 301). In April 1660, just before the Restoration, Milton still argued, in Skinner's paraphrase: 'Accepting the rule of king . . . is strictly equivalent to deciding to enslave oneself' (ibid., 305).

In another essay, Skinner considers Hobbes's thesis in *Leviathan* that an education that teaches the work of Greek and Latin authors has led to 'a habit (under a false shew of Liberty,) of favouring tumults' (ibid., 308). Against traditional views, Skinner argues that this Hobbesian thesis, indeed, can be supported by contemporary evidence, especially due to the availability of translations of classical texts in English. He does not deny that the common law theorists had a view of liberty, but emphasizes the Roman origins of their favourite arguments (cf. esp. Skinner 2002e and f).

Remarkable in Skinner's analysis of Cicero and other Roman authors is the identification of *civitas libera* with the *free state* among the English seventeenth-century authors. This does not, of course, mean that he would now project the modern concept of state to the Romans, but, on the contrary, that when seventeenth-century English authors use that expression, they emphasize the difference between the status of freedom and that of slavery as a qualification of a regime. It is in such terms that Skinner interprets the 1642 struggle on the 'negative voice' of the King against Parliament. The Parliament was even 'attempting to apply the vocabulary of Roman republicanism to the English polity', and the case of appealing to Roman theories was even more explicit in the pamphlet literature. Skinner concludes that 'it is striking that Parliament itself and many of its supporters preferred to justify their decision to go to war in neo-classical rather than in contractarian terms' (Skinner 2002b, 327).

In the conceptual history of liberty, the Machiavellian and the contractarian variations on the neo-Roman conception of liberty differ in their relation to politics in noticeable respects. The British seventeenth-century thinkers understood the political exclusively in terms of the polity. Individual liberty itself seems among them entirely to lack the dimension of contestation and virtuosity so characteristic of Machiavelli.

In his latest essays, Skinner has sketched the fate of the neo-Roman concept of liberty and its critiques as far as the nineteenth and twentieth centuries. He has added the dimension of 'an awareness of living in dependence on arbitrary power', explicitly present in Locke's critique of Filmer (Skinner 2002e). He has particularly raised attention to J. S. Mill's assertion that a new danger to liberty appeared from the conformity of custom and opinion, in which 'Mill implicitly rejects the assumption that freedom is necessarily interpersonal in character, arguing instead that we ourselves may be among the agents capable of undermining our own liberty' (ibid.). Skinner connects this to the Marxian view of 'false consciousness' – although he could here also have invoked what he previously said about Machiavelli and the need for 'affirmative action' to support the freedom of the individual.

Skinner's discussion of the history of the concept of liberty illustrates the fact that the fate of certain theories does not primarily depend on their inherent merits. Of at least equal significance are the political struggles about the concept of liberty, by different rhetorical means and related to the special conditions as well as of the singular facticities of the situations. Skinner's thesis is that the hegemonic position of the strict coercion view is itself a contingent product of skilled rhetoric, monopolizing a certain interpretation to the wider concept of 'negative liberty' under the conditions of suitable general political and intellectual trends.

How far Skinner considers a Benjaminian (1940) 'actualization' of the 'lost treasury' in matters of liberty to be possible, remains an

open question. More important to Skinner is that the very historical reality of republican and neo-Roman conceptions of liberty in
the past and the rhetorical redescription of the conceptual struggle
around them are sufficient to raise question marks to the hegemony
of the narrow interpretation of negative liberty. It is in this perspective that we have to look closely at Skinner's remarks on the
contemporary debate on liberty.

Intervention in the Contemporary Debate

To give a background to Skinner's remarks on his contemporaries'
views on liberty, I shall briefly present three of them. The most
famous is Isaiah Berlin's 'Two Concepts of Liberty' (1958); the
concept of liberty is also discussed in a separate chapter in John
Rawls's *A Theory of Justice* (1971); whereas Philip Pettit's *Republicanism* (1997) represents a view explicitly indebted to Skinner. Then
I shall return to Skinner's comment on them, mostly presented in
footnotes in his work (a fine and extensive discussion of Skinner's
views in relation to the contemporary debate can be found in Marco
Geuna's introduction (2000) to the Italian edition of *Liberty before
Liberalism*).

Isaiah Berlin's inaugural lecture at Oxford in 1958, 'Two Concepts
of Liberty', is perhaps the most quoted text in British post-war
political theory. In retrospect it looks essayistic, neither strictly
philosophical nor properly historical, and its cult status is hard to
understand. Even the claim that when liberty is evoked in the political debate there is not a single concept but two different ones is
neither new nor provocative, although remarkable as a simplifying
move in a debate. It seems to me, rather, that the very speech act of
calling the (for Berlin) 'higher' liberty 'negative' and the 'lower'
liberty 'positive', inverting the ordinary normative sign, is the
provocative act.

Considered from a purely heuristic approach, we can rather
doubt that Berlin has really distinguished two different concepts
of liberty, simply on the grounds that one is regarded as the
proper concept and the other as improper. For a conceptual
historian, Berlin's argument has an essentialist tone: 'Everything is
what it is; liberty is liberty' (Berlin 1958, 125). Thus, Berlin's main
interest seems a purely philosophical clarification, but what he is
doing at the same time is to introduce a highly partisan
political move in the guise of making a key distinction. Berlin

initially proposes a clear-cut distinction, without justifying his choice of names:

> The first of these political senses of freedom or liberty . . . I shall call the 'negative' sense, is involved in the answer to the question 'What is the area within which the subject – a person or group of persons – is or should be left to do or be what he is able to do or be, without interference by other persons?' The second, which I shall call the positive sense, is involved in the answer to the question, 'What, or who, is the source of control or interference that can determine someone to do, or be, this rather than that?' (ibid., 121–2)

In this formula, freedom is reduced to a question of interference or control, and the opposition between the two freedoms to that of existence of a sphere of freedom and source of freedom. In other formulations Berlin takes up different aspects, such as the distinction between 'freedom from' and 'freedom to' (ibid., 127) and the opposition between (negative) liberty and law (ibid., 148). 'Positive liberty' is further explicated in terms of the 'wish on the part of the individual to be his own master' (ibid., 131) or being 'the possessor of reason and will' (ibid., 135), 'autonomy' (ibid., 136), 'self-realization' (ibid., 141) or 'sovereignty' (ibid., 166). Indeed, it seems to me that for Berlin formulations do not matter, they only serve as illustrations of a conceptual opposition judged to be central and indicating some internal variation within the main poles. Such a usage serves the legitimating purpose in favour of his asymmetric conceptual pair.

A definite point for Berlin, however, is to insist on the independence of conceptions of liberty from the form of the polity. The key passage concerning the relations between liberty and polity is presented as follows:

> It is that liberty in this sense is not incompatible with some kinds of autocracy, or at any rate with the absence of self-government. . . . Just as a democracy may, in fact, deprive the individual citizen of a great many liberties which he might have in some other form of society, so it is perfectly conceivable that a liberal-minded despot would allow his subjects a large measure of personal freedom. (ibid., 129)

If the formula 'some kinds of autocracy' still indicates a relation between negative liberty and the type of the polity, this relation is considered as empirical and not conceptual: 'Self-government may, on the whole, provide a better guarantee of preservations of civil liberties than other regimes, and has been defended as such by libertarians. But there is no necessary connection between individual liberty and democratic rule' (ibid., 130).

In the Introduction to the collection *Four Essays on Liberty*, Berlin later clarified some of his views. In particular, he stresses, against Erich Fromm, Bernard Crick (and implicitly, Hannah Arendt), that to him: 'The freedom of which I speak is opportunity for action, rather than action itself' (Berlin 1969, xlii). Or, in another formula: 'The extent of a man's negative liberty is, as it were, a function of what doors, and how many, are open to him; upon what prospects they open; and how open they are' (ibid., xlviii). In relation to Weber's concept of *Chance*, Berlin's freedom-as-opportunity is passive: liberty either is already there or it is not, whereas to Weber there are always some *Chancen* and whether a specific *Chance* is realizable depends on the agent's insight into the situation and on her experiment in trying to realize it. Compared with Weber in particular the dimension of liberty as resistance, opposition, confrontation, subversion, provocation and so on is lacking in Berlin's identification of the sphere of non-inference by the authorities.

John Rawls's discussion of liberty is, of course, related to his 'theory of justice'. He follows Berlin's line in defining negative liberty in terms of coercion, following Gerard MacCallum's triadic explication of the concept. 'Therefore I shall simply assume that liberty can always be explained by a reference to three terms: the agents who are free, the restrictions or limitations which they are free from, and what it is that they are free to do or not to do' (Rawls 1971, 202).

Conceptually, what is most important is that Rawls speaks like Berlin of 'restrictions' or 'limitations' as 'constraints' and liberty as liberty 'from interference' (ibid.). In a rather Hegelian manner, however, Rawls considers 'that the basic liberties must be assessed as a whole, as a system' (ibid., 203), and in this sense he writes: 'While rules of order limit our freedom, since we the cannot speak whenever we please, they are required to gain the benefits of this liberty' (ibid.). This has nothing to do with Machiavelli's 'affirmative action' for liberation from quasi-natural inclinations. It can rather be seen as an attempt to include liberty in a system, to functionalize individual liberty to liberty as a characteristic of a specific order: 'liberty is represented by the complete system of the liberties of equal citizenship, while the worth of liberty is proportional to their capacity to advance their ends within the framework the system defines' (ibid., 204). Thus, Rawls instrumentalizes individual liberty as a criterion between systems, clearly differentiating from the neo-Roman view of freedom in the polity as a necessary condition of individual liberty.

Philip Pettit's 'republican' conception of liberty is largely sketched with Skinner's and Pocock's historical views in the background, although written in the style of a philosophical system-builder. Pettit's point of departure for the conceptualization is to present a 'third' concept of liberty, 'freedom as non-domination'. His point of departure is the thesis: 'Domination . . . is exemplified by the relationship of master and slave or master and servant' (Pettit 1997, 22). He thus uses the same paradigm for the lack of freedom as Skinner's neo-Roman authors, but names the counter-concept 'domination' (cf. esp. ibid., 52), also referring to Weber. However, as Weber scholars know, this *domination* is a mistranslation of the idiosyncratic Weberian concept of *Herrschaft*.

In Weber's usage the concept does not refer to such stable relations of rule or authority as master vs. servant, but it is nominalized to concern any relation of asymmetric power-shares. In a letter to Michels commenting on the latter's *Zur Soziologie des Partei-wesens in der modernen Demokratie*, Weber insists that he and his shoemakers each have some shares of *Herrschaft* (*Briefe 1909–1910* (1994), 761). More generally, *Herrschaft* as a variant of *Macht*, is like all Weberian concepts a *Chance*-concept, namely, *Herrschaft* does not exist as facticity but only as opportunity, and as such it is, as I have discussed above, always in need of legitimation. The lack of *Herrschaft* is by no means an ideal situation, it would rather be a sign of powerlessness and stagnation. In particular, democracy does not mean a lack of *Herrschaft*, but a competition for temporally limited shares of *Herrschaft*.

Interestingly, Pettit's view of liberty, so far as it is applied to constitutional politics, is not based on consent, as in the contractarian views, but on contestability.

> . . . it must always be possible for people in the society . . . to contest the assumption that guiding interest and ideas really are shared, and, if the challenge proves sustainable, to alter the pattern of the state activity. Unless such a contestability is assured, the state may easily represent a dominating presence for those of a certain marginalized ethnicity or culture or gender. (Pettit 1997, 63)

The formulation as well as the proposals for institutionalizing contestability (ibid., 185–202) indicate, however, that liberty is by no means seen in the contesting act, but is only a Lockean style veto-power in relation to the consensual order. The very idea of insti-tutionalizing contestability into the service of a good order domesticates the acts of contestation.

Returning to the work of Skinner, his remarks on Isaiah Berlin have a tone of respect, although Berlin obviously is not enough of a historian for Skinner's taste, as can be inferred from this remark in a book review: 'It is surely going too far to say that Machiavelli "completely ignores the concepts of categories" of other thinkers of the age' (Skinner 1979b, 830). More specifically, Skinner shares with Berlin not only the acceptance of the idea of negative liberty but in addition its formulation in terms of 'the mere non-obstruction of individual agents in the pursuit of their chosen ends' (Skinner 1984, 197), or 'as the absence of impediments to the realisation of our chosen ends' (Skinner 1986, 247). Skinner draws, however, different consequences for what such claims signify for the concept of liberty, as discussed above for example in the relationship between liberty and law and liberty and service as well as the relations between individual and public liberty.

Skinner is thus defending Berlin against a narrow Hobbesian manner of opposing liberty to coercion (cf. Skinner 1990b, 299n.) and also uses, as just quoted, some formulations resembling those used by Berlin about the meaning of negative liberty. Still, Skinner remains critical of the speech act that Berlin has used in thematiz-ing the concept of liberty. This holds for the range of attitudes towards liberty: 'Berlin in effect equates (or confuses) the "negative" idea of liberty with the classical liberal understanding of the concept' (Skinner 1998, 114n.). In other words, Skinner criticizes Berlin for not reflecting upon the possibility that the range of refer-ence for the negative liberty could be wider than what he allows it to be, and, indirectly, for supporting a 'hegemonal' conception. Skinner illustrates by means of historical case studies the claim that a number of positions excluded or neglected by Berlin can still be made compatible precisely with the concept of negative liberty. The key difference is put forward in *Liberty before Liberalism* as follows:

> What the neo-roman writers repudiate *avant la lettre* is the key assumption of classical liberalism that force or the coercive threat of it constitute the only forms of constraint that interfere with individ-ual liberty. The neo-roman writers insist, by contrast, that to live in a condition of dependence is in itself a source and a form of constraint. (ibid., 84)

Skinner extends the concept of negative liberty by denying that coercion is the only form of constraint (ibid., 116, 118 n. 29) and insisting that dependence should also be considered as one. Indeed, Skinner does not commit himself to this neo-Roman view, but rather to the plurality of views, which he, as already quoted, will leave 'to ruminate' (ibid., 118).

I think Skinner has, in his recent essay on Milton, further pinpointed the difference in terms of arguing that Milton 'reformulates with exceptional clarity the classical assumption that freedom is to be contrasted not with actual but with possible constraints' (Skinner 2002b, 291). Thus, he specifies the hierarchy between interference and dependence to be comprehensible within a single conceptual horizon. Perhaps we could make a further distinction in the concept of 'possible', distinguishing the ancient concept of *potentia* from the Weberian concept of *Chance*, which then could allow us to speak of 'degrees' of threats to freedom and reinterpret both interference and dependence as chances. This would also allow an understanding that constraints are not a political analogy to necessities, but that even they leave some degree of *Chancen* to act differently.

In his recent Isaiah Berlin Memorial Lecture, Skinner clarified that 'Berlin's essay represents a belated but recognisable contribution to a long-standing debate about the merits of philosophical Idealism that had continued to resonate in the Oxford of his youth' (Skinner 2002f). He has also detected the origins of Berlin's concept of 'positive liberty' in the works of T. H. Green and Bernard Bosanquet and their ideal of freedom as self-perfection. He then identifies 'positive liberty' in terms that acknowledge this view as a legitimate possibility, while making clear that Skinner himself does not subscribe to it: 'what underlies these theories of positive liberty is the belief that human nature has an essence, and that we are free if and only if we succeed in realising that essence in our lives' (ibid.). Furthermore, he enumerates variants of possible liberty, maybe too rapidly including Arendt with her identification of freedom as politics, while not considering Arendt's key distinction between politics as contingent action and fabrication, to which only the ideal of self-perfection is applicable. Skinner also affirms the opportunity character of negative liberty more explicitly than before: 'I happen to agree with Berlin that there are many different ends that we can equally well pursue' (ibid.).

In comparison with the comments on Berlin, what Skinner says on Rawls is much more critical. In his Machiavelli essay of 1983 Rawls is presented as the paradigmatic example of a 'gothic' thinker of 'liberty as a natural right, of coercion as the antonym of liberty and of the duty to maximize liberty as the chief (perhaps the sole) duty of enlightened governments' (Skinner 1983, 3). Machiavelli is opposed to Rawls as someone who defends liberty without recourse to rights. Rawls's revised contractarianism is, above all, understood as a search for an Archimedean point: 'For a contemporary philosopher like Rawls . . . the aim is of course to stand at an Archimedean point outside history, with the result that he prefers to reflect on his intuitions about justice at an imagined "constitutional convention" in order to elucidate the legal foundations of a free society' (ibid., 10).

Quentin Skinner is too much of a historian to believe in the benefits of such an approach, although he later appreciates Rawls's *Theory* as 'a utopian treatise' (Skinner 1998, 79 n. 47) and relativizes the divide between republicans and contractarians. However, he has 'some doubt, perhaps, whether Rawls has really succeeded in freeing himself from the imaginative constraints imposed by history in the way his thought experiment claims' (Skinner 1983, 11), and he is also too much an anti-foundationalist to question the desirability of building such ahistorical systems. Or, to put it the other way round, Skinner prefers the historical approach to constructing philosophical systems precisely for the reason that he always finds them liable to parochialism, whereas the historical approach enables us to question even more radically the notion that some contemporary ideas (of any period) could serve as basis for an acceptable system. Perhaps we could say that the very idea of a good order appears to Skinner to be questionable (cf. in this respect his Habermas essay, Skinner 1982a).

The main specific target of Skinner's criticism of Rawls is the use of 'rights' as 'natural' instances that are not only beyond history and politics but are used as a shelter of individual freedom against them. He not only doubts that Rawls manages in his contractarianism to avoid the fallacies of natural law thinking, but also puts a question mark on the political consequences Rawls and other contemporary contractarians draw from it. In 1992 Skinner formulated the point as follows:

I fully endorse his sense that the right way to think about the relationship between individual citizens and the powers of the state is to emphasize the equal right of all citizens to pursue their chosen goals so far as possible. I merely wish to question whether Rawls and (especially) his more enthusiastic followers are right to assume that

the best way to secure and maximize that value is necessarily to treat
the calls of social duty as so many 'interferences'. (Skinner 1992b, 215)

Although Rawls, unlike Berlin and others, clearly acknowledges
that individual liberty has political implications, Skinner argues
that Rawls is liable to interpret rights in a narrow and legalistic
manner. Not acknowledging a 'common good' easily leads citizens
to be too passive, not critical enough towards the temptation of
politicians to make 'decisions in line with their own interests and
those of powerful pressure-groups instead of the interests of the
community at large' (ibid., 223). At this point Skinner, in my view,
too easily projects Machiavellian arguments to present-day parliamentary government, in which it is anachronistic to speak of a
common good beyond the political controversies.

One main reason why Skinner in *Liberty before Liberalism* replaces
the epithet republican with neo-Roman is that the seventeenth-
century authors he studies are not strict anti-monarchists (Skinner
1998, 22–3, 55). It is, moreover, a move away from Pettit's attempt
to include him under the umbrella of fellow republicans, when it
can be seen that Skinner now speaks even of Machiavelli as a neo-
Roman theorist of liberty (in the essays of Skinner 2002b).

The footnotes referring to Pettit in *Liberty before Liberalism* indicate Skinner's grounds for such a move. They have a common point
of departure in the opposition of freedom to slavery, and Skinner
even attributes to Pettit his own shift to the opinion that maybe,
after all, the differences concern the very concepts of liberty
(Skinner 1998, 70n.). Despite this, Pettit's and Skinner's interpretations vary at remarkable points (as also pointed out by Geuna
2000, xxiii–xxvii and Springborg 2001). Skinner never uses Pettit's
emphatic 'freedom as non-domination' but prefers 'dependence' as
an antonym to freedom. In particular, Skinner does not share Pettit's
view that non-interference and non-domination would refer to 'an
alternative account of unfreedom' (Skinner 1998, 82n.), but argues
that 'unfreedom can be produced either by interference or by
dependence' (ibid., 84n.).

A tacit reason for Skinner's demarcation from Pettit views can
perhaps be found in the latter's tendency to turn 'republicanism'
into a coherent theory. Pettit is a system-builder similar to Rawls,
and he raises the same suspicion in Skinner as a historically
oriented thinker. Although Pettit in the subtitle understands non-
domination 'as a political concern', he then claims that it 'is not an
ideal that should be left to individuals to pursue in a decentralized
way' and even claims it to be 'a neutral political ideal' (Pettit 1997,

95, 97). Skinner would never use such expressions and would consider such a 'political ideal' to be rather unpolitical, not leaving much space for politicking save politicization, similarly to Rawls's *Political Liberalism* (1993) (cf. Palonen 2002c). In consequence, Skinner does not subscribe to Pettit's view that the 'republican' liberty also contains 'positive elements', but continues to insist on the negativity of the neo-Roman concept of liberty (Skinner 2002e).

Skinner remains cautious in his own comments on the contemporary debate. In the lecture on Berlin he none the less refers to the fact that Berlin clearly realized that the negation of dependence played a role in the debates about decolonization, but rejected any suggestion 'to call the demand for recognition and status a demand for liberty in some third sense', whereas Skinner emphasizes how the 'distinctive claim they defend is that a mere awareness of living in dependence on the goodwill of an arbitrary ruler *does* serve in itself to restrict our options and thereby limit our liberty' (Skinner 2002f). Skinner's remarks on contemporary authors contribute to his individual profile with a definite *Wertbezug* on the value and significance of (negative) liberty, implying a research programme for the history of the concept. In the final page of the lecture on Berlin he affirms the wider political point of such historical studies on contested concepts:

> With terms at once so deeply normative, so highly indeterminate, and so extensively implicated in such a long history of ideological debate, the project of understanding them can only be that of trying to grasp the different roles they have played in our history and our own place in that narrative. But the more we undertake this kind of study, the more we see that there is no neutral analysis of any such keywords to be given. The history is all there is. (ibid.)

A Profile on the History and Theory of Liberty

Considered historically, what Quentin Skinner has written on the concept of liberty since the early 1980s does not result from a research programme, but, rather, from a series of case studies which have grown into a long-term personal research programme. The essays on Machiavelli and negative liberty in the 1980s seem to have been rather an illustrative history in Skinner's style to criticize contemporaries by the means of historical counter-examples, limited to his own main research interests.

In the 1983 essay on Machiavelli, departing from Harrington's critique of 'gothic' theorists on natural liberty, Skinner's tone is that

of a cultural pessimist deploring the hegemony of the contemporary 'gothics'. Maybe this tone was the impulse to dig deeper into
the history of the concept and to make the hegemonization itself a
result of political struggle, the history of which should be written,
as Skinner proposes to do in the above quoted *TLS* statement. Since
then the historical studies have been widely extended and nuanced
and at the same time the allegedly hegemonic view has received its
own nuances.

Departing from Machiavelli, Skinner has extended his case
studies to Lorenzetti and other pre-humanist thinkers, to Hobbes,
to the neo-Roman writers critical of Hobbes, to Milton and to the
debates around the struggle between Parliament and Charles I in
1642, in his most recent essays dealing also with nineteenth- and
twentieth-century thinkers. Extending the case studies has also
increased the variation of views on liberty: although the Roman references have become ever more important to Skinner, the distinction from the contractarian views has been relativized, when other
theorists than Hobbes have been subjected to a detailed analysis. As
in the case of legitimating Protestantism, it seems that Skinner now
realizes better than in the 1980s that the controversies on liberty are
not directly related to philosophical commitments or traditions
of thought, but acute struggles on legitimation, such as those in
England in 1642 and 1649, may modify philosophical commitments
on concepts such as liberty on political grounds.

Koselleck's thesis that the concepts are 'pivots' around which the
debates turn (Koselleck 1996, 65) clearly holds also for Skinner's
studies on the concept of liberty. Neither does Skinner always
depart from a debate in a limited historical context, but analyses
debates around a key conceptual theme that has been actualized at
various contexts. But, of course, his studies on the history of the
concept of liberty are studies on its 'uses in argument' and his main
interest remains the 'linguistic action' to which the competing con-
ceptualizations of liberty are related.

As I have already indicated, Skinner explicitly acknowledges that
his studies on the concept of liberty have a more definite contemporary reference than his other studies (Skinner 1998, 107–9). Still
his contemporary focus is on rather narrow Anglophone debates:
for a Weber and Sartre scholar, for example, it may be hard to understand what sense there is in debating with Rawls, Berlin and Pettit
(although I have tried to overcome this prejudice). On some occasions, especially in his reviews, Skinner opens up the discussions
towards wider debates on liberty.

From this perspective Skinner's discussion of Charles Taylor's *Sources of the Self* is interesting, although not dealing directly with Taylor as a defender of 'positive liberty'. I was especially pleased with Skinner's polemic against marriage, relating feminist critiques to a topic to the opposition between freedom and dependence (cf. also Skinner 2001a). The key passage is this one:

> The feminist case is thus that the traditional family has served more than any other institution to prevent women from attaining the liberal goals of self-realization and moral self-development. Although the charge is by now a familiar as well as a deeply troubling one, Taylor makes no mention of any such tensions in 'our' visions of the values inherent in ordinary life. . . . Once again it begins to look as though 'we' may be male. (Skinner 1991b, 141)

Analogous to this is Skinner's polemic against Taylor's reliance on the church and religious belief: 'Speaking as a modern unbeliever, I do not feel in the least inclined to concede that those who embrace theism must be acknowledged to have a fully adequate source for their moral beliefs' (ibid., 148). Skinner also doesn't believe in Taylor's 'prospect of reincorporating the promise of theism into a genuine pluralistic social philosophy' (ibid., 149) and writes in more general terms: 'Like Durkheim, what Taylor fears above all is loss of meaning, a fear he appears to experience almost as a phobia' (ibid., 142). A clearly 'existential' dimension of liberty, analogous to Sartre's view of being condemned to freedom, is contained in Skinner's declaration: 'since there is no God, we shall somehow have to manage on our own' (ibid., 149).

Thus, although dealing in his academic studies with a rather narrow dimension of negative liberty, Skinner's review of Taylor illustrates that, when speaking about liberty today, he is highly sensitive to the 'existential' dimensions of liberty. I think these views are by no means unconnected to the opposition between freedom and dependence.

There are, of course, numerous tendencies towards an increasing 'dependence' today: commercialization, industrialization, bureaucratization, specialization, technologization and mediatization, to name just a few of them. Hardly anybody can avoid being 'dependent' on them. Such a dependence does not *a priori* mean an equally radical loss of liberty as in the limit-situations of slavery, serfdom, absolutist monarchy, or modern totalitarian regimes, and almost any of the tendencies can also be turned into an instrument that liberates individuals from certain old chains, such as those of marriage and church. Thus, does this render Skinner's historical case studies and the discussion of liberty irrelevant for today's discussion?

One aspect to claim so would be to remark how the neo-Roman critique of dependence relies on the concept of will. In post-Nietzschean thought, voluntarism has been become suspicious, while the concept of will has been transformed itself into a kind of metaphor of energy. To some extent, for example, the metaphors of play and game, present in the history of conceptions of politics, such as in the negativist Sartrean version of outplaying (*déjouer*, cf. Palonen 1992) could serve in the analysis of ambiguous situations with mixtures of dependence and opportunity and the possibilities of intervention better than the will-vocabulary.

Still, I think Skinner has good grounds to deny that non-dependence would, as such, be an archaic and voluntaristic ideal. In *Liberty before Liberalism*, a key insight into the critique of present-day views by studies of the past is legitimated in the following terms:

> The intellectual historian can help us to appreciate how far the values embodied in our present way of life, and our present ways of think-ing about those values, reflect a series of choices made at different times between different possible worlds. This awareness can help to liberate us from the grip of any hegemonal account of those values and how they should be interpreted and understood. Equipped with a broader sense of possibility, we can stand back from the intellec-tual commitments we have inherited and ask ourselves in a new spirit of enquiry what we should think of them. (Skinner 1998, 116–17)

Such a broad sense of possibility could now be applied to the tendencies seeming to produce an increasing dependence and analysing them, not in terms of 'either freedom or dependence', but within a horizon of possible actions and effects in this respect. Skinner's understanding of dependencies as possible constraints, especially as specified in the Weberian terms of *Chancen*, could be relevant to a research programme dealing with more recent con-ceptual history of liberty than what Skinner has explicitly done.

An insight into the possible, linking the topics of freedom and politics together, is also explicit in Skinner's Introduction to *Regard-ing Method*. He concludes with a confidence regarding the use of language as a resource and presents his 'political plea': 'We may be freer than we sometimes suppose' (Skinner 2002a, 7).

6

From Philosophy to Rhetoric

The Rise of Rhetoric

'First the "linguistic turn," then the "interpretative turn," and now the "rhetorical turn".' These were the words of Richard Rorty at the 1984 Iowa Symposium on The Rhetoric of the Human Sciences (Simons 1990, vii). Such a dateline indicates when rhetoric began to regain a wider acceptance in the human sciences.

The slogan 'new rhetoric' had been launched much earlier. In his books *A Grammar of Motives* (1945) and *A Rhetoric of Motives* (1950), Kenneth Burke legitimated a rhetorical perspective; moreover, American speech communication departments continued teaching rhetorical practices; and, in the 1950s, the *Quarterly Journal of Speech* had already turned to political topics. In Europe, a 'new rhetoric' was introduced through Chaïm Perelman and Lucie Olbrechts-Tyteca in *Traité de l'argumentation. La nouvelle rhétorique* (1958) and elsewhere. Also in 1958, Stephen Toulmin published a book called *The Uses of Argument*, later used as a further expression of the 'new rhetoric'. Roland Barthes (1970) underlined the omnipresence of rhetoric in European culture.

Since the 1980s, the rhetorical reinterpretation of various thinkers has highlighted new aspects in the work of allegedly well-known authors, including Hobbes and Machiavelli. Perhaps the best example of this trend are the studies on Nietzsche (Kremer-Marietti 1992; Kopperschmidt & Schanze 1994; Thomas 1999). Nietzsche's Basel lectures on ancient rhetoric have been recently edited and a historical link between his works and the rhetoric and Sophistic of the ancient Greeks has been established (*Werke. Kritische Gesamt-ausgabe*, 2/4). In addition, a new interest in the history of ancient and Renaissance rhetoric as a wider cultural phenomenon, challenging the conventional view on the legitimacy of 'superseding' rhetoric by philosophy and science, is obvious. Books such as Marc Fumaroli's *L'âge de l'éloquence* (1980) or Brian Vickers's *In Defence of Rhetoric* (1989) have played a pioneering role in this respect.

The chapter 'Rhetoric and Liberty' in Quentin Skinner's *The Foundations* has independent roots: he treats rhetoric as a language of political theory, oriented towards the liberty of city-republics. In Skinner's work, it is also connected to his thesis that it is the Roman heritage of Cicero, Sallust and Quintilian that played a key role in the formation of a 'republican' political theory in the *regnum italicum* from the thirteenth century. After *The Foundations* the historical role of Roman rhetorical thinking has gained more prominence in Skinner's studies on Lorenzetti, Machiavelli and other Italian thinkers. The next step for Skinner was then to study the presence of Roman rhetorical thinking in the English Renaissance and in the debates surrounding the Civil War, especially in the work of Hobbes.

In this chapter I shall first focus on implicit connections to rhetoric in Skinner's philosophical background and then discuss his turn towards a critique of philosophy around 1980. I take up the role of rhetoric in recent Hobbes studies and Skinner's response to it. His analysis of the rhetorical culture of the English Renaissance is connected with his studies on political theory. Finally, I assess the role of Skinner's 'rhetorical turn' in his critique of contemporary political theorizing and in constructing a new, rhetorical, perspective on conceptual change.

Rhetorical Philosophy: Wittgenstein and Austin

What was the relationship of Ludwig Wittgenstein and J. L. Austin to rhetoric? I have not found any systematic discussion of how related Wittgenstein's work since the late 1920s was to ancient or modern rhetoric. Neither the biographical studies on Wittgenstein nor works on him from the perspective of the history of philosophy seem to speak of rhetoric. For example, in Mark Bevir's *The Logic of the History of Ideas* (1999) Wittgenstein is explicitly turned into a representative of grammatical 'logic', contrary to historical and rhetorical approaches (cf. remarks in Palonen 2000a).

Still, Chaïm Perelman and his students, as well as the American rhetoricians of human sciences, regularly invoke the name of Wittgenstein and, for example, the metaphor of language games. Michel Meyer of the Brussels school directly connects Austin to Aristotle in a table, rendering parallel the illocutionary dimension of language with *ethos*, the locutionary with *logos* and the perlocutionary with *pathos* (Meyer 1993, 23).

When rereading Wittgenstein's *Philosophische Untersuchungen* I found the tone very similar to the ancient sophists' critique towards the philosophies of Plato and Aristotle. Wittgenstein, in particular, opposes categorical classifications and clear-cut distinctions through counter-examples and thought experiments. By doing so, he refuses to subscribe to the 'realist' idea that things and phenomena 'are' something independent of the language by which there are spoken. He clearly is arguing *in utramque partem*, aiming to make simple and evident states of affairs look more complicated, to show the limits of some commonly used paradigmatic examples. For Wittgenstein, 'Untersuchung aber richtet sich nicht auf die *Erscheinungen*, sondern, wie man sagen könnte, auf die "*Möglichkeiten*" der Erscheinungen' (Wittgenstein 1953/1958, § 90).

In a key passage, Wittgenstein clearly shares the rhetorical insight that we should 'radikal mit der Idee brechen, die Sprache funktionere immer auf *eine* Weise, diene immer dem gleichen Zweck' (ibid., § 129). If there are no strict rules for the proper use of language, we obtain a range of choice for the various modes of using language – an idea then invoked by Austin in his distinction between the constative and performative uses of language. This contingency of language can also be detected in the Wittgensteinian metaphor of language games (*Sprachspiele*). The 'playability' of any language, the differentiation between the various games as well as the malleability and interpretability of the rules in concrete cases can be understood as dimensions of such contingency, tending to make the use of language immediately interesting.

One of the most famous sentences of *Philosophische Untersuchungen*, frequently quoted by Skinner, is an expression Wittgenstein used in passing: 'Die Bedeutung eines Wortes ist sein Gebrauch in der Sprache' (ibid., § 43, cf. § 30). The so-called ordinary language philosophers have tended to trivialize questions of meaning, whereas Wittgenstein himself speaks on the multidimensionality of meaning as a condition of understanding of a concept, as expressed in the following paragraphs:

531. Wir reden vom Verstehen eines Satzes in dem Sinne, in welchem er durch einen andern ersetzt werden kann, der das Gleiche sagt, aber auch in dem Sinne, in welchem er durch keinen anderen ersetzt werden kann. (So wenig wie ein musikalisches Thema durch ein anderes.)

In einem Fall ist der Gedanke des Satzes, was verschiedenen Sätzen gemeinsam ist; im anderen, etwas, was nur diese Worte, in diesen Stellungen ausdrücken. (Verstehen eines Gedichts.)

532. So hat also 'verstehen' hier zwei verschiedene Bedeutungen? – Ich will lieber sagen, diese Gebrauchsarten von 'verstehen' bilden seine Bedeutung, meinen *Begriff* des Verstehens.

Denn ich *will* 'verstehen' auf alles das anwenden. (ibid., 176)

The multidimensional 'meaning of a concept' that Wittgenstein indicates here includes both semantics and vocabulary. A further dimension concerns words as deeds. For example, Wittgenstein writes on negation: 'Das Zeichen der Verneinung ist eine Veranlassung etwas . . . zu tun' (ibid., § 549), and more generally: 'Die Sprache ist ein Instrument. Ihre Begriffe sind Instrumente' (ibid., § 569), and further: 'Begriffe leiten uns zu Untersuchungen. Sind der Ausdruck unserer Interessen, und lenken unser Interesse' (ibid., § 570).

Wittgenstein is, however, hardly interested in the historical and political dimensions of using concepts and playing language games. An insight that could encourage such studies can, however, be found in the volume *Über Gewissheit*: 'Wenn sich die Sprachspiele ändern, ändern sich die Begriffe, und mit den Begriffen die Bedeutungen der Wörter' (Wittgenstein 1970, § 25). Concepts exceed here the meaning of words and, more specifically, conceptual changes are rendered dependent on the context of the language games in which they are used.

Although Austin's *How to Do Things with Words* is a technical work in philosophy, the links to rhetoric are explicit in its mode of argument. Austin was seemingly relying rather on the grammarians, from whom the philosophers should learn how to treat language. In rhetorical terms, the speech acts refer to different dimensions of rhetoric: perlocutions allude to acceptance in the audience, whereas illocutions refer to the qualifications of the acts as moves.

Wittgenstein and Austin introduced an action perspective to language that was as critical towards the *vita contemplativa* tradition of philosophy as the sophistic and rhetorical criticism of the ancient philosophy. Such an action perspective is able to render the contingency of politics intelligible, without *a priori* reducing it, offering a critical perspective to the sociological approaches that dominated academic debates of the 1960s and 1970s.

It is by this moment of contingency that Skinner invoked his distance from the conventional history of ideas. Wittgenstein and Austin offered him the first tools for the critique of philosophy. Skinner's move from speech acts to 'ancient theorists of eloquence who originally spoke of rhetorical redescription' meant that he has 'come to share their more contingent understanding of normative concepts' (Skinner 1999c, 67). This can be understood as an inclusion of the speech act vocabulary in the wider perspective of rhetoric.

Skinner's Critique of Philosophy

Although Skinner has turned history into an argument against purely philosophical approaches in textual interpretation, he regarded history as being complementary to philosophy. In the Wittgensteinian atmosphere at Cambridge in the 1960s, Skinner still revered the philosophers: 'We were waiting for the philosophers to tell us' (Skinner to KP, September 2001). His critique of the Laslett formula illustrates such a reliance on the necessity of philosophy as a master discipline.

Towards the end of 1970s, Skinner's views began to change. This change can be documented best through his review articles for the *New York Review of Books*. These reviews originally underpinned the writing of a book on hermeneutics for Cambridge University Press (Skinner to KP, April 1999), a plan that was never realized, although fragments of it were incorporated into 'A Reply to My Critics' (1988c).

We can take as point of departure Skinner's admiring review of Richard Bernstein's *The Restructuring of Social and Political Theory*. He criticizes the author for overstressing the dominance of positivism when, for example, he tends 'to overlook the important role played by the study of history in undermining positivist confidence' (Skinner 1978c, 26). Bernstein's heroes are the Frankfurt school, the starting point of which appears to Skinner as dubious: 'Doesn't it begin to look as if the project of "critical theory" amounts to little more than a version of the Indian rope-trick?' (ibid., 28). Skinner's key point, specifically directed against Habermas, is the following:

If there is one lesson we have thoroughly learned from Quine, Kuhn and the post-empiricists, it is that the evidence we cite in favor of our beliefs is not sufficient to determine them. What we are prepared to count as evidence depends on the beliefs we already hold. But this appears to leave us in a world of rival and perhaps incommensurable systems of thought, each of which will be susceptible of rational defence, while none of them will be capable of being appraised from a genuinely neutral point of view. (ibid.)

To Skinner what matters is that within analytical philosophy itself a main assumption of classical philosophy, a rational determination of beliefs, has been convincingly demonstrated to be a hopeless task. For Skinner this does not lead to 'irrationalism' but rather to a 'semantic holism', to an insight into the interdependence of beliefs. A 'neutral point of view' is beyond human powers. In other words, Nietzschean and Weberian perspectivism – an underestimation of Weber's role is Skinner's further argument against Bernstein (ibid., 26–7) – can, according to Skinner, be legitimated within the province of analytical philosophy. Habermas's ultra-rationalism or Martin Hollis's claim 'that a rational man must choose and occupy his roles in a rational style' (criticized in Skinner 1978b, 67) appear to him as not having taken such a critique seriously.

The converse side of this inevitability of competing perspectives consists in the acceptance of a political dimension, in the sense of both contingency and controversiality, as present in philosophical controversies. To Skinner this is no remnant but a liberating instance, allowing discussion of different philosophical views with regard to their political content and significance. This politics of philosophy – I owe this phrase to Tuija Pulkkinen – is explicit in Skinner's essay 'Habermas's Reformation'. He makes an unconventional move when connecting Habermas explicitly to the contractarian line of thought:

These claims may at first appear strange and arbitrary, but in fact Habermas is merely updating one of the most familiar conceptual devices associated with the traditional discussion of the 'social contract' in political thought. . . . But in essence this basic suggestion remains strictly analogous to the ideal of a 'state of nature' developed by such early contractrarians as Locke and Rousseau, and revived by such avowed disciples of their approach as John Rawls in *A Theory of Justice*. The proposal is simply that if potentially repressive institutions are rightly to be regarded as legitimate, it must be possible to imagine their creation under conditions of freedom and equality, and their acceptance by the unforced consent of all those subsequently liable to be affected by their behavior. (Skinner 1982a, 36)

Similar to Skinner's comments on Rawls, the main target is the depoliticizing move of the contractarians, appearing in the work of Habermas as the idea of 'unforced consent'. To Skinner such a reliance on the force of consent appears anachronistic in the contemporary situation: 'It is hard to think of a single living philosopher who subscribes to the obviously absurd belief that any proposition not capable of being scientifically grounded must represent nothing more than the statement of an arbitrary preference' (ibid., 38). Skinner's point is directed against Habermas's naïve and ahistorical view on the resolution of conceptual controversies: 'Does Habermas really mean that *everyone* in the ideal speech situation would arrive at exactly the same moral as well as cognitive judgments? . . . Is it really plausible to suppose that all of us would agree what counts as coercion and what as true liberty?' (ibid.).

Here Skinner touches the Achilles' heel of all contractarian arguments, namely their inability to consider concepts as historical, changing and controversial. Habermas and Rawls retain such an essentialist tendency in so far as they assume that the name for a concept would induce a greater agreement about its content. In contrast to this attitude, conceptual historians have realized that such an assumption only transfers the controversy one step forward, to concern the interpretation of the concept used in the argument (cf. also Palonen 2002c).

Skinner's further argument concerns Habermas's underestimation of the normative force of facticity: 'If an institution has been accepted as legitimate over any period of time, it will inescapably have acquired a life and momentum of its own which could well enable it to survive for a considerable period even after everyone has ceased to believe in its legitimacy' (Skinner 1982a, 38). Although delegitimation is a crucial aspect of political change to Skinner, he does not – unlike Habermas – consider it to be sufficient, but as something that requires additional political moves at the level of institutional changes. Politics cannot be reduced to theory politics.

An enthusiastic review of Richard Rorty's *Philosophy and the Mirror of Nature* entitled 'The End of Philosophy?' contains perhaps Skinner's most remarkable critique of philosophy. He objects to philosophers' traditional self-interpretation of their field as 'queen of the disciplines', which is questioned more radically than ever by Rorty: 'Ever since Aristotle declared that philosophy is "the first and last of the sciences," philosophers have tended to take a very exalted view of the importance of their subject. They will find it much harder to do so after reading Professor Richard Rorty's disturbing and brilliantly argued book' (Skinner 1981b, 46).

Subscribing to this critique, Skinner does not share Rorty's view on the impending end of philosophy – 'the suggestion that we may be "in a fair way to dispensing with philosophy" is surely a considerable overstatement' (ibid., 47). He is not ready to disqualify the 'central traditions of philosophy', such as the work of Bertrand Russell (ibid., 46), a political hero of the young Skinner (Skinner 2002d, 35–6). He regards Rorty's triad of favourites – Wittgenstein, Heidegger and Dewey – as 'a shock tactic' (Skinner 1981b, 46) and insists that among those contributing to the 'project of deconstruction' the name of Collingwood should be mentioned. He quotes the latter's view from 1924 on 'the philosopher as an "international boundary commissar"' (ibid.) and summarizes the Collingwoodian criticism of philosophy as follows:

> There are thus no ultimate categories of thought for the metaphysician to lay bare. There are only shifting paradigms, changing questions, new sets of answers, all inevitably limited by the scope of the prevailing disciplines. Those are precisely the arguments that Rorty's heroes mount, so it is surprising that he never mentions Collingwood's work. (ibid.)

It is the disciplinary hierarchy that is the target of Skinner's criticism, as inspired by Collingwood's and Rorty's antifoundationalism. It is paraphrased by Skinner as follows: 'the search for the indubitable foundations of our thought is no more likely to succeed than the search for the unicorn, and ought immediately (and for the same reason) to be called off' (ibid., 47). Rorty's critique can be directed against the professional ideology of philosophers, the 'assumption that philosophers already know the answer to basic "conceptual" questions' (ibid., 48). Skinner concludes that such claims can be turned against the philosophers themselves: 'While posing as the vigilant guardian of rationality, such philosophers expose themselves to the perpetual danger of elevating our local and fallible canons of argument into a set of imperishable truths' (ibid.).

In addition to Rorty and Collingwood, Skinner relies on the post-analytical philosophers. He appreciates Quine's 'denying that any categorical distinction can be drawn between matters of definition and matters of fact.' According to Quine, Skinner writes, 'allegedly "analytical" truths may simply be those for which no one has yet given us any interesting alternatives that might lead us to question them' (ibid., 47). Thus, contingency in the intellectual world also concerns the naming of the units and the making of distinctions, which are no more based on 'the nature of things' than, say, street names or the parliamentary left–right distinction. Here, once again, Skinner comes, equipped with modern academic instruments, to a conclusion that corresponds precisely to Weber's view: 'Ein System der Kulturwissenschaften auch nur in dem Sinne einer definitiven, objektiv gültigen Fixierung der *Fragen* und *Gebiete*, von denen sie zu handeln berufen sein sollen, wäre ein Unsinn in sich' (Weber 1904, 185).

Rorty also practises a variant of intellectual history that inverts legitimation stories. 'History, he proposes, may be capable of serving as a therapy: by returning to the historical moments at which our current epistemological delusions arose, we may be able to liberate ourselves from their grasp' (Skinner 1981b, 46). Skinner appreciates Rorty's attempts to identify the point at which philosophers deluded themselves. Strictly speaking, this is not Skinner's own view: Rorty's belief in the self-healing forces of such a historiography looks one-dimensional, in comparison with Skinner's disillusioned history of the losers.

For Skinner the crucial conclusion he draws from Rorty's critique of philosophy is to understand that it must be an illusion to suppose 'that physics is "objective" in some way in which poetry or politics may not be' (ibid., 48). It is at this moment that Skinner regards Rorty's anti-foundationalist and anti-hierarchical conception as 'salutary':

> It reminds us that there is indeed a crucial sense in which the work, say, of a political theorist may be strongly analogous to that of an experimental scientist. . . . both are 'ways of coping', and both are subject to stringent pragmatic tests. A good theory of mechanics enables us to construct bridges which are not likely to collapse; a good theory of politics enables us to construct states of which the same may be said with similar confidence. (ibid.)

The last sentence should also be read as a mark of ironic distance. As I already mentioned, Skinner has nothing against utopian authors like Rawls, but he does not construct such utopias himself nor take them at their face value. His review article of Rorty marks a definite break with Skinner's expectations that philosophers should or could resolve conceptual questions for others. Perhaps this also alludes to Skinner's work towards engaging himself in reflecting changes in political concepts.

As a critique of philosophy we should also count Skinner's Introduction to the volume *The Return of Grand Theory in the Human Sciences*. This volume, I think, should be read as a sensitive move towards current intellectual tendencies, while Skinner himself retains a detached attitude towards contemporary debates. He has not given up his doubts about the possibility of a 'grand theory', showing in the Introduction a definite distance towards the revival of a classicist style of theorizing in the works of Rawls, Habermas and Althusser particularly. I just want to quote one further judgement on Habermas and those who slightly later were labelled communitarians, whom he provocatively connects with neoconservatives, such as Roger Scruton in Britain:

> It is a striking fact that, although Habermas presents this diagnosis from a Marxist perspective, a number of political writers from the so-called New Right have lately developed a remarkably similar attack on the moral limitations of *laissez-faire* capitalism, defending a form of conservatism founded not on free markets and the minimal state, but rather on an almost Hegelian sense that the values of community, loyalty and deference must be prized and cultivated above all. (Skinner 1985a, 9)

In line with his critique of philosophy is a certain reading of the new theoretical interests that render the epithet 'grand theory' rather paradoxical. The common feature of these thinkers is 'a willingness to emphasize the importance of the local and the contingent, a desire to underline the extent to which our concepts and attitude have been shaped by particular historical circumstances, and a corresponding strong dislike – amounting almost to hatred in the case of Wittgenstein – of all overarching theories and singular schemes of explanation' (ibid., 12). It is clear that this judgement does not concern Rawls or Althusser, but rather those 'anti-theorists' that have 'been engaged in theorizing at the same time' (ibid., 12–13), such as Foucault, Derrida or Feyerabend. As is the case with Rorty, the work of such anti-theorists has clearly inspired Skinner's critique of the authority of philosophy and supported his growing interest in conceptual change (a topic he attributes to Foucault, ibid., 13, cf. also Skinner 1985b).

The critique of philosophy is continued in Skinner's 'A Reply to My Critics'. I have already referred to his position concerning 'truth' and 'relativism'. This critique should not be mixed with an episte-mological naïvety à la Minogue (1981), but is a 'self-conscious reflec-tion' that favours the mutual enrichment between theory and practice (Skinner 1988c, 233). He is not content with merely expli-cating what 'ordinary historians' are already doing, but what he himself is doing in his methodological writings 'has been to articu-late some general arguments about the process of interpretation itself, and to draw from them a series of what I take to be method-ological implications' (ibid., 234).

While claiming that the question of truth 'does not arise' in the kind of historical investigations that he is conducting (ibid., 256), Skinner argues against equating 'the holding of false beliefs with lapses of rationality' (ibid., 240). Even concerning rationality the danger of anachronism is imminent, and to counter it Skinner insists: 'The golden rule is that, however bizarre the beliefs we are studying seem to be, we must try to make the agents who accepted them appear [in Hollis's phrase] to be as rational as possible' (ibid., 246). Although 'all forms of histories are bound to be "whiggish"'' in so far as it is the historian who poses the questions, this does not mean a licence to dismiss something in the context of the agents as *a priori* irrelevant (ibid., 248). The historians cannot determine 'whether the belief in question is rational according to their own . . . standards of rationality' (ibid., 244). Skinner admits that there are cases in which, when the explanations conflict with the self-explanations of past agents, 'ours must be regarded as superior ones' (ibid., 254). But the point of this 'is to say no more than that one of our beliefs is that our stock of social explanation has become enriched over the course of recent centuries' (ibid.).

In short, Skinner's view is a further expression of his 'semantic holism' of beliefs. To speak of 'rationality' is possible only in rela-tion to one's other beliefs, and it has, as in the case of Weber, nothing to do with the substance of the beliefs defended. More interestingly, Skinner now seems to claim that 'concepts' have gained a key posi-tion in the interrelation between beliefs.

The beliefs we form, the judgements we make, will always be medi-ated by the concepts available to us for describing what we have observed. And to employ a concept is always to appraise and clas-sify our experience from a particular perspective and in a particular way. What we experience and report will accordingly be what is brought to our attention by the range of concepts we possess and the nature of the discriminations they enable us to make. We cannot hope to find any less winding a path from experience to belief, from observational evidence to any one determinate judgement. (ibid., 249)

Skinner simultaneously argues against both epistemological empiricism and conceptual realism. More explicitly than ever he joins the perspectivist view of knowledge and classification by claiming that 'our concepts are not forced upon us by the world' (ibid., 250). Additionally, it becomes clear that Skinner shares the view of Koselleck on concepts as 'pivots' (1996, 65) and disagrees with Pocock's view (1996) that concepts are just one instance in the language or discourse.

One consequence of this position is to show the limits of a dictionary-like one-to-one translation, without committing oneself to linguistic determinism, in style of the Shapir–Whorf hypothesis. Already with the trivial case of the Latin *imber* and the English rain, Skinner is ready to conclude: 'I am merely contending that it will always be a mistake for an historian to assume that the task of explicating an alien concept can be reduced to that of finding a counterpart in his own language for the term that expresses it' (Skinner 1988c, 252). With Machiavelli's famous concept of *virtù*, he criticizes existing interpretations for rejecting the possibility 'that Machiavelli may have been using the term with perfect consistency to express a concept so alien to our own moral thought that we cannot hope nowadays to capture it except in the form of an extended and rather approximate periphrasis' (ibid., 253). The interconnection of concepts and vocabularies also means that 'it generally will be fatal to revise the terms in which they are expressed' (ibid., 255).

One aspect of Skinner's critique of the monopolistic claims of philosophers is paradoxical in so far as this has piqued his interest in concepts as key instances of argumentation. It is here, however, that the traditional philosophical style of speaking of concepts becomes fatal and is replaced by Skinner with a historical, political and rhetorical mode of using concepts.

To summarize, what Skinner has been doing when turning towards a critique of philosophy is not directed against the activity of philosophizing. He, on the contrary, claims that Minogue's defence of methodological naïvety 'is itself a philosophical argument' (ibid., 234). It is the philosopher's claims on authority and superiority over other disciplines, on attributing a specific place to questions and on relying on a ready-made classification of categories and unhistorical conceptual 'clarification' that Skinner characterized as an 'insufficient puzzlement' (ibid., 282).

Such a critique corresponds to Weber's critique of his own discipline, of unproblematized normative and ahistorical commitments in the political economy of his day: 'Aber die Eigenart jener Weltanschauung mit ihrem optimistischen Glauben an die theoretische und praktische Rationalisierbarkeit des Wirklichen, wirkte wesentlich insofern, als sie *hinderte*, daß der problematische Charakter jenes selbstverständlich vorausgesetzten Gesichtspunkts entdeckt wurde' (Weber 1904, 185). Such a programme was, with the analysis of the rhetorical tradition during the Renaissance, actualized in the next phase of Skinner's work. This was recently emphasized by Skinner himself responding to an interview with following words:

> But I certainly used to show an insufficient awareness of the extent to which the writers of the texts we study are in less than full control of what they write. Here I have been influenced by what I take to be one of the most valuable insights of deconstructionist criticism. The insight I have in mind is that what passes for argument in philosophical texts often proves on more sceptical inspection to amount to little more than a tissue of metaphors and other rhetorical devices employed to lend authority to what is asserted. This helps to explain why, since the 1980s, I have spent so much time studying the classical and Renaissance art of rhetoric. (Skinner 2002d, 50)

Rhetoric and Philosophy in Hobbes

Skinner's rhetorical studies have several interrelated dimensions. He interprets the history of Hobbes's political theory in terms of its relationship to rhetoric against the background of an extensive discussion of the rhetorical culture of the English Renaissance, which also leads him to a historical reinterpretation of the political thought of that period. To my query about the origins of his extensive studies on English Renaissance rhetoric, Skinner replied:

> I had originally envisaged a short book about Hobbes in which I drew on the secondary literature about the reception and teaching of classical rhetoric in Renaissance England, and showed how far Hobbes was nurtured in, and reacted against, that training. But I found that no such general study existed, and in the end I had to do my best to write such a survey myself. This added several years to

the writing of my book on Hobbes, and made it twice as long as I (and the CUP) had originally envisaged. (Skinner to KP, January 2002)

As with the conceptual history of liberty, Skinner's discussion on rhetoric also has contemporary political relevance. It continues his critique of philosophy, with the rhetorical idea of arguing *in utramque partem* as a style opposed to the authoritative claims of philosophy. More specifically, the discussion of ancient and Renaissance rhetoric has enabled Skinner to generalize the perspective on conceptual change by incorporating the vocabulary of speech acts in that of *ars rhetorica*.

New styles of Hobbes studies arose after Skinner left the topic in the early 1970s. Perhaps the most prominent among them was to stress the role of scepticism in Hobbes's thinking. Richard Tuck, for example, in his Introduction to the Cambridge edition of *Leviathan*, considered scepticism as 'the central theme of the Renaissance in the late sixteenth century', with Michel de Montaigne its main exponent. 'This was the culture to which Hobbes contributed his first publication, his translation of Thucydides' (Tuck 1991, xiii; cf. also Tuck 1993, esp. 285–98).

Hobbes's humanist education and the presence of rhetorical elements in his early work, such as the edition of Thucydides' *Peloponnesian War* and translation of parts of Aristotle's *Art of Rhetoric*, is commonly recognized. Hobbes scholars used, however, to pay no particular attention to his early work, and this is also the case with the young Skinner, who in a footnote writes: 'Recent commentaries on Hobbes (my own included) have been woefully insensitive to the importance to this rhetorical background for an understanding of Hobbes's thought' (Skinner 1991a, 4).

The rhetorical interest in Hobbes studies was raised by David Johnston's *Rhetoric of Leviathan* (1986). Johnston's work has its origins in Sheldon Wolin's seminar, in which the author had the opportunity 'to articulate some arguments against Quentin Skinner's interpretation of Hobbes and receive the benefit of Professor Skinner's response' (Johnston 1986, x). Departing from Hobbes's interpretation of Thucydides and considering his minor publications, Johnston's key historical thesis is to deny the role of Hobbes's sudden conversion in favour of the continuous presence of rhetoric in his later work:

But this new fascination with the axiomatic method and its explanatory potential did not in any sense constitute a rejection of the rhetorical tradition that had shaped Hobbes's thinking during the first forty years of his life. The ideas and interests he had inherited from that tradition continued to contribute to the formation of his political thought throughout the rest of his life. (ibid., 23)

Johnston is, of course, not insensitive to the militantly anti-rhetorical argumentation in Hobbes's *Elements of Law* and *De Cive*, as opposed to the *Leviathan*. Johnston interprets this opposition in terms of differences between Latin and vernacular audiences, reading *Leviathan* as a book 'intended for a large, public audience and aimed to shape popular opinion directly' (ibid., 89). His specific attention concerns the changing role of metaphor: 'But if the aim of *Leviathan* is less to demonstrate the truth of his political doctrines than to imprint them upon the minds of his readers, then metaphors, along with many other literary devices that have no place in a strict scientific demonstration, are entirely in place' (ibid., 91). In a broader sense, Johnston regards Hobbes as an advocate of a 'Politics of Enlightenment' and sees here a difference between *The Elements of Law* and *Leviathan*: 'The opposition between logic and rhetoric, between the rational use of language and its abuse ... gives way in *Leviathan* to a new and broader opposition between knowledge, reason, and science on the one hand and ignorance, superstition and magic on the other' (ibid., 108–9).

Skinner acknowledges his debt to the study of Johnston (for example, in Skinner 2001b, 17) and it was from Johnston's subtitle that he adopted the phrase 'Reason and Rhetoric'. Despite this, Skinner regards Hobbes as being much more deeply embedded in the rhetorical culture than Johnston does. He objects that Johnston 'employs the word [rhetoric] principally to refer to Hobbes's literary strategies and more particularly to ask what political point Hobbes may have been performing in *Leviathan*' (Skinner 1996a, 6). The latter remark seems to allude to the mode in which Skinner himself treated Hobbes in the early phase of his studies. In *Reason and Rhetoric in the Philosophy of Hobbes*, Skinner, however, sets a different objective.

By contrast, when I speak of Hobbes's rhetoric in *Leviathan* I employ the word in the way that Hobbes himself would I believe have understood it. I use it, that is, to describe a set of linguistic techniques ... derived from the rhetorical doctrines of *inventio, dispositio* and *elocutio*, the three principal *elementa* in classical and Renaissance theories of written eloquence. (ibid.)

Such an expression accentuates Skinner's aim to avoid anachronisms when speaking of Hobbes's rhetoric. Now, I think this view has a definite point when employed just to Hobbes and his relationship to the Renaissance English *ars rhetorica*. In his debate with the French philosopher Yves Zarka, Skinner presents his point as follows: 'I am less interested in Hobbes as the author of a philosophical system than in Hobbes as the contributor to a series of debates about the concept of *scientia civilis* within the Renaissance' (Skinner 2001b, 20, cf. 1996a, 6). Or, as he puts it in the first sentence of *Reason and Rhetoric*: 'This book examines the central aspiration of Hobbes's civil philosophy, the aspiration to convert the study of moral and political theory into a scientific discipline' (Skinner 1996a, 1).

Thus, it is neither Hobbes's 'doctrine of rhetoric' nor the content of his rhetoric as such that interests Skinner, but the presence and absence of rhetoric in Hobbes's *scientia civilis* marks the main point. He argues in particular against the scepticism thesis: 'I see little evidence, however, that Hobbes was much interested in Pyrrhonism . . . in any of his treatises on civil science. He was not primarily responding to a set of epistemological arguments. Rather he was reacting against the entire rhetorical culture within which the vogue of scepticism had developed' (ibid., 9, cf. also Skinner 1994b, 269).

Skinner thus argues that Johnston 'could have carried his argument much further' (Skinner 1993a, 78). Furthermore, 'it is misleading to suggest that Hobbes had set his concern with the rhetorical tradition "to one side" by the time he came to write these works, and still more misleading to add that he became "less and less interested" in "the formal study of rhetoric"' (ibid., 80). In order to understand its role to Hobbes – both as a target of criticism and as an instrument – we have to construct a much more detailed understanding of the practices of this rhetorical culture. 'Hobbes's world is so rich and strange that, if we turn to it merely for answers to our own questions, we shall needlessly impoverish our own intellectual lives' (Skinner 1996a, 15). Once again Skinner inveighs against 'insufficient puzzlement', against the lack of a sufficiently radical distance to the present as a condition to understand the point of past moves.

> I attempt to show, however, that to think of Hobbes's prose as a clear window through which we can gaze uninterruptedly at his thought is a serious mistake. Hobbes's thought in *Leviathan* is mediated by a prose in which the techniques of *ornatus* are used to produce a large

number of deliberately ambiguous effects. To fail to recognise this is to fail to recognise what kind of a work we have in our hands. (ibid., 13)

In order to understand this, it is necessary to become familiar with the rhetorical culture of the English Renaissance oneself and to present a comprehensive picture of it to readers. Skinner's main move in *Reason and Rhetoric* is to open up an academic, literary and political world that had been hardly considered, except by specialists. In fact, the world of the Tudor rhetoricians was dealt with by Skinner in chapters on the 'Northern Renaissance' in *The Foundations* (Skinner 1978a I, 213–48). He deals in particular with Thomas Elyot and his *The Book Named the Governor*, but also names such as Roger Ascham, Richard Mulcaster and Philip Sidney are already mentioned, although not as rhetoricians. The study of school curricula and English rhetorical handbooks, such as Thomas Wilson's *The Arte of Rhetorique*, together with the work of several students and colleagues of Skinner (for example, Peltonen 1995), opened up a new culture also to Skinner himself.

To speak of 'rhetorical culture' also refers to a further implication of Skinner's interpretive principles, namely his rejection of the divide between literary and other historical texts. 'The canon of leading treatises in the history of philosophy is at the same time a canon of major literary texts' (Skinner 1996a, 14). His explicit aim is to deepen the cultural context that he considers necessary to understand Hobbes's views on *scientia civilis*. 'I see no prospect of understanding his thought unless we treat this wider discourse as the primary object of our research' (ibid., 8). As opposed to his interpretation of the Renaissance as a break with the ancient world, Skinner now concedes that this does not unconditionally hold true for Renaissance rhetoricians:

What is striking . . . is the extent to which they nevertheless lack any sense of the past as a foreign country. Having dusted down the ancient texts, they exhibit almost no interest in reconstructing their historical contexts as a way of making better sense of them. On the contrary, they approach them as if they are contemporary documents with an almost unproblematic relevance to their own circumstances. This in turn means that there is nothing unhistorical about yoking Cicero and Quintilian together with the vernacular rhetoricians of Tudor England . . . and treating them as if they were all contributing to the same argument. To do so is simply to reflect the extraordinary strong sense of cultural unity with which the Tudor humanists confronted their classical authorities. (ibid., 40)

Here Skinner's emphasis on historical discontinuity is toned down in order to understand the specificity of the debates and arguments in a context in which the ancient writings were understood to contribute. The 'contemporaneity' is not to be measured by the calendar but by the range of authors, debates and arguments treated as contemporaries in the texts. The context of Hobbes's work has been extended into an entire rhetorical culture.

Making a 'wider discourse as the primary object of our research' relativizes the divide between texts and contexts. The genre of *Reason and Rhetoric* is double-edged. Skinner's point is not only to present the five initial chapters as preliminaries to a study on Hobbes, but equally to use the chapters on Hobbes as illustrative contexts that improve our understanding of the chapters on Renaissance rhetorical culture. As a contribution to theory politics, beyond the 'Hobbesiologists', it is just such an inversion of the roles of text and context that seems to me the main point of Skinner's *Reason and Rhetoric*. In consequence, I will here depart from Skinner's thesis on Hobbes and then extend the assessment of his discussions to the political significance of Renaissance rhetorical culture.

Skinner's historical revision consists in a definite thesis about the periodization of the role of rhetorical culture to Hobbes. The first step is to emphasize the depth of Hobbes's humanist *Bildung*, invoking his largely unknown early works, such as the *Horae subscivae* from 1620, which according to Skinner probably also contains studies by Hobbes (as well as by his pupil William Cavendish). In addition, the poem *De Mirabilibus Pecci* (1627) as well as the translation and introduction to Thucydides and an edition of parts of Aristotle's *Rhetoric* are written in a 'rhetorical style' (Skinner 1996a, 238–49). Even those of Hobbes's writings which attack rhetoric and the humanist programme of *scientia civilis*, in particular *Elements of Law* and *De Cive*, follow in this same attack with classifications, distinctions, vocabularies and even examples of Roman and Renaissance rhetoric (ibid., 250–326).

Against this background Skinner is able to specify in which respect Hobbes, after 1647 and in particular in *Leviathan* (published in 1651), partly rehabilitated rhetoric. Skinner's point is that Hobbes returned to the Ciceronian programme *ratio atque eloquentia*, viewing reason and rhetoric as equally indispensable parts of the *scientia civilis*. 'Although he never came to view the *ars rhetorica* with positive favour, he undoubtedly came to believe in the inescapable need for an alliance between reason and eloquence, and hence between the art of rhetoric and the methods of science' (ibid., 346).

The later Hobbes's use of rhetoric remained strictly instrumental, marking a distance from the principles of rhetorical culture. Skinner illustrates, however, that this does not make him less brilliant in using rhetorical instruments for his own purposes. In the final chapters of *Reason and Rhetoric*, he analyses in detail how the different components of the Roman and Renaissance rhetorical programme, in particular various techniques of *ornatus* as well as the ironic and satirical use of tropes and figures, were used by Hobbes in his two-edged political criticism of both the Catholics and the 'enthusiast' Protestants. In a later article, Skinner also closely analyses the provocation of laughter and the use of some non-classical tropes (Skinner 2001d).

The value of the *ars rhetorica* in Hobbes studies remains hotly disputed in reviews and polemics. Not only do philosophers such as Zarka (2001) tend – even more radically than the critics of Skinner's 'contextualist' studies on Hobbes in the 1960s and 1970s – to denounce Skinner's 'historicism', but also some rhetoric specialists, such as Nancy Struewer (1998), propose a different conception of rhetoric. Others, such as Patricia Springborg (1997) and Karl Schuhmann (1998), on the contrary, regard Skinner's work as inspiring and thought-provoking. As a study of Hobbes's debt to rhetorical culture as well as on his use of rhetorical classifications and techniques, *Reason and Rhetoric* marks a major novelty within the Skinnerian *œuvre*.

The Rhetorical Culture of the Renaissance

The thematization of the rhetorical culture of the Renaissance in Britain adds, as I have already indicated, a new dimension to the political thought of the period. In *The Foundations*, Skinner's interest, as far he goes to the second half of the sixteenth century, was focused on the political struggles surrounding the Reformation. The authors working within the already established Tudor Anglican regime did not merit special interest.

In *Reason and Rhetoric*, Skinner admits that the rise of Tudor vernacular rhetoric took place among the Protestant scholars (Wilson, Fenner, Peacham), and *ars rhetorica* partly served as skills in preaching (Skinner 1996a, 67). Despite this, he regards the role of secular Roman rhetoric as decisive in this context.

> . . . the schoolboys of late Tudor and early Stuart England continued
> to be drilled in a basically Roman tradition of secular rhetoric,

according to which the point or purpose of studying the ars rhetorica was civic and political character. Without a mastery of this art, it
was argued, no one can hope effectively to discharge the most important duties of nobility or citizenship. (ibid.)

This political dimension of rhetoric allows Skinner to concentrate
on topics different from those he dealt with in *The Foundations*: the
formation of the state did not play a role with Tudor and Stuart
rhetoricians. No break with secular antiquity was made, and 'any
grammar school pupil of Hobbes's generation would have studied
the views of Cicero and Quintilian on the nature of *scientia civilis*
more closely than that of anyone else' (Skinner 2000b, 28).

Pocock's interpretations of Harrington (in Pocock 1975 and elsewhere) and later studies, such as Markku Peltonen's *Classical
Humanism and Republicanism in English Political Thought 1570–1640*
(1995), also contributed to the relativization of the monarchy–
republic divide by considering the presence and significance of local
self-government. Peltonen invokes the role of such lesser known
figures as Richard Beacon and Thomas Scott and reads republican
elements also in the work of Francis Bacon which idealizes civic
greatness. He does not, however, explicitly thematize the specific
rhetorical element in this republicanism.

The opposition between republic and monarchy was played
down in Renaissance rhetoric in favour of opposing styles of life-
conduct. The political ideal of citizenship, connected to the *negotium*
style of life, was preferred to the Christian *otium* ideal. This *negotium*
was not, as Machiavelli's, militantly atheistic, nor strictly republican in the sense of Italian city-republics. The place for secular foren-
sic rhetoric remained in the courts and in the deliberative role of the
counsellor of princes (Skinner 1996a, 72–3). According to Skinner,
'the humanists we have been considering were conspicuously successful at claiming a place in public life on their own behalf' (ibid.,
73). The idea of *vir civilis* is then described in the following terms:
'besides being a wise man capable of reasoning aright, the true *vir
civilis* must be a man of the highest eloquence, capable of persuading his listeners by the sheer force of his "winning" speech to
acknowledge the truths that his reason brings to light' (ibid., 83).

The *scientia civilis* of Renaissance rhetoricians thus followed the
Ciceronian ideal of *ratio atque eloquentia*. Oratory is a power that
wins the audience to the side of 'reason', which alone is insufficient:
'a *vir civilis* who dedicates himself to the execution of his principal
duties will at the same time be acting as an exponent of the rhetori-

cal arts' (ibid., 87). Francis Bacon speaks of a '"politic part of eloquence", the force of which derives from its capacity to help a speaker to adjust his arguments to suit to different audiences' (ibid., 97).

It is such a *negotium* ideal of *vir civilis* as a politically engaged orator (speaker or writer) in the classical and Renaissance *scientia civilis* that is vigorously opposed by Hobbes, especially in *The Elements of Law* and *De Cive*. 'His discussion is mainly aimed at stigmatising the art of rhetoric as a cause of the dissolution of commonwealths' (ibid., 285). The classical distinction was based on the distinction 'between citizens and mere subjects' (ibid.) and Skinner draws an interesting conclusion regarding the rhetorical move against the *vita activa* ideal Hobbes undertakes:

> . . . it seems clear that Hobbes's purpose in calling his first treatise on politics *De Cive*, or *The Citizen*, must have been to arouse a number of expectations with the intention of disappointing them. The essence of his argument – couched in what must have struck his original readers as a pure oxymoron – is that citizens and subjects are one and the same. (ibid., 286)

Such a view is, of course, coherent with Hobbes's contractarian assumption that allows both a natural liberty and a liberty of subjects, but no liberty to choose the form of the polity.

One of the similarities between Roman and Renaissance rhetoric lies in the so-called Grand Style, a style of high *ornatus* of 'the weapons an orator must learn to wield if he is to have any prospect of winning the war of words and thus of gaining victory for his side of the argument' (Skinner 1996a, 49). (For a French discussion cf. Fumaroli 1980.) Operating with such a style meant the maximum use of tropes and figures. The mastery of rhetoric 'alone enables us to speak with eloquence, while eloquence alone enables us to hold the attention of an audience' (ibid., 86). The power of the orator consists in his 'capacity to shift or move an audience' (ibid., 89). Still, persuasion and eloquence are not necessarily connected to one another (ibid., 100) and the appeal to the emotions of the audience remained controversial also among Renaissance rhetoricians.

The need for 'moving' the audience, in the double sense of the word, refers to definite aspects of the Roman and Renaissance *scientia civilis* as a discipline that studied the possibilities of changing the current state of affairs. The *ratio* referred to a normative judgement of *salus publica* that was always understood to deviate from the existing state of affairs and which could be threatened by mere eloquence (for Cicero cf. ibid., 83–4). The rhetorical moment dealt with the means of achieving this desired state. Perhaps we could also say that *ratio* referred to the moral criteria of judgement, whereas *eloquentia* referred to the policy needed to make change. One of Skinner's main points is that it was the latter aspect that was experienced as problematic among Roman and Renaissance scholars of civil science, and therefore the rhetorical dimension practically gained the upper hand over the less controversial moral dimension. 'By defining the good orator as someone who forces us to do what reason commands the Roman rhetorical theorists presented him as a figure of almost magical potency' (ibid., 91).

What appeared as *ratio* or *sapientia* to ancient and Renaissance rhetoricians seems to have been a variant of *prudentia* rather than the only true morality or judgement. It becomes clear from Skinner's account that a basis for Hobbes's rejection, in his anti-rhetorical phase, of the possibility of combining reason and eloquence consists in a much more strict conception of reason. This is expressed in such formulations as 'the one and only road to *scientia* is by way of *definitions*' or 'beginning with the most evident principles', as Skinner paraphrases his view in English (ibid., 295). Such principles then appear to Hobbes as 'inexpugnable' (ibid., 300), whereas the *salus publica* remained to Cicero and his followers always a matter of judgement and interpretation.

Thus, the opposition between Hobbes and the rhetorical views on *scientia civilis* which remained also after Hobbes's readoption of rhetoric as an instrument for his own purposes was analogous to the opposition between Plato and the sophists. It concerned the need for and value of a singular and incontestable 'evident' criterion of judgement as opposed to the *dissoi logoi*, to the Protagorean thesis: 'On every subject there are two *logoi* [speeches or arguments] opposed to one another' (quoted from Diogenes Laërtius in the translation of Gagarin & Woodroff 1995, 187).

Skinner renders this principle of eloquence in the Latin form of arguing *in utramque partem*. He paraphrases Cicero's views referring to Carneades as a model for such a mode of arguing:

> Carneades managed on a famous occasion to argue convincingly in favour of justice on one day and no less convincingly against it on the day following. He thereby demonstrated that, even when discussing the virtues, it will always be possible to uphold the central contention of rhetorical theory, the contention that there are two sides

to every question, and thus that one can always argue *in utramque partem*. (Skinner 1996a, 9–10)

I think here we arrive at the heart of rhetorical culture. A controversy about a subject matter is, in the rhetorical perspective, not due to a lack of reason or wisdom, but an inherent part of any judgement in *scientia civilis*. Skinner refers to the views of Cicero and Quintilian as arguing 'that the idea of a fully demonstrative *scientia civilis* is nothing more than an oxymoron. An orator can never hope to prove or demonstrate his conclusions beyond doubt (*demonstrare*); he can only hope to discuss and debate the rival merits of different points of view (*disserere*)' (ibid., 103). Or, as Quintilian underlined, 'in politics . . . we can only hope to arrive at conclusions "worthy being debated"' (ibid., 302). The point is, as accentuated by Skinner: 'neither Cicero nor Quintilian ever seriously doubts that the *ars rhetorica* is a genuine art' (ibid., 103) – or *scientia civilis* a genuine *scientia*, we could add.

Now, we may conclude that a rhetorical culture, both in ancient Rome and in Renaissance England, is a culture of debate, dispute, controversy, contestation and – if an anachronism is allowed – of politics. In the Renaissance reception of rhetoric this was, in the monarchist regimes, perhaps played down into set-piece school dialogues or narrowly academic or law court disputes (cf. ibid., 27–30), but even then it contained a 'republican' potential to extend the contestation to public matters and politically crucial controversies.

In connection with Skinner's previous work on Lorenzetti and Machiavelli, we can now claim that the explication of the rhetorical culture opens up new political dimensions in the 'Northern Renaissance' and also republican (or neo-Roman) aspects in English politics, not so radically different from the Italian city-republics. In particular, Marc Fumaroli (1980) has insisted that an *age of eloquence* was also present in the French culture of the sixteenth and late seventeenth century, but rather in a legal and clerical dimension.

Thus, we may further speculate about the political implications of Skinner's thesis on English rhetorical culture. Why was it in England and not France that a revolt against a monarchical regime arose in the seventeenth-century Parliament? Was this due to the fact that the Huguenots were domesticated by the Edict of Nantes, whereas in England the Anglican Church was never equally successful against the sectarian Christians? Or was the reason rather that a centralized state apparatus was already in place in France, whereas in England local powers were sturdier? Or was it, after all, the Parliament, with a real debating culture, that was adopting a rhetorical mode of political action already in the sixteenth century (cf. Redlich 1905, 41–70), thus enabling England to differ from France, where *les états généraux* remained much more marginal? In a recent essay on the origins of Parliament's revolt against Charles I, Skinner underlines the significance of the Roman classics also for leading parliamentarians, such as Henry Parker (Skinner 2002b, ch. 12).

It is a commonplace to stress feudal and common law origins of the English Parliament, originally considered as a High Court, like the French *parlements*. The Italian city-republics, their assemblies and their ancient models are also imperfect as an analogy. Skinner's studies on English rhetorical culture in the Renaissance, combined with the role of neo-Roman authors in Parliament's revolt against Charles, indicate a programme of further studies that analyse the changing character of the Parliament since the Elizabethan era. It seems surprising how little attention is devoted to the character of the English Parliament as a distinctive *locus* of deliberative rhetoric and of arguing *in utramque partem* and of the development of definite practices corresponding to this purpose (cf. however remarks in Kelley 1993). I think we can assume that Skinner's *Reason and Rhetoric* will inspire studies of the rhetorical dimension in parliamentary history.

In relation to *The Foundations*, the invocation of Renaissance rhetorical culture provokes me to question Skinner's thesis on the formation of the state as the only central issue in political theories of the age. The decline of a rhetorical culture surely was partly due to the formation of the state as a centralized instance, the legitimacy of which was seen to be beyond question. The rhetorical culture, in particular the practice of arguing *in utramque partem*, indicated an opposing tendency within the state, as affirmed in the powers of Parliament and in the legitimization of the opposition in the eighteenth century (cf. Skinner 1974a). When accentuating the rhetorical dimension and its incarnation in Parliament, we may also reconsider Skinner's thesis on the roles of the absolutist and the republican dimension in the formation of the state (in Skinner 1989b). From this perspective, the deliberative role of Parliament as a rhetorical element in the modern state can be viewed as opposed to the administrative element. This dimension is commonly underplayed in the republican emphasis on popular participation.

I have speculated about the implications Skinner left unthematized in his *Reason and Rhetoric*. His aim was to analyse the Renaissance rhetorical culture in order to understand better Thomas Hobbes's civil science and the changing roles attributed to rhetoric in it. Here I have accentuated the implications of the rhetorical culture in relation to Skinner's own previous work as well as sketched outlines for further studies on Renaissance English political theory. If the role of rhetorical practices of debate and contestation are so deeply embedded in the thought and practices of the period as claimed by Skinner, their relationship to the role and character of the Parliament surely deserves a fresh look. More generally, the histories of the European parliaments should be revisited by considering the role of the rhetorical culture in their daily activities, and, similarly, histories of 'parliamentarism' require reconsideration as rhetorical regimes par excellence (on the French Third Republic cf. Rousselier 1997).

Like Skinner's conceptual history of liberty, his history of Renaissance rhetoric is also one of lost possibilities. The role of Thomas Hobbes in the struggle against this culture, in particular his claim to have superseded the rhetorical by a scientific style of reasoning and replaced the argument *in utramque partem* with an evident unitary 'reason', may be regarded as remarkable (cf. Skinner 1996a, esp. 299–302). To Hobbes, 'the English revolution appears as a victory for the irrational but overwhelming power of neo-classical and antinomian rhetoric over the small power of science and rationality' (ibid., 435). Such arguments could rely on established commonplaces, against which the rhetorical style was directed, such as the priority of unity over plurality, of concord over contest, of *otium* over *negotium*. Skinner's history of the rhetorical culture of the Renaissance helps us to understand that such an anti-rhetoric can itself be used as a successful rhetorical means, and that the decline of rhetorical culture was a product of a political struggle.

Rhetoric and the Critique of Philosophy

In comparison with his theses on liberty, Quentin Skinner remains more cautious in connecting his historical rehabilitation of ancient and Renaissance eloquence with his critique of contemporary philosophy. At the end of the Introduction to *Reason and Rhetoric* he, none the less, makes suggestions regarding the significance of his discussion of the rhetorical culture, wanting 'to highlight the divisions between three rival views about the character of moral and political argument' (ibid., 15). In addition to the anti-rhetorical and instrumentally rhetorical views of Hobbes, Skinner presents 'the still more rhetorically minded views associated with Renaissance humanism: that our watchword ought to be *audi alteram partem*, always listen to the other side' (ibid.). This position is then described in a manner not restricted to the context of the Renaissance:

> This commitment stems from the belief that, in moral and political debate, it will always be possible to speak *in utramque partem*, and will never be possible to couch our moral or political theories in deductive form. The appropriate model will always be that of a dialogue, the appropriate stance a willingness to negotiate over rival intuitions concerning the applicability of evaluative terms. We strive to reach understanding and resolve disputes in a conversational way. (ibid., 15–16)

Although the Habermasian or Oakeshottian tones in this passage may mitigate the politicizing possibility of contesting every authoritative claim in a debate, this possibility nevertheless remains obvious. In the final passage of the Introduction Skinner explicitly turns, continuing his work from the 1980s, to the critique of contemporary philosophy for neglecting the contestational perspective:

> This humanist vision has by now been so widely repudiated that the very idea of presenting a moral or political theory in the form of a dialogue has long since lost any serious place in philosophy. I hope, however, that I may have succeeded in presenting more sympathetically the values of the early modern rhetorical culture against which the practice of modern philosophy was to rebel so successfully. I hope I may at the same time have conveyed something of the attractions of its strongly contrasting accounts of rationality and moral argument. I even hope that, by focusing on the historical juncture at which the shift from a dialogical to a monological style of moral and political reasoning took place, I may have succeeded in raising anew the question of which style is more deserving of our intellectual allegiances. (ibid., 16)

Here his project of rescuing 'lost treasures' is invoked. Although Skinner leaves the contest of intellectual styles open, his own sympathies are on the side of the rhetorical culture, although he does not formulate a programme about what it could mean in the contemporary world.

In the final pages of *Reason and Rhetoric*, Skinner also discusses the significance of Hobbes to British philosophy. Hobbes's teaching succeeded with a specific 'tone of voice':

... in teaching philosophy to speak English, Hobbes at the same time taught it a particular tone of voice. As we have seen, the tone is very much that of the sane and moderate *savant* beset on all sides by fanaticism and stupidity. We cannot expect reason to triumph, the tone implies, since the foolish and ignorant will always be in a majority. But we can at least hope to discomfit them by wielding the weapons of ridicule, deriding their excesses, sneering at their errors, drawing our readers into a scornful alliance against their general benightedness. (Skinner 1996a, 436)

Skinner's own tone here does not lack admiration for the rhetorical skills of ridicule, but is hardly in favour of the 'moderate *savant*'. Referring to Bertrand Russell's mode of writing the history of philosophy as ironic distance winning the upper hand, Skinner writes: 'It remains the tone in which Hume's latter-day admirers – Bertrand Russell provides an eminent example – have continued to write the history of philosophy, presenting it as a sequence of more or less ludicrous misconceptions finally unmasked by their unanswerable blend of civilised satire and unimpeachable rationality' (ibid., 437). Lazy readers have assimilated Skinner's own view in this tradition (cf. Miller & Strong 1997). It is, however, against such a reliance on the 'rationality' of the winners over the losers that Skinner's entire programme of intellectual historiography is directed.

The Skinnerian perspective on rhetoric allows us to understand his critiques of philosophy and normative political theory better. The contractarian views of Rawls or Habermas – the latter's pathos of discussion is restricted by the presumption of a consensus as a condition of discussion – rely on a similarly monistic basis as Hobbes's, and any claims to have exhaustively defined concepts such as liberty appear similarly as dubious in a rhetorical perspective. Even philosophers closer to Skinner, such as Hollis and Pettit, remain far from arguing *in utramque partem*.

Roland Barthes's critical thesis on the omnipresence of the rhetorical elements in our culture has been turned by Skinner into an instrument of recovery. It is in this perspective that Skinner, through his studies on rhetoric, has recontextualized the works of Collingwood and Rorty, Weber and Nietzsche, as well as Wittgenstein and Austin as contributions indebted to the styles and practices of a rhetorical culture.

The anti-foundationalist character of rhetoric is not limited to the possibility of arguing *in utramque partem* concerning normative principles, but can also be detected in manoeuvres concerning the interpretation of situations. In other words, as opposed to the English tradition, Skinner sees in the rhetorical culture resources against 'the cult of fact' (cf. the renaming of Skinner 1997a in Skinner 2002a). Already in Roman rhetoric, a number of resources and techniques to obtain the desired change in the audience, to 'move' the audience in the double sense of the word, were constructed. These techniques were available to all sides of a contest and could be used for different purposes. One of Skinner's main points is to illustrate how in his later work, Hobbes instrumentalized these techniques for anti-rhetorical political purposes, a possibility that hardly appeared to be evident to Roman or Renaissance rhetoricians.

In *Reason and Rhetoric*, Skinner presents in detail the resources of rhetorical culture that were available in the Roman and Renaissance contexts to change the views of the audience. My point is that such techniques can be also used either for politicking or for interpreting the moves of politicking by linguistic means. No such repertoire has been presented in contemporary political science, which is surprisingly uninterested in modes of politicking. In the rhetorical analysis of politics, however, the establishment of ethos and the pathos of the arousal of emotions, are commonplaces, and rhetorical theorists, such as Chaïm Perelman, also discuss the strategies of *logos*, such as the invocation of commonplaces and the amplification of arguments.

More original is Skinner's discussion of 'the uses of imagery'. The first aspect, 'turning auditors to spectators', is related to Quintilian's thesis that '[a] good orator will not only state or narrate his case; he will "hold forth" the facts so that they can be, as it were, visually inspected' (Skinner 1996a, 185). In the English Renaissance, such a use of figures and tropes 'eventually came to be described simply as "imagery"' (ibid., 187). Skinner's point is to suggest that it was not a maximum but an optimum of imagery that was rhetorically appropriate: 'we must always take care to temper and adjust our language to suit the time, the place and the persons concerned' (ibid., 192). Perhaps the political point of combining these principles could be summarized by saying – with Nietzsche – that we cannot make a distinction between 'plain' and 'figurative' language, but only between different modes, styles and degrees of figuration in a political argument.

The aspect in the imagery that was most systematically used by Hobbes was provocative laughter and scorn. Skinner has discussed Renaissance theories of laughter, which appears political in so far as laughter is always connected with contempt and derision, 'a uniquely powerful weapon of moral and political debate' (Skinner

2001d, 439). One of the aspects in which Renaissance rhetoricians transcended the resources of their ancient authorities concerned the tropes and schemes that expressed mockery or scorn. Skinner's discussion concerned such lesser known tropes as *aestismus, charientismus, diasyrmus* and *mycterismus* and such figures as *synchoresis, aposiopesis, tapinosis, leptotes* and *apodixis* (Skinner 1996a, 206–11, for Hobbes's uses 403–25; Skinner 2001d, 442–7). Any one of them can serve as a specific resource in the analysis of contemporary political rhetoric, although Skinner insists that the decline of rhetoric was accompanied by the delegitimation of open laughter as a means in politics: 'laughter has been wholly outlawed from civilized life' (Skinner 2001d, 447). However, a rehabilitation of the rhetorical culture of arguing *in utramque partem* could perhaps mean a replacement of the *esprit de sérieux*, as criticized by Jean-Paul Sartre, or the insight that laughter always remained an instrument of parliamentary politics.

Conceptual Change Through Rhetorical Redescription

I have reserved a separate treatment for the problematics of Skinner's fourth chapter of *Reason and Rhetoric* on the techniques of redescription. What Skinner says here and in parallel passages (esp. Skinner 1991a, 1993a, 1994a and b) on the scheme *paradiastole* and of rhetorical redescription in general contains a perspective on conceptual change that extends and reformulates his views from the 1970s, especially as developed in 'Some Problems' and 'The Idea of a Cultural Lexicon' (1974c and 1979a). He occasionally has recourse to the vocabulary of speech acts in *Reason and Rhetoric*. Thus, to Skinner there is no absolute dividing line between the two 'dialects' of rhetorical redescription, a concept already mentioned in his Austinian essays.

Among the Roman rhetoricians, the point was that 'a mastery of *inventio* can help us to stretch the truth in the required ways' (Skinner 1996a, 138). The idea of 'stretching the truth' illustrates the singularity of the rhetorical orientation towards changing the views of the audience. 'Truth' is not anything fixed but has a certain range of variation that can be used in argument and either in a narrower (*reductio*) or a wider (*amplificatio*) direction.

From questions like this, Skinner returns to the strategies of renaming and revision of meaning, presented as tasks of the 'innovating ideologist' in 'Some Problems' (see chapter 3 above, sixth section). He has noticed that such strategies were present already among 'the classical theorists of eloquence' in order 'to excite the emotions of our listeners and enlist them on our side' through the simple means of 'offering a redescription of an action or state of affairs' (ibid., 139–40).

The first strategy concerns claims that 'one or other of the terms used . . . has been misleadingly defined' (ibid., 140). This strategy is already present in Aristotle's *Art of Rhetoric* and Cicero's *De inventione*. The naming controversies arise when the facts are agreed upon and the question remains, as Skinner quotes Cicero, 'by what name the fact should be described' (ibid.). The ancients regularly repeated a limited number of examples regarding the moral qualification of deeds, the value of which was not in dispute. 'The rhetorical significance of the proposed redefinition is that it serves to place the action in a new moral light' (ibid., 141). Disputes about naming or definition could concern either 'the technique of "elevating" or "depreciating" actions' or 'to augment or extenuate the alleged significance of a particular action or state of affairs' (ibid.). It is either the value or the significance that is the subject of controversy. These distinctions can be regarded as parallel to what Skinner in 'The Idea of a Cultural Lexicon' distinguishes between the range of attitudes and range of reference of the concepts (cf. chapter 4 above, fifth section).

In recontextualizing his views from the 1970s, Skinner claims that Roman rhetoricians already recognize how 'the manipulations of definitions obviously constitutes a somewhat crude and inflexible rhetorical device' (Skinner 1996a, 142). It would have been interesting to hear more about such occasions in which controversies surrounding proper names or the practices of naming authorities in ancient Rome came to the fore of political disputes.

The same questions about value and significance, as Skinner already indicated in the 1970s, equally well concern, as he put it in 'The Idea of a Cultural Lexicon', the criteria of the application of a concept. He now presents this second mode in the following rhetorical terms: 'We can argue, they claim, that a given action has been wrongly assessed not because the terms used to describe it have been misdefined, but rather because the action itself has a different moral complexion from that which the terms used to describe it suggest' (Skinner 1996a, 142).

In such cases there is an agreement on the names, but 'we ought . . . to speak of substituting one thing for another, *res pro re*', as

Skinner refers to Quintilian (ibid., 144). The point seems to be that in the Roman context conflicts on the 'descriptive' meaning of the concepts played a lesser role than the normative questions of the value and significance of the concepts. As Skinner paraphrases Quintilian: 'if we can manage to challenge the description of a given action or state of affairs, we can often manage *eo ipso*, to challenge its moral appraisal at the same time' (ibid.) or 'the proposed redescriptions serve in every case to re-evaluate what was done' (ibid., 145).

As compared with Skinner's previous work, what is remarkable is the revised insight on the history of the speech acts involved in the redescription of concepts. It is not Austin or Searle, but Aristotle, Cicero, *Ad Herennium* and Quintilian to whom we owe the use of 'descriptive-evaluative terms': 'there is no categorical distinction ... between descriptive and evaluative terms: some descriptions serve at the same time to evaluate' (ibid.). In Roman rhetoric such terms are commonplaces used fluently within a rhetorical culture. It is in this respect that Skinner has also given up an assumption that he used in the 1970s, namely the 'standard meaning' of concepts. He explicitly acknowledges this in the essay 'Rhetoric and Conceptual Change':

> Since then, however, I have immersed myself in the writings of the ancient theorists of eloquence who originally spoke of rhetorical redescription, and have come to share their more contingent understanding of normative concepts and the fluid vocabularies in which they are generally expressed. As a result, I have found myself adopting their assumption that it makes little sense to speak of evaluative terms as having accepted denotations that can either be followed or, with varying degrees of disingenuousness, effectively manipulated. Rather, as the ancient rhetoricians put it, there will always be a sufficient degree of 'neighbourliness' between the forms of behaviour described by contrasting evaluative terms for those terms themselves to be susceptible of being applied in a variety of conflicting ways. It now seems to me, in short, that all attempts to legislate about the 'correct' use of normative vocabularies must be regarded as equally ideological in character. Whenever such terms are used, their application will always reflect a wish to impose a particular moral vision upon the workings of the social world. (Skinner 1999c, 67)

The metaphor of 'neighbourliness' is used to refer to the above-mentioned possibility of 'stretching the truth', that is, of the possibility that a concept has no criteria of 'proper' or 'ordinary' use, significance and evaluation. In all these respects there is a range of variation in the uses that cannot be fixed in advance by any dictionary or other authoritative source, but the uses remain disputable according to situations and purposes. Perhaps we could qualify it as a characteristic of a rhetorical culture that such a degree of contingency, contestability and historical variation in the use of concepts is experienced as appropriate. It is in such a culture that language can be considered as a resource of action and thought, and Wittgensteinian views on the determination of the meaning of concepts through their use would be properly intelligible.

Roman rhetoricians understood that the possibilities of rhetorical redescription contain a powerful tool in all rhetorical genres. In particular, this is the case with deliberative oratory, as Skinner summarized the view in the rhetoric of *Ad Herennium*: 'By means of such redescriptions we can hope to discredit whatever policies are being advocated' (Skinner 1996a, 147). In principle, the device of rhetorical redescription is open to both revaluing and devaluing acts, but in the Roman context the possibility to dethrone any policy was experienced as a more dramatic move. This seems to concern the shared scale of values, whereas an *Umwertung der Werte* (to use Nietzsche's expression) was hardly possible before Machiavelli (cf. Skinner 1999c, 69–70).

The main novelty in Skinner's rhetorical studies is a special technique, the trope or scheme of rhetorical redescription called *paradiastole*. It is not commonly mentioned in rhetoric textbooks or dictionaries. This Greek word survives only in Latin rhetorical texts, with the first mention in Rutilius Lupus's list of rhetorical *schemata* (Skinner 1991a, 5). An explication connected to the *topoi* discussed by Skinner is given to *paradiastole* by the rhetorics of *Ad Herennium*: 'We must seek to ensure that the virtues – those qualities of action which will show us to be in the right – are amplified if we are recommending them, but attenuated if we are proposing that they be ignored' (ibid., 7). This scheme seems have to been, according to Skinner, amply used among Renaissance rhetoricians (Skinner 1996a, 150–3).

In other words, *paradiastole* seems to offer an exemplary scheme of how to operate with a concept in relation to its neighbourhood. This concerns especially the normative concepts, 'virtues', and the scheme makes use of a key principle of the Aristotelian moral theory, the 'doctrine of the mean', in which virtues and vices appears as neighbours to each other, and 'every good quality will be found to have a "neighbouring" or "bordering" vice' (ibid., 154). Under such a condition, 'a clever orator can always hope to challenge the proffered description of an action or state of affairs with some show of plausibility' (ibid., 156).

In principle the scheme can be used both to devalue virtues and to excuse (if not revalue) vices. According to Skinner, in both ancient and Renaissance eloquence there was a tendency to favour the second, and 'a number of Tudor rhetoricians were led to conclude that the figure of paradiastole can actually be *defined* as a method of excusing the vices by redescribing them as virtues' (ibid., 163). An inversion seems, according to Skinner, to have taken place in the early seventeenth century due to translations of Plutarch and Machiavelli. Skinner's point is that in *Il Principe* the technique of rhetorical redescription 'is used specifically as a means of depreciating and undermining the so-called "princely" virtues of clemency and liberality' (ibid., 170).

Even among Renaissance rhetoricians, the use of *paradiastole* remained contested, the search for applying evaluative terms without ambiguity (ibid., 172) was a commonplace, and the question of the overreaching of rhetoric arose also among its practitioners (ibid., 179). This can be taken as an expression of the decline of a specifically rhetorical culture in favour of one in which ambiguity and the revisability of concepts were already commonly regarded as vices. Hobbes was, in this respect, not a special case: 'As with so many of his contemporaries, the main danger he foresees is that a world of complete moral arbitrariness will be conjured up' (ibid., 282), which did not prevent him from using the scheme, for example when denying the difference between *civis* and *subditus*. Hobbes was in search of a 'science of virtue and vice', that is, his instrumentalization of moral concepts to the given and quasinatural criterion of 'civil peace' (ibid., 317).

The critique of 'complete moral arbitrariness' can, however, be countered by the argument that it was only specific 'neighbouring' vices and virtues to which the concepts could be stretched, and it is in only in this sense that the borderline between vices and virtues remains ambiguous. To those arguing against rhetorical culture and the possibility of stretching concepts in general such nuances did not play any role; and with the decline of rhetoric, the reason for stretching concepts and the political point of such a use seem to have been lost. If such arguments were to gain the upper hand, we would arrive back at the Fregean ideal of timeless concepts, as criticized by Skinner already back in 1969 (cf. also Skinner 2002d, 38).

Against this *mainstream* of the twentieth-century academic concept formation, various opposing tendencies have arisen. One aspect of this is the thesis on the contestability of concepts in political language and related topics, originally introduced by W. B. Gallie, Skinner's predecessor in the Cambridge political science chair.

Melvin Richter has, in an important article, emphasized the depth and width of the contestability of political concepts. He first 'indicates that disputes about such concepts as "democracy" involved their central rather than their marginal meanings', then notes that 'in "contestable" concepts, disagreements form an indispensable part of the meaning' – for example in the case of freedom – and infers that 'this is to suggest that the meaning of some concepts derive from controversy rather than from any consensus about their meaning. Certain concepts are valuable, not despite disputes about their meaning, but just because of such disagreements' (Richter 2000, 138). He, furthermore, claims that there are several types of contested concepts (ibid., 138–40), or perhaps more precisely, several respects in which a concept may be contestable.

Both the argument *in utramque partem* and the paradiastolic rhetorical redescriptions are, in the 'democratized' Western political cultures at least, inherent parts of using political concepts and instruments of activities of politicking and politicization. The idea of stable and unambiguous concepts has at least partially lost its prominence and even come to be viewed with suspicion (cf. Bauman 1991). Political agents have taught us to use ambiguous concepts and stretch their meaning to new phenomena or strange contexts as an inherent instrument of politics. Even the frequent claims among politicians of reaching a consensus about concepts are to be regarded as rhetorical moves within the contested use rather than an end to it. A conceptual regimentation would curtail the chances of democratic politics.

Skinner's distinctive merit in the 'rhetorification' of contemporary academic culture consists in actualizing the resources of Roman and Renaissance rhetoric for interpreting conceptual change. As opposed to the rather vague discussion on the contestability of concepts he has both justified the point of contestation through the argument *in utramque partem* and generalized his speech act theoretical views in rhetorical terms.

> The more we succeed in persuading people that a given evaluative term applies in circumstances in which they may never have thought of applying it, the more broadly and inclusively we shall persuade them to employ the term in the appraisal of social and political life.

> The change that will eventually result is that the underlying concept will come to acquire a new prominence and a new salience in the moral arguments of the society concerned. (Skinner 1999c, 71)

Thus, in Skinner's perspective on conceptual change through the transfer to new situations, the question never concerns the criteria of use for a concept or that of different conceptions of the same concepts alone, but the normative dimensions of evaluation and significance that are always present. In the *Cogito* interview he specifies the degrees of conceptual change into two main types: 'I am inclined to make a distinction here between change of meaning of the terms that express the key concepts, which actually seems to me quite rare, and change in the relationships of concepts to each other, which seems to happen all the time' (Skinner 1997c, 73).

This formula indicates that the normative dimension of a concept is irreducibly connected with the relations between concepts – corresponding to Skinner's 'semantic holism' – that are changed by the rhetoric of everyday usage. Contrary to this, there are certain more dramatic changes, such as the formation of such new concepts as the state and the fate of the 'neo-Roman' concept of liberty as a counter-concept to dependence. Skinner's own histories of concepts are concentrated – as are Koselleck's, although in a different sense – on the latter types of conceptual changes.

It is obvious that to Skinner both types of conceptual changes are intelligible in terms of rhetorical redescriptions. The schema *paradiastole* appears, however, in slightly different forms in the two cases. In simple and everyday cases, the disputes with actual audiences are at the forefront, and conceptual changes can be rendered intelligible as the results of successful persuasions concerning the normative 'neighbourhoods' of the concepts. In the more radical types, conceptual change can be regarded as the result of a mixed product of competing views, as Skinner's claim on the formation process of the concept of the state as a joint product of republican and anti-republican projects. We cannot regard the almost complete disappearance of the neo-Roman concept of liberty as a result of successful propaganda alone; as Skinner argues in *Liberty before Liberalism*, the changing conditions of political culture also contributed to this result. In cases like this it is rather, as Skinner emphasizes when speaking on conventions between historical periods, that the lack of understanding of the original meaning, its normative connotation and range of reference, unintentionally contributes to conceptual change.

However, it seems to me to be erroneous to draw a strict line between the intended and unintended forms of rhetorical redescription. Rather, the opposition between omnipresence and rarity of types of conceptual change alludes to the poles of a scale in the use of rhetorical redescription. The illocutionary force of such descriptions always remains uncontrollable, and the unanticipated uses of a concept may give occasion to new intended turns in the use of a concept. The two limit-situations of conceptual change may also indicate strategic alternatives: are some new political aims attainable through the means of modifying the relations of a concept to others, or is a more radical reconceptualization to be proposed in order to oppose effectively some hegemonic views?

In this perspective, the omnipresence of conceptual change by no means signifies a breakdown of the entire conceptual horizon, but continuous modifications in the current horizon concern only a few aspects of it at one time. Such continuous modifications of concepts are, within the rhetorical perspective, intelligible in terms of 'neighbourhood relations', without an assumption of a unchanging 'core' for each concept or the existence of a consensus about a 'standard meaning'. No given view on the direction of conceptual changes is needed, but all this is a part of rhetorical struggles that can be regarded as no less contingent than, for example, electoral struggles.

A radical reconceptualization, such as the introduction of a new concept, the transvaluation of values (as a simultaneous devaluation of established and revaluation of depreciated values) or a 'horizon shift' introducing a new concept with the old name (for *die Geschichte* Koselleck 1967a, 1975, for politics Palonen 1985, 1990, 1993 and forthcoming) is a different matter. It seems to require styles of rhetorical redescription that may differ from what is presented in Skinner's microscopic analyses on conceptual change both in the 1970s and in the rhetorical language of the 1990s. The point seems to be less that of persuading the actual users than in indicating new and different modes of using the concept: new horizons can be 'drawn' only in a partial and fragmentary fashion, making use of specific new chances, without knowing in advance how to get rid of the old ones and what will ensue when a certain *topos* is followed. Every step in such a process of reconceptualization is intelligible in rhetorical terms, but the rhetoric of invention and legitimation can well be something beyond the scope of imagination for Roman and Renaissance rhetoricians. For example, Koselleck's thesis on the temporalization of concepts (cf. e.g. Koselleck 1972b, 1988a) can then be understood as a definite instrument for rhetorical redescription for such comprehensive conceptual changes.

The advantage of Skinner's rhetorical perspective on conceptual changes is that either the 'microscopic' or 'macroscopic' quality can be regarded in the nominalist and contingent character of such changes. As such, conceptual changes are not only analogous to political changes but rather intelligible as dimensions of political changes in themselves. I think this is a generalization of Skinner's key insight that political thought is an aspect of political life in the rhetorical language.

Skinner and Rhetoric Studies Today

'I had always been interested in it' was Quentin Skinner's response to my question about the origins of his turn towards rhetoric (Skinner to KP, January 2002). This interest has been documented historically since *The Foundations*, but Skinner does not, as Pocock does in *Politics, Language and Time* (1971, 17–18), speak of rhetoric in his methodological essays of the 1960s and 1970s or in 'A Reply to My Critics'. When revising his essays for the three volumes of *Visions of Politics*, he has not explicitly shifted to a rhetorical vocabulary (cf. however Skinner 2002a, ch. 8 with 1974c). Thus, we may ask how Skinner's work is related to contemporary rhetorical culture.

Rhetoric studies are now so fashionable that Skinner wisely does not want to be simply identified with them. His rhetoric-related studies have nothing to do with the media or communication rhetoric. Skinner's historical studies also have no explicit connection to the work of theorists of the new rhetoric, such as Perelman or Burke and their contemporary followers. Skinner's study on rhetorical *scientia civilis* seems to have not yet received more detailed notice in the rhetorical studies of academic disciplines.

Rather surprising is the lack of connection between Skinner and the rhetorical historiography practised by Hayden White (1973, 1978) and Frank Ankersmit (1994) in particular. Skinner's work is not close to the specialist histories of rhetoric, although he makes use of Brian Vickers's work, for example. He is not interested in 'school rhetoric', although he deals with the changing classifications of rhetoric during the Renaissance. To Skinner, rhetoric is always connected with politics, both political practices and the *scientia civilis*. It is no wonder that historians specializing in rhetoric tend to find in Skinner's book something other than what they themselves do.

Skinner also takes a distance from the practice of rhetorical reading, as exemplified in the case of Johnston, through an explicitly historical connection to the *ars rhetorica* and its internal classifications. It is only in this perspective of making Hobbes as much of a context for rhetorical culture as vice versa, that the genre of Skinner's *Reason and Rhetoric* becomes intelligible. The common critique of the book among those reviewers who are specialists on Hobbes (cf. Vaughan 1997; Martinich 1998; Rowe 1997) concerns the dispensability or auxiliary role of the first part of the book, which can be said to miss one of Skinner's main points.

In *The Foundations*, Skinner presented rhetoric in a manner that corresponds to Pocock's 'language of political theory' (cf. esp. Pocock 1971, 1987) that is present in the Renaissance context. Already in his Lorenzetti study Skinner seems, however, to regard rhetoric as a comprehensive alternative to the scholastic 'philosophy', and in *Reason and Rhetoric* he speaks of Roman and Renaissance rhetorical culture. It is in this sense that the rhetorical *scientia civilis* might be regarded as a particular intellectual style in writing about Renaissance politics in wide 'cultural' terms rather than as a substantial language related to the constitutional politics.

Skinner's turn towards rhetoric does not mean a conversion to a new jargon, but he continues to use the vocabularies of rhetoric and speech acts in a parallel fashion. His rhetorical interests continue his critique of philosophy by other means. It is at this level that Skinner's immersion in the resources of rhetoric has further sharpened his profile in contemporary theory politics.

One of the main aspects in Skinner's rehabilitation of classical and Renaissance eloquence consists in the recontextualization of the work of Wittgenstein and Austin on linguistic action into a rhetorical perspective. Skinner now shares with the ancient theorists of eloquence 'their more contingent understanding of normative concepts and fluid vocabularies' (Skinner 1999c, 67, full quotation in preceding section), which clearly has both increased Skinner's interest in conceptual change and given him new resources to deal with it. The concern with the normative dimension of concept and the strictly nominalist perspective of linguistic action have, combined with rhetorical resources, unwittingly contributed to the comprehensive perspective that Skinner has reached on conceptual change.

As such, his rhetorical perspective is partly complementary, partly competitive with others, such as Koselleck's (cf. Palonen 1999b). In 'Rhetoric and Conceptual Change', Skinner describes this programme in terms explicitly indebted to Weber (Skinner 1999c, 62, quoted above in chapter 3, third section). He turns the intelligibility of the contingency, controversiality and historicity of concepts into a heuristic instrument. Rhetoric is the name for the orientation towards the world which makes such an approach possible, at the same time fully acknowledging the constitutive role of politics in conceptual changes.

Bonnie Honig has in her *Political Theory and Displacement of Politics* spoken of *virtue* and *virtù* theorists of politics. Characteristic of the first is an attempt towards the 'elimination from a regime of dissonance, resistance, conflict and struggle' and confining politics to 'tasks of stabilizing moral and political subjects, building consensus, maintaining agreements, or consolidating communities and identities' (Honig 1993, 2). The *virtù* theorists 'see politics as disruptive practice that resists the consolidations and closures of administrative and juridical settlement for the sake of the perpetuity of political contest' (ibid.).

Readers of this book should have no difficulty in situating Quentin Skinner on the side of the *virtù* theorists of politics. As in the case of Max Weber, Skinner seems never to worry about the maintenance of order, system or 'society', whereas he clearly is worried about too much of them. Most militantly he advocates this view in his two latest essays on liberty. He ends the essay 'States and the Freedom of Citizens' as follows:

> It is partly the acceptance of the view that freedom is undermined only by coercion that allows such systems of power to flourish and seem defensible. The effect has been to shift the balance away from the liberty of citizens and towards increasingly arbitrary forms of state authority. If we believe in democracy, we shall want to shift the balance back again. We could do much worse than begin by reconsidering what it means to enjoy our freedom as citizens of modern states. We have no need to accept the conveniently meagre answer that our rulers and their apologists currently offer us. (Skinner 2002e)

Here we can, I think, once again, find a link between rhetoric and liberty. The rhetorical attitude of questioning all authorities and theory monopolies and arguing in a mode making the weaker *logos* stronger can be understood as a strong resource against all depoliticizing claims in the name of order and in the name of truth as well.

More offensively considered, the rhetorical resources also induce a questioning of commonplaces, established 'facts' and the standardized meanings of concepts, to politicize the situation by indicating a presence of *Spielräume* for contingency and controversy where none of this is commonly believed to exist.

7

Quentin Skinner as a Contemporary Thinker

Imagine that Max Weber would today, in 2003, 'rise from his grave' as he says of the 'many old gods' in 'Wissenschaft als Beruf' (Weber 1919b, 17). Whom could he count among those worth reading today? Surely not the Weberologists – myself included. Even less the economists, among whom he was once counted, or sociologists, who have tended to monopolize him since World War II. My guess is that Quentin Skinner would be among the first ten contemporary authors whom Weber would count as readable. He is both thematically and methodologically close to Weber, a more consistent nominalist and perspectivist than anyone else today, and at the same time a rather similar decathlete of the human sciences as Weber himself.

The Intellectual Profile

The work of Weber and Skinner is something that hardly anyone starting an academic career today can imitate. Such a profound knowledge of Latin as Skinner received at school in the 1950s has become a real rarity. Ever more specialized and time-bound undergraduate and doctoral studies and the burden of heavier loads of teaching and administrative duties on professors prevent anyone even thinking about attempting to create a work like Skinner's. His individual profile of combining the vocations of a specialist intellectual historian on certain topics and periods and his orientation as a wide-ranging theorist of politics, historiography and related fields is admirable because it has become almost unattainable. In order to get our students to understand something of the work of such authors as Weber or Skinner, we have to vitalize, despite all administrative obstacles, aspects of *Bildung* and independent study.

As the *TLS* list of 1995 indicates, Quentin Skinner is among the most quoted and reviewed political theorists-cum-intellectual historians since 1970. Sometimes he has been a favourite target of critics. After *The Foundations* the polemical reviews and comments no longer dominate as earlier, but a more comprehensive understanding of his views nevertheless remains rare.

Skinner's interpretations of Machiavelli, Hobbes or the history of the concepts of state and liberty remain partly a matter for specialists. Within a perspectivist conception, any 'results' of studies will regularly be overthrown and even the procedures to obtain them may be questioned: 'irgendwann wechselt die Farbe,' wrote Max Weber with a chemical metaphor on the replacement of a perspective (1904, 214). Skinner's work shall, thus, be valued by the moves to dethrone existing views and to construct alternative perspectives that are at least of equal importance.

Characteristic of Skinner's work is his double strategy of distancing past and present. The discontinuity between past and present is used mainly to criticize the present through the past, but serves also to underline that the past he analyses has a contemporary significance. That Skinner's studies always have double references and audiences is almost regularly missed by his critics.

This may be partly due to his precise and cautious self-identification. For example he writes: 'I am not myself a first order political theorist but merely (or at least mainly) an historian of the subject' (Skinner 2001a, 15). I think, however, that the words in parenthesis are here crucial. My thesis in this book (and in Palonen 2002c) is that in his singular manner of being a historian of political theory Skinner also becomes a first-order political theorist himself.

Skinner has always been both a *homo politicus* keenly commenting on contemporary politics and a spectator, who prefers to take a stand in favour of the plurality of views rather than commit himself to a singular one. Sometimes he becomes engaged in contemporary struggles, occasionally with a tone of cultural pessimism (cf. the characterization 'we live in reactionary times' (Skinner 2002d, 59) and the final parts of Skinner 2002e and 2002f), whereas in other situations it is the distance of a cool historian that retains the upper hand.

Such ambiguities are part of Skinner's own intellectual profile. As a historian of political thought and concepts he analyses theory politics rather than actual events and the contingent 'realization' of some possibilities (cf. his declining to say anything specific about 'the world itself', Skinner 2001a, 15). The events do matter, but they are taken as challenges to the existing horizon of the possible. Studying the possibilities and their changing horizons in the rhetoric of controversies and conceptual changes appears to be the most interesting aspect of politics. In the face of the existential commitments of a politician, Skinner remains an occasional politician.

I have called the Skinnerian revolution the inversion of perspective in the study of 'political thought' from the application of thought to politics to thinking as a dimension of politics. In rhetorical terms, this can be regarded as a further instance of changing the normative colour of a description, a revaluation of politics-as-activity as well as a reversal of the common academic priority of *vita contemplativa* over *vita activa*.

How far the Skinnerian revolution has been successful remains, of course, a matter of dispute. Skinner in his recent reflections highlights that the intellectual situation in the 1950s and 1960s was entirely different from today. This can be regarded as an acknowledgement of a certain 'illocutionary force' in his work when producing 'perlocutionary effects' that have changed the intellectual horizon.

The question remains, however, how far such a success is worth celebrating. Today 'the Cambridge school' is sometimes regarded as a 'mainstream' in the Anglophone study of political thought and intellectual history. Attempts to return to an older, more philosophical form of the 'history of ideas' have been recently formulated by young scholars, such as Mark Bevir (1999). Though I acknowledge Bevir's originality as a daring builder of a new 'system' with many fruitful insights into the process of interpretation, his project is constructed on a misleading polemic which lacks a grasp, for example, of the significance of rhetoric and, in particular, of Skinner's revolutionary inversion of the relations between thought and politics (cf. Palonen 2000a).

In this book I have kept Skinner separate from 'the Cambridge school' and publications in the *Ideas in Context* series. Disciples are indeed often more dogmatic than their teachers in so far as they adopt certain positions as already accepted, whereas a person like Skinner had to fight hard for certain theses that today may appear as commonplaces. A vulgarization of one's own ideas can be regarded as a sign that one has to nuance or even change one's views in some respect, as Skinner has done in particular through his turn towards rhetoric.

In my view, the studies frequently included in 'the Cambridge school of intellectual history' almost regularly fall short of the Skinnerian revolution. Moreover, someone like Richard Rorty explicitly continues to regard politics as a separate public sphere and refuses to reflect upon the political implications of critiques of philosophy. John Dunn in his *The Cunning of Unreason* attempts to 'make sense of politics' in a dualist view as both an 'activity' and a 'field' (Dunn 2000, 4–5), which already turns politics into only a specific subject matter and not also an instrument of the intelligibility of aspects of activity and thought.

Perhaps here we should consider the fact that during the periods of Skinner's specialized studies, the distinction between politicians and thinkers was not yet drawn. So, it is always possible to read Machiavelli and Lorenzetti, Luther and Erasmus, Hobbes and Milton as politicians. Skinner interestingly treats twentieth-century theorists similarly, reading Collingwood and Rorty, Rawls and Habermas, Taylor and Pettit as theory politicians, whose work reaches beyond strictly academic provinces.

In the analysis of contemporary political thought we have an occasion to carry Skinner's programme further and to try to treat politicians as theorists of politics as well. Employing Skinnerian tools, I have, for example, used the analysis of the normative dimension of conceptual change through rhetorical redescription for the apologies of politicians, claiming to detect here a neglected genre of political theorizing (Palonen 2002d).

To adhere to the Skinnerian revolution in the study of political thought and concepts by no means requires a subscription to Skinner's approach for such a study. The inversion of the relationship between thought and action is compatible with various approaches and perspectives on the study. A continuation of the Skinnerian revolution through other means than those used by Skinner himself is an obvious and legitimate possibility.

A Vision of Time

In this volume I have presented Quentin Skinner's profile on the study of intellectual history and theory politics in five roughly successive theses. In the first step, he turns history into a critical instance in textual interpretation, both as a heuristic condition of intelligibility of thought and as a normative criterion for the assessment of interpretations. In the second step, he adopts the perspective of linguistic action both for textual interpretation and for the intelligibility of politics in general. In the third step, he then inverts the academic commonplace on the priority of political thought over political action, not only giving priority to action but interpreting political thought as a politics on the level of possibilities. It is here he introduces a decisive break that I have called the Skinnerian revolution. In the fourth step, Skinner then applies the thought-as-politics perspective to the concept of liberty, at the same time rewriting its history and turning this revision of history into a critical instance in contemporary discussion. In a fifth step, Skinner rehabilitates the rhetorical culture of the Renaissance and by this very move revalues controversies as a political dimension of all scholarship and thus turns rhetorical redescription into a definite perspective on conceptual change.

Each of these theses contains a remarkable novelty in the study of history and politics. They do not indicate conversions, but rather complications of Skinner's approach and repertoire. Taken together they give to Skinner an intellectual profile of remarkable individuality. Such a profile is difficult to understand in its historical complexity, and the Skinner of the commentators appears tame in comparison with the original.

It is characteristic of Skinner's work that it is always moving towards new directions that are not predictable in advance. While this movement is still ongoing, it may be already an expression of a mythology of coherence to claim that all of the main theses of Skinner's research programme can be made intelligible as moves making use of a specific vision of time. Skinner himself has never explicated his temporal commitments, being rather suspicious of my previous suggestions in this direction (cf. Palonen 1999b and Skinner 1999c, 65, 71–2). In this respect I remain, however, obstinate and will finish this book with speculations about Skinner's temporal vision.

The identity of a historian and the use of 'historical' as an argument signifies for Skinner – and opposes him to the 'professional conservatism' of most historians – an explicit emphasis on discontinuity, in the sense of both regarding the past as a foreign country and considering the present as a contingent and fragile by-product of past struggles. This discontinuity also concerns conventions, for to Skinner the most interesting conventions are those so different from those of the present that they are difficult to identify as conventions regulating the actions and thought of past agents.

The perspective of linguistic action is a further dimension of Skinner's interest in discontinuity, and politics can be regarded as a paradigmatic example of it. In Skinner's nominalistic view, by complementing Weber with the new tools of Wittgenstein and Austin, linguistic action is not only limited to extraordinary *kairos* situations in the pivots of synchronic structures. On the contrary, we can detect speech acts everywhere and when directing our attention to them the structures appear to dissolve into contingent conventions.

The priority of political life over political thought also indicates an instance of discontinuity. Skinner has given a key role to events and to the breakdowns of processes, to political moves, changing constellations, not least to crises, dead ends, *faits accomplis*, and so on, which may suddenly render much of previously accepted or even unproblematic thought obsolete and which pose challenges to rethink. Understood as a dimension in politics, political thought is regarded by Skinner from the perspective of responses to such challenges, whereas movements towards routine, tradition and convention are analysed mainly from the perspective of the chances of their breakdown. Skinner analyses the conceptualization of the state, for example, not as a process to habituate a new vocabulary, but rather, as a conceptual innovation with plural origins that converge.

Skinner's conceptual history of liberty is a good illustration of historical discontinuities, their political origins and consequences. He does not limit this to writing the history of lost treasures, but has also dissolved the 'hegemonic' views of negative and, most recently, also of positive liberty (cf. Skinner 2002f and g) into a wide variety of different conceptions. In particular, the history of liberty is intertwined with contemporary debates by using the past and strange views as instruments to deconstruct the seemingly given conditions of a debate and by bringing up a variety of unrealized possibilities that require also a revision of the conditions of the current debate.

Actualizing of historically realized alternatives to the present-day debate can already be understood as a move in favour of a rhetorical culture, in which arguing for and against any view is, as in Nietzschean and Weberian perspectivism, considered as a condition not only of politics but also of knowledge. Maybe we could, like Hayden White, also regard the *paradiastole* as the 'master trope' of Quentin Skinner's argument. Any concept with a range of variation can rhetorically be used for a variety of different political purposes and, at the same time, can also be interpreted as a heuristic instrument in the understanding conceptual changes. The very fluidity of the trope illustrates the presence of discontinuities and the corresponding possibilities for operating with them and for distinguishing variants of them both in political activity in general as well as in theory politics.

The main figure of Skinner's use of historical discontinuity is temporal distance, especially between past and present, but also between pasts and between presents. The presence of such a distance commits him to argue against the comprehensive philosophies of history or 'the History'. He argues, and this is one of his similarities with Koselleck (cf. Palonen 2002c), against the philosophical pathos of History, for example in the Enlightenment, Hegelian and Marxist traditions. But Skinner's views equally differ from the implicit framework of history in the empiricist historiography, such as those who like to quote the Rankean *wie es eigentlich gewesen* thesis. His perspectivist view of history is critical of all claims of *Eigentlichkeit*.

Pointillism can be used as a metaphor of Skinner's nominalist conception of history. I do not refer so much to a specific doctrine in the history of art around 1900, but rather to his insistence that there is already a distance between events (including events in thought). In the case of Skinner we have to add here the very idea of marking a 'point', an emphasis that distinguishes what is considered remarkable from the background.

Such a pointillism links Skinner to the distinction of the *kairos* time from that of the *khronos*, as in the sophist perspective to temporality (cf. Cassin 1995, esp. 466–70). The metaphor of pointillism finely illustrates how to Skinner the 'texture' of history does not consist of a single and dramatic kairotic instance, but that the opposition between chronological and kairotic elements is a regular feature both in political action and in historical interpretation. Skinner's linguistic action is a paradigmatic example of a kairotic move in the texture of history. It signifies a moment of presence that marks a break with the lapse of the chronological time, both in the current present or in the past present. Thus, Skinner's underlining of the role of linguistic action marks the present moment of the illocutionary act as a political moment *par excellence*, in relation to the past conventions and future effects.

When dealing with theory politics, however, Skinner thematizes in a Weberian manner possibilities in an open horizon that are real or realizable for the acting politicians in the present, thus differing also from locating the possible in the future, as for example Heidegger and Sartre tend to do. Skinner's project of recovering lost treasures indicates an enrichment of the present horizon of the possible by possibilities actualized in the past. Such an actualization of past possibilities remains, as we have seen, to Skinner a procedure for increasing the available alternatives, without suggesting to political agents which of the alternatives should be chosen. Such a presentation of past possibilities means an extension of the present towards the past, or, in Koselleckian terms, a widening of the space of experience available to the agents in the present.

When Skinner's vision of time is focused on the relationships between present(s) and past(s), the dimension of the future is seldom if ever thematized by him in a more detailed manner (cf. however his 'gloomy' prediction of an increase of religious or national parochialism in Skinner 2001a, 23–4). This may be to some extent due to his professional ideology as a historian. More crucial, it seems to me, is maybe his acknowledgement of the radical contingency of history, of the regular presence of unexpected consequences in any politically and historically interesting action. Thus, in his historical studies, Skinner dispenses with speaking about the future in general terms and any general discussion about the future appears politically dubious to him. This silence about the future is one of the strengths of Skinner's approach, both methodologically and politically.

I thus consider Quentin Skinner to be a 'contemporary thinker' in a pre-eminent sense. To him the moment of the present has a certain priority over both past and future. The fragile and contingent presence of action over both conventions and effects, both in the past and in the present, further accentuates his contemporaneity.

References

Publications of Quentin Skinner

(1961): The Whitbread Papers from Southill. *The House of Whitbread* 21/1, 18–21.

(1962): John Bunyan. *The House of Whitbread* 21/4, 14–17.

(1962–3): Sheridan and Whitbread at Drury Lane 1809–1815. *Theatre Notebook* 17, 40–6, 74–9.

(1963): Samuel Whitbread II at Drury Lane. *The House of Whitbread* 23/1, 6–9.

(1964): Hobbes' 'Leviathan'. Review article. *The Historical Journal* 7, 321–33.

(1965a): History and Ideology in the English Revolution. *The Historical Journal* 8, 151–78.

(1965b): Hobbes on Sovereignty, *The Listener* 2 September, 418–20.

(1965c): Hobbes on Sovereignty: An Unknown Discussion. *Political Studies* 13, 213–18.

(1965d): Old Nick. Review of W. H. Greenleaf, *Order, Empiricism and Politics* and Felix Raab, *The English Face of Machiavelli. A Changing Interpretation 1500–1700. The Spectator* 8 January.

(1965e): On Two Traditions of English Political Thought. Review of W. H. Greenleaf, *Order, Empiricism and Politics. The Historical Journal* 8, 136–9.

(1965f): Christopher Hill and the 'Intellectual Origins of the English Revolution'. *Cambridge Review* 22 May.

(1966a): The Ideological Context of Hobbes's Political Thought.

182 *References*

The Historical Journal 9, 286–317. Revised version entitled The Context of Hobbes's Theory of Political Obligation, in Skinner 2002c, 264–86.

(1966b): The Limits of Historical Explanations. *Philosophy* 41, 199–215.

(1966c): Thomas Hobbes and his Disciples in France and England. *Comparative Studies in Society and History* 8, 153–67. Abbreviated and revised version in Skinner 2002c, 308–23.

(1966d): Review of *Crisis in Europe 1560–1660*, ed. Trevor Aston. *English Historical Review* 81, 791–5.

(1967a): More's *Utopia*. Review article. *Past and Present* 38, 153–68.

(1967b): Science and Society in Restoration England. Review article. *The Historical Journal* 10, 286–93.

(1967c): Review of George R. Abernathy, *The English Presbyterians and the Stuart Restoration. English Historical Review* 82, 170–1.

(1967d): Review of *Hobbes Studies*, ed. Keith C. Brown. *Journal of Political Economy* 73, 102.

(1968): 'Don Pasquale' at the Arts. *Cambridge Review* 11 October, 23.

(1969a): Meaning and Understanding in the History of Ideas. *History and Theory* 8, 3–53. Reprinted in *Meaning and Context*, ed. James Tully, Cambridge: Polity 1988, 29–67. Abbreviated and revised version in Skinner 2002a, 57–89.

(1969b): Thomas Hobbes and the Nature of the Early Royal Society. *The Historical Journal* 12, 217–39. Revised and extended version entitled Hobbes and the Politics of the Early Royal Society, in Skinner 2002c, 324–45.

(1970a): Conventions and the Understanding of Speech Acts. *The Philosophical Quarterly* 20, 118–38. Reprinted in *The History of Ideas*, ed. Preston King, London: Croom Helm 1983, 259–84.

(1970b): Cromwell and God. Review of Christopher Hill, *God's Englishman. The Listener* 30 July, 155–6.

(1970c): Revolting Students. Review of the new editions of Hobbes's *Behemoth* and *Elements of Law* by Ferdinand Tönnies. *The Listener* 15 January, 91–2.

(1970d): Review of John Dunn, *The Political Thought of John Locke. American Historical Review* 75, 489–90.

(1971): On Performing and Explaining Linguistic Actions. *The Philosophical Quarterly* 21, 1–21.

(1972a): Conquest and Consent. Thomas Hobbes and the Engagement Controversy. In *The Interregnum: The Quest for Settlement*, ed. G. E. Aylmer, London: Macmillan, 79–98. Revised version in Skinner 2002c, 287–307.

(1972b): Motives, Intentions and the Interpretations of Texts. *New Literary History* 3, 393–408. Reprinted in *Meaning and Context*, ed. James Tully, Cambridge: Polity 1988, 68–78. Revised, fused with Skinner 1996b and entitled Motives, Intentions and Interpretations, in Skinner 2002a, 90–102.

(1972c): 'Social Meaning' and the Explanation of Social Action. In *Philosophy, Politics and Society*, Fourth Series, ed. Peter Laslett, W. G. Runciman and Quentin Skinner, Oxford: Blackwell, 136–57. Reprinted in *Meaning and Context*, ed. James Tully, Cambridge: Polity 1988, 79–96. Abbreviated and revised in Skinner 2002a, 128–44.

Laslett, Runciman and Skinner (1972): Introduction. In *Philosophy, Politics and Society*, Fourth Series, ed. Peter Laslett, W. G. Runciman and Quentin Skinner, Oxford: Blackwell, 1–7.

(1973): The Empirical Theorists of Democracy and Their Critics. A Plague on Both Their Houses. *Political Theory* 1, 287–304.

(1974a): The Principles and Practice of Opposition: The Case of Bolingbroke versus Walpole. In *Historical Perspectives*, ed. N. McKendrick, London: Europa Publications, 93–128. Abbreviated, revised and entitled Augustan Party Politics and Renaissance Constitutional Thought, in Skinner 2002b, 344–67.

(1974b): The Role of History. *Cambridge Review*, March, 102–4.

(1974c): Some Problems in the Analysis of Political Thought and Action. *Political Theory* 2, 277–303. Reprinted in *Meaning and Context*, ed. James Tully, Cambridge: Polity 1988, 97–118. Revised version entitled Moral Principles and Social Change, in Skinner 2002a, 145–57.

(1974d): Reasonable Prospects. Review of John Passmore, *Man's Responsibility for Nature*. *Times Literary Supplement* 14 June, 638–9.

(1974e): Review of Stanley Fish, *Self-consuming Artifacts*. *Modern Philology*, August, 92–6.

(1975): Hermeneutics and the Role of History. *New Literary History* 8, 209–32.

(1976a):   Projectors and Practitioners. Review of Charles Webster, *The Great Instauration. Times Literary Supplement* 2 July, 810–12.

(1976b):   Standards of Living. Review of Ronald L. Meek, *Social Science and the Ignoble Savage. Times Literary Supplement* 13 February, 155–6.

(1976c):   Review of *Handbook of Political Science*, vol. I, ed. Fred I. Greenstein and Nelson W. Polsby. *Political Theory* 3, 385–8.

(1978a):   *The Foundations of Modern Political Thought*. Vol. I, *The Renaissance*. Vol. II, *The Age of Reformation*. Cambridge: CUP.

(1978b):   Action and Context. *Proceedings of the Aristotelian Society* 52, 57–69.

(1978c):   The Flight from Positivism. Review of Richard Bernstein, *The Restructuring of Social and Political Theory. New York Review of Books* 15 June, 26–8.

(1978d):   The Lessons of Thomas More. Review of *The Complete Works of Thomas More. New York Review of Books* 24 August, 57–60.

(1978e):   Milton, Satan and Subversion. Review of Christopher Hill, *Milton and the English Revolution. New York Review of Books* 23 March, 6–9.

(1979a):   The Idea of a Cultural Lexicon. *Essays in Criticism* 29, 205–24. Reprinted as Language and Social Change, in *Meaning and Context*, ed. James Tully, Cambridge: Polity 1988, 119–32 and as Language and Political Change, in *Political Innovation and Conceptual Change*, ed. Terence Ball, James Farr and Russell N. Hanson, Cambridge: CUP 1989, 6–23. Revised version with the original title in Skinner 2002a, 158–74.

(1979b):   Inside Story. Review of Isaiah Berlin, *Against the Current. New Statesman* 9 June, 830–1.

(1979c):   Taking off. Review of Andre Gunder Frank, *World Accumulation 1492–1789*, Geoffrey Parker and Lesley M. Smith (eds), *The General Crisis of the Seventeenth Century* and Reinhard Bendix, *Kings or People. New York Review of Books* 22 March, 15–16.

(1980a):   The Origins of the Calvinist Theory of Revolution. In *After the Reformation*, ed. Barbara Malament, Manchester: Manchester University Press, 309–30. Revised version entitled Humanism, Scholasticism and Popular Sovereignty, in Skinner 2002b, 245–63.

(1980b): Duellist. Review of J. H. Hexter, *Reappraisals in History* and *On Historians*. *New York Review of Books* 24 January, 39–40.

(1980c): The Language of the Historian of Ideas. In *XVe congrès international des sciences historiques, Bucarest, 10–17 août 1980. Rapports I. Grands thèmes et méthodologie*, Bucarest: Editura Academiei Republicii Socialiste Románia 1980, 414–19.

(1981a): *Machiavelli*. Oxford: OUP.

(1981b): The End of Philosophy? Review of Richard Rorty, *Philosophy and the Mirror of Nature*. *New York Review of Books* 19 March, 46–8.

(1981c): Machiavelli's Lessons of Diplomacy. *The Times Higher Education Supplement* 15 May, 12.

(1981d): The World as a Stage. Review of Clifford Geertz, *Negara*. *New York Review of Books* 16 April, 35–7.

(1981e): Quentin Skinner Replies (to Robert R. Sullivan concerning 1981b). *New York Review of Books* 5 November, 62.

(1982a): Habermas's Reformation. *New York Review of Books* 7 October, 35–8.

(1982b): Review of J. C. Davis, *Utopia and the Ideal Society*. *The Times Literary Supplement* 29 January, 96.

(1983): Machiavelli on the Maintenance of Liberty. *Politics* 18, 3–15. Reprinted in a revised form as Two Views on the Maintenance of Liberty, in *Contemporary Political Theory*, ed. Philip Pettit, New York: Macmillan 1991, 35–58. Revised version entitled Machiavelli on *virtù* and the Maintenance of Liberty, in Skinner 2002b, 160–85.

(1984): The Idea of Negative Liberty: Philosophical and Historical Perspectives. In *Philosophy in History*, ed. Richard Rorty, J. B. Schneewind and Quentin Skinner, Cambridge: CUP, 193–221. Revised version entitled The Idea of Negative Liberty: Machiavellian and Modern Perspectives, in Skinner 2002b, 186–212.

Rorty, Schneewind and Skinner (1984): Introduction. In *Philosophy in History*, ed. Richard Rorty, J. B. Schneewind and Quentin Skinner, Cambridge: CUP, 1–14.

(1985a): Introduction: The Return of Grand Theory. In *The Return of Grand Theory in the Human Sciences*, ed. Quentin Skinner, Cambridge: CUP, 1–21.

(1985b): After Structuralism: The Return of Grand Theory. *The Listener* 5 April, 14–15.

(1985c): What is Intellectual History? *History Today* 35, 50–2.
(1985d): Ms. Machiavelli. Review of Hanna Fenchel Pitkin, *Fortuna is a Woman*. *New York Review of Books* 14 March, 29–30.
(1985e): Preface. In *The Return of Grand Theory in the Human Sciences*, ed. Quentin Skinner, Cambridge: CUP, vii–viii.
(1986):   The Paradoxes of Political Liberty. In *The Tanner Lectures on Human Values* VII, Salt Lake City: University of Utah Press, 225–50.
(1987a): Ambrogio Lorenzetti: The Artist as Political Philosopher. *Proceedings of the British Academy* 72, 1–56. Revised version entitled Ambrogio Lorenzetti and the Portrayal of Virtuous Government, in Skinner 2002b, 39–92.
(1987b): Sir Thomas More's *Utopia* and the Language of Renaissance Humanism. In *Languages of Political Theory in Early-Modern Europe*, ed. Anthony Pagden, Cambridge: CUP, 123–57. Revised version entitled Thomas More's *Utopia* and the Virtue of True Nobility, in Skinner 2002b, 213–44.
(1988a): Introduction. In Niccolo Machiavelli, *The Prince*, ed. Quentin Skinner and Russell Price, Cambridge: CUP, ix–xxiv.
(1988b): Political Philosophy. In *The Cambridge History of Renaissance Philosophy*, ed. Charles B. Schmitt and Quentin Skinner, Cambridge: CUP, 389–452. Revised version in two parts entitled The Rediscovery of Republican Values, and Republican Virtues in an Age of Princes, in Skinner 2002b, 10–38, 118–59.
(1988c): A Reply to My Critics. In *Meaning and Context*, ed. James Tully, Cambridge: Polity, 231–88. Revised version in two parts entitled Interpretation, Rationality and Truth, and Interpretation and the Understanding of Speech Acts, in Skinner 2002a, 27–56, 103–27.
(1988d): Warrender and Skinner on Hobbes. A Reply. *Political Studies* 36, 692–5.
(1988e): Preface. In *The Cambridge History of Renaissance Philosophy*, ed. Charles B. Schmitt and Quentin Skinner, Cambridge: CUP.
(1988f): Introduction. In *The Cambridge History of Renaissance Philosophy*, ed. Charles B. Schmitt and Quentin Skinner, Cambridge: CUP.
(1989a): Il concetto inglese di libertà. *Filosofia politica* 3, 77–102.
(1989b): The State. In *Political Innovation and Conceptual Change*, ed.

Terence Ball, James Farr and Russell N. Hanson, Cambridge: CUP, 90–131. Revised and extended version entitled From the State of Princes to the Person of the State, in Skinner 2002b, 368–413.

(1989c): The Missing History: a Symposium. *The Times Literary Supplement* 23 June, 690.

(1990a): Machiavelli's *Discorsi* and the Pre-humanist Origins of Republican Ideas. In *Machiavelli and Republicanism*, ed. Gisela Bock, Quentin Skinner and Maurizio Viroli, Cambridge: CUP, 121–41. Reworked into The Rediscovery of Republican Values, in Skinner 2002b, 10–38.

(1990b): The Republican Ideal of Political Liberty. In *Machiavelli and Republicanism*, ed. Gisela Bock, Quentin Skinner and Maurizio Viroli, Cambridge: CUP, 293–309.

(1990c): Hobbes on the Proper Significance of Liberty. *Transactions of the Royal Historical Society* 40, 121–51. Revised version in Skinner 2002c, 209–37.

(1990d): The Past in the Present. Review of Stephen Toulmin, *Cosmopolis*. *New York Review of Books* 12 April, 36–7.

(1991a): Thomas Hobbes: Rhetoric and the Construction of Morality. *Proceedings of the British Academy* 76, 1–61. Revised version entitled Hobbes on Rhetoric and the Construction of Morality, in Skinner 2002c, 87–141.

(1991b): Who are 'We'? Ambiguities of the Modern Self. *Inquiry* 34, 133–53.

(1992a): The Italian City Republics. In *Democracy. The Unfinished Journey 508 BC to AD 1993*, ed. John Dunn, Oxford: OUP, 57–69.

(1992b): On Justice, the Common Good and the Priority of Liberty. In *Dimensions of Radical Democracy*, ed. Chantal Mouffe, London: Verso, 211–24.

(1992c): Liberty and Legal Obligation in Hobbes' *Leviathan*. In *Cambridge Essays in Jurisprudence*, ed. Ross Harrison, Cambridge: CUP, 231–56.

(1993a): *Scientia civilis* in Classical Rhetoric and in the Early Hobbes. In *Political Discourse in Early Modern Britain*, ed. Nicholas Phillipson and Quentin Skinner, Cambridge: CUP, 67–93. Revised version entitled Hobbes's Changing Conception of Civil Science, in Skinner 2002c, 66–86.

(1993b): Two Concepts of Citizenship. *Tijdschrift voor filosofie* 55, 403–19.

188   *References*

Philipson and Skinner (1993): Preface. In *Political Discourse in Early
          Modern Britain*, ed. Nicholas Phillipson and Quentin
          Skinner, Cambridge: CUP, xii–xiii.
(1994a):   Modernity and Disenchantment: Some Historical Reflec-
          tions. In *Philosophy in the Age of Pluralism*, ed. James Tully,
          Cambridge: CUP, 37–48 (revised version of 1991b).
(1994b):   Moral Ambiguity and the Renaissance Art of Eloquence.
          Essays in Criticism 44, 267–92. Revised and extended
          version in Skinner 2002b, 264–85.
(1994c):   The Study of Rhetoric as an Approach to Cultural
          History: the Case of Hobbes. In *Main Trends in Cultural
          History. Ten Essays*, ed. Willem Melching and Wyger
          Velema, Amsterdam: Rodopi, 17–53.
(1995):   The Vocabulary of Renaissance Republicanism: a Cultural
          longue durée? In *Language and Images of Renaissance Italy*,
          ed. Alison Brown, Oxford: Clarendon Press, 87–110 (a
          variant of 1990b).
(1996a):   *Reason and Rhetoric in the Philosophy of Hobbes.* Cambridge:
          CUP.
(1996b):   From Hume's Intentions to Deconstruction and Back.
          Journal of Political Philosophy 4, 142–54. Fused into
          Motives, Intentions and Interpretations, in Skinner 2002a,
          90–102.
(1996c):   Thomas Hobbes' Anti-Liberal Theory of Liberty. In
          Liberalism Without Illusions, ed. Bernard Yack, London:
          University of Chicago Press, 149–69 (a variant of 1990c).
(1996d):   Bringing Back a New Hobbes. Review of *The Correspon-
          dence of Thomas Hobbes, Three Discourses: A Critical Modern
          Edition of Newly Identified Work of the Young Hobbes. New
          York Review of Books* 4 April.
(1997a):   Deux interprétations de Hobbes et Actualité de Hobbes:
          Yves Zarka et Quentin Skinner. *Le débat*, septembre,
          92–120 (Skinner 100–8, 115–20) (French version of 2001b).
(1997b):   Sir Geoffrey Elton and the Practice of History. *Transactions
          of the Royal Historical Society* 47, 301–16. Revised, extended
          version entitled The Practice of History and the Cult of
          the Fact, in Skinner 2002a, 8–26.
(1997c):   An Interview with Quentin Skinner. *Cogito* 11, 69–76.
(1998):   *Liberty before Liberalism.* Cambridge: CUP.
(1999a):   Ambrogio Lorenzetti's *buon governo* Frescoes: Two Old
          Questions, Two New Answers. *Journal of the Warburg and
          Courtauld Institute* 62, 1–28. Revised version entitled

Ambrogio Lorenzetti on the Power and Glory of Republics, in Skinner 2002b, 93–117.

(1999b): Hobbes and the Purely Artificial Person of the State. *The Journal of Political Philosophy* 7, 1–29. Revised version in Skinner 2002c, 177–208.

(1999c): Rhetoric and Conceptual Change. *Finnish Yearbook of Political Thought* 3, 60–73. Revised version entitled Retrospect: Studying Rhetoric and Conceptual Change, in Skinner 2002a, 175–87.

(1999d): Thomas Hobbes and the Renaissance *studia humanitatis*. In *Writing and Political Engagement in Seventeenth-Century England*, ed. Derek Hirst and Richard Strier, Cambridge: CUP, 69–88. Revised, extended version entitled Hobbes and the *studia humanitas*, in Skinner 2002c, 38–65.

(1999e): The Advancement of Francis Bacon. *New York Review of Books* 4 November.

(2000a): *Machiavelli. A Very Short Introduction*. Oxford: OUP (revised version of 1981a).

(2000b): John Milton and the Politics of Slavery. *Prose Studies* 23, 1–22. Revised and extended in Skinner 2002b, 286–307.

(2000c): Thomas Hobbes's Changing Conception of Civil Science. In *Enlightenment, Passion, Modernity. Historical Essays in European Thought and Culture*, ed. Mark S. Michale and Robert L. Dietle, Stanford: Stanford UP, 27–43.

(2001a): Political Theory after the Enlightenment Project. In *Schools of Thought. Twenty-five years of Interpretative Social Science*, ed. Joan W. Scott and Debra Keates, Princeton: Princeton UP, 15–24.

(2001b): Quentin Skinner on *Reason and Rhetoric in the Philosophy of Hobbes*. In *Hobbes. The Amsterdam Debate*, ed. and introd. Hans Blum, Hildesheim: Olms, 17–24, further contribution to the debate with Yves Zarka, 25–30 (English original of 1997a).

(2001c): The Rise of, Challenge to, and Prospects for a Collingwoodian Approach to the History of Political Thought. In *The History of Political Thought in National Context*, ed. Dario Castiglione and Iain Hampsher-Monk, Cambridge: CUP, 175–88 (revised version of 1996b).

(2001d): Why Laughing Mattered in the Renaissance. *History of Political Thought* 22, 418–47. Revised, extended version entitled Hobbes and the Classical Theory of Laughter, in Skinner 2002c, 142–76.

(2001e): La philosophie et le rire. *Le monde* 13 Juin.
(2001f): Liberté politique et corruption. Propos recueillis et traduits de l'anglais par Marie Gaille-Nicodimo. *Magazin littéraire* 397, Dossier Machiavel aujourd'hui, 62.
(2002a): *Visions of Politics*. Vol. 1, *Regarding Method*. Cambridge: CUP.
(2002b): *Visions of Politics*. Vol. 2, *Renaissance Virtues*. Cambridge: CUP.
(2002c): *Visions of Politics*. Vol. 3, *Hobbes and Civil Science*. Cambridge: CUP.
(2002d): On Encountering the Past. An Interview with Quentin Skinner by Petri Koikkalainen and Sami Syrjämäki 4.10.2001. *Finnish Yearbook of Political Thought* 6, 34–63.
(2002e): States and the Freedom of Citizens. Forthcoming in *States and Citizens*, ed. Quentin Skinner and Bo Stråth, Cambridge: CUP.
(2002f): A Third Concept of Liberty. Forthcoming in *Proceedings of the British Academy* 87.
(2002g): A Third Concept of Liberty. *London Review of Books* 4 April, 16–18 (abridged version of 2002f).
(2002h): Visions of Civil Liberty. In *The Future of the Past. Big Questions in History*, ed. Peter Martland, London: Pimlico, 104–12.
(2002i): Political Philosophy: The View from Cambridge. A conversation convened by Quentin Skinner at the invitation of the Editor of *The Journal of Political Philosophy* and held in Cambridge on 13 February 2001. *Journal of Political Philosophy* 10, 1–19.

Other Literature

Anderson, Perry (1974): *Lineages of the Absolutist State*. London: NLB.
Ankersmit, Frank (1994): *History and Tropology*. Berkeley: University of California Press.
Anter, Andreas (1995): *Max Webers Theorie des modernen Staates*. Berlin: Duncker & Humblot.
Arendt, Hannah (1958/1960): *Vita activa*. München: Piper 1981.
Arendt, Hannah (1968): *Between Past and Future*. Harmondsworth: Penguin 1977.

Ashcraft, Richard (1981): Review of *The Foundations. Journal of History of Philosophy* 19, 388–92.

Austin, J. L. (1962): *How to Do Things with Words*, ed. J. O. Urmson and Marina Sbisà. Oxford: OUP 1980.

Aylmer, G. E. (1979): Review of *The Foundations. English Historical Review* 95, 139–42.

Barthes, Roland (1970): L'ancienne rhétorique. Aide-mémoire. In *L'aventure sémiologique*, Paris: Seuil 1985.

Bauman, Zygmunt (1991): *Modernity and Ambivalence*. Cambridge: Polity.

Beetham, David (1980): Excavating the Foundations of Political Theory. *Government and Opposition*, 15, 235–40.

Benjamin, Walter (1940): Über den Begriff der Geschichte. In *Illuminationen*, Frankfurt/M: Suhrkamp 1980, 251–62.

Berlin, Isaiah (1958): Two Concepts of Liberty. In *Four Essays on Liberty*, Oxford: OUP 1969, 118–72.

Berlin, Isaiah (1969): Introduction. In *Four Essays on Liberty*, Oxford: OUP 1969.

Bevir, Mark (1999): *The Logic of the History of Ideas*. Cambridge: CUP.

Brunner, Otto (1939/1942): *Land und Herrschaft*. Brünn: Rohrer.

Burke, Kenneth (1945): *A Grammar of Motives*. Berkeley: University of California Press 1969.

Burke, Kenneth (1950): *A Rhetoric of Motives*. Berkeley: University of California Press 1969.

Cassin, Barbara (1995): *L'effet sophistique*. Paris: Gallimard.

Clausewitz, Carl v. (1832): *Vom Kriege*. Frankfurt/M: Ullstein 1980.

Coleman, Janet (1980): Reasonings of State. *Cambridge Review* 5 December, 50–5.

Coleman, Janet (2000): *A History of Political Thought*. Vol. 1, *From Ancient Greece to Early Christianity*. Vol. 2, *From the Middle Ages to the Renaissance*. Oxford: Blackwell.

Collingwood, R. G. (1939): *An Autobiography*. Oxford: Clarendon Press 1978.

Collingwood, R. G. (1946): *The Idea of History. Revised Edition with Lectures 1926–1928*, ed. Jan van der Dussen. Oxford: OUP 1994.

Connolly, William E. (1988): *Political Theory and Modernity*. Ithaca: Cornell University Press.

Crick, Bernard (1962): *In Defence of Politics*. Harmondsworth: Penguin 1976.

Crick, Bernard (1968): Politics as Freedom. In *Philosophy, Politics and*

Society, Third Series, ed. Peter Laslett and W. G. Runciman, Oxford: Blackwell, vii–xv.

Dunn, John (1968): The Identity of the History of Ideas. *Philosophy* 43, 85–104.

Dunn, John (1969): *The Political Thought of John Locke*. Cambridge: CUP.

Dunn, John (1979): The Cage of Politics. *The Listener* 15 March.

Dunn, John (2000): *The Cunning of Unreason. Making Sense of Politics*. London: Harper & Collins.

Fairlie, Henry (1968): *The Life of Politics*. London: Methuen.

Figgis, John Neville (1907): *Studies in Political Thought from Gerson to Grotius*. Cambridge: CUP 1931.

Freeden, Michael (1996): *Ideologies and Political Theory. A Conceptual Approach*. Oxford: Clarendon Press.

Fumaroli, Marc (1980): *L'âge de l'éloquence*. Paris: Albin Michel.

Gagarin, Michael and Woodroff, Paul, eds (1995): *Early Greek Political Thought from Homer to the Sophists*. Cambridge: CUP.

Geuna, Marco (2000): La libertà esigente di Quentin Skinner. In *Quentin Skinner. La libertà prima del liberalismo*, Torino: Einaudi, vii–xli.

Gunnell, John (1979): *Political Theory. Tradition and Interpretation*. Cambridge/Mass: Winthrop.

Hampsher-Monk, Iain (2001): The History of Political Thought and the Political History of Thought. In *The History of Political Thought in National Context*, ed. Dario Castiglione and Iain Hampsher-Monk, Cambridge: CUP, 159–74.

Honig, Bonnie (1993): *Political Theory and Displacement of Politics*. Ithaca: Cornell UP.

Ivison, Duncan (1997): *Self at Liberty*. Ithaca: Cornell UP.

Jellinek, Georg (1900): *Allgemeine Staatslehre*. Berlin: Häring.

Johnston, David (1986): *Rhetoric of Leviathan*. Princeton: Princeton UP.

Kelley, Donald R. (1970): *Foundations of Modern Historical Scholarship. Language, Law and History in the French Renaissance*. New York: Columbia UP.

Kelley, Donald R. (1979): Review of *The Foundations. Journal for the History of Ideas* 40, 663–73.

Kelley, Donald R. (1993): Elizabethan Political Thought. In *Varieties of British Political Thought*, ed. J. G. A. Pocock, Cambridge: CUP, 47–79.

Kopperschmidt, Josef and Schanze, Helmut, eds (1994): *Nietzsche oder 'Die Sprache ist Rhetorik'*. München: Fink.

Koselleck, Reinhart (1959): *Kritik und Krise. Eine Studie zur Pathogenese der bürgerlichen Welt.* Frankfurt/M: Suhrkamp 1973.

Koselleck, Reinhart (1967a): Historia Magistra Vitae. Über die Auflösung des Topos im Horizont neuzeitlich bewegter Geschichte. In *Natur und Geschichte. Karl Löwith zum 70. Geburtstag,* ed. H. Braun and M. Riedel, Stuttgart: Kohlhammer, 196–219.

Koselleck, Reinhart (1967b): Richtlinien für das Lexikon politisch-sozialer Begriffe der Neuzeit. *Archiv für Begriffsgeschichte* 11, 81–99.

Koselleck, Reinhart (1972a): Einleitung. In *Geschichtliche Grundbegriffe,* Bd. I, XIII–XXVIII, Stuttgart: Klett.

Koselleck, Reinhart (1972b): Über die Theoriebedürftigkeit der Geschichtswissenschaft. In ed. Werner Conze, *Theorie der Geschichtswissenschaft und Praxis des Geschichtsunterrichts,* Stuttgart: Klett, 10–28.

Koselleck, Reinhart et al. (1975): Geschichte, Kap. I, V–VII. In *Geschichtliche Grundbegriffe,* Bd. II, Stuttgart: Klett-Cotta, 593–5, 647–718.

Koselleck, Reinhart (1979): *Vergangene Zukunft. Zur Semantik geschichtlicher Zeiten.* Frankfurt/M: Suhrkamp.

Koselleck, Reinhart (1988a): Begriffsgeschichtliche Anmerkungen zur Zeitgeschichte. In *Die Zeit nach 1945 als Thema kirchlicher Zeitgeschichte,* ed. Victor Conxenius, Martin Greschat and Hermann Kocher, Göttingen: Vandenhoek & Ruprecht, 17–31.

Koselleck, Reinhart (1988b): Erfahrungswandel und Methodenwechsel. Eine historisch-anthropologische Skizze. In *Historische Methode,* ed. Christian Meier and Jörn Rüsen, München: DTV, 13–61.

Koselleck, Reinhart (1994): Some Reflections on the Temporal Structure of Conceptual Change. In *Main Trends in Cultural History,* ed. Willem Melching and Wyger Velema, Amsterdam: Rodopi, 7–16.

Koselleck, Reinhart (1996): A Response to Comment on the *Geschichtliche Grundbegriffe.* In *The Meaning of Historical Terms and Concepts. New Studies on* Begriffsgeschichte, ed. Hartmut Lehmann and Melvin Richter, Washington: German Historical Institute, 59–70.

Kremer-Marietti, Angèle (1992): *Nietzsche et la rhétorique.* Paris: PUF.

Laslett, Peter (1956): Introduction. In *Philosophy, Politics and Society,* ed. Peter Laslett, Oxford: Blackwell, vii–xv.

Laslett, Peter (1960): Introduction. In *John Locke, Two Treatises on Government.* Cambridge: CUP (Student Edition 1988).

Laslett, Peter and Runciman, W. G. (1962): Introduction. In

Philosophy, Politics and Society, Second Series, ed. Peter Laslett and W. G. Runciman, Oxford: Blackwell, vii–xv.

Laslett, Peter and Runciman, W. G. (1968): Introduction. In *Philosophy, Politics and Society*, Third Series, ed. Peter Laslett and W. G. Runciman, Oxford: Blackwell, vii–xv.

Laslett, Runciman and Skinner (1972): see previous section, Publications of Quentin Skinner.

Leslie, Margaret (1970): In Defence of Anachronism. *Political Studies* 18, 433–47.

Luhmann, Niklas (2000): *Die Politik der Gesellschaft*. Frankfurt/M: Suhrkamp.

Lyotard, Jean-François (1984): *Le différend*. Paris: Minuit.

Macpherson, C. B. (1962): *The Political Theory of Possessive Individualism*. Oxford: OUP 1971.

Martinich, A. P. (1998): Review of *Reason and Rhetoric*. *Journal of Modern History* 70, 149–53.

Massingham, K. R. (1981): Skinner is as Skinner does. *Politics* 16, 124–9.

Meinecke, Friedrich (1924): *Die Idee der Staatsräson in der neueren Geschichte*. München: Oldenbourg 1960.

Merleau-Ponty, Maurice (1947): *Humanisme et terreur. Essai sur le problème communiste*. Paris: Gallimard 1980.

Mesnard, Pierre (1936): *L'essor de la philosophie politique au XVIe siècle*. Paris: Boivie.

Meyer, Michel (1993): *Questions de rhétorique*. Paris: Librairie générale française.

Miller, J. D. B. (1958): *Politicians. An Inaugural Lecture*. University of Leicester.

Miller, J. D. B. (1962): *The Nature of Politics*. London: Duckworth.

Miller, Ted and Strong, Tracy B. (1997): Meanings and Contexts. Mr Skinner's Hobbes and the English Mode of Political Theory. *Inquiry* 40, 323–55.

Mills, C. Wright (1959): *The Sociological Imagination*. Harmondsworth: Penguin 1975.

Minogue, Kenneth (1981): Method in Intellectual History. In *Meaning and Context*, ed. James Tully, Cambridge: Polity 1988, 176–93.

Namier, Lewis B. (1955): *Personalities and Powers*. Hamilton: Greenwood Press.

Nelson, John S., Megill, Alan and McCloskey, Donald N., eds (1987): *The Rhetoric of the Human Sciences*. Madison: University of Wisconsin Press.

Nicolet, Claude (1982): *L'idée républicaine en France*. Paris: Gallimard.
Nietzsche, Friedrich (1887): *Zur Genealogie der Moral*. In *Werke*, ed. Schlechta, Bd. II, Frankfurt/M: Ullstein 1981, 763–900.
Nietzsche, Friedrich (1981): *Aus dem Nachlaß der achtziger Jahre*. In *Werke*, ed. Schlechta, Bd. III, Frankfurt/M: Ullstein.
Nietzsche, Friedrich: *Werke. Kritische Gesamtausgabe* 2/4. Berlin: de Gruyter 1995.
Oakeshott, Michael (1962/1991): *Rationalism in Politics and Other Essays*. New and expanded edition, foreword by Timothy Fuller, Indianapolis: Liberty Press 1991.
Oakeshott, Michael (1975): *On Human Conduct*. Oxford: Clarendon Press 1991.
Oakeshott, Michael (1980): Review of *The Foundations of Modern Political Thought*. *The Historical Journal* 23, 449–55.
Palonen, Kari (1985): *Politik als Handlungsbegriff. Horizontwandel des Politikbegriffs in Deutschland 1890–1933*. Helsinki: Societas Scientiarum Fennica.
Palonen, Kari (1990): *Die Thematisierung der Politik als Phänomen. Eine Interpretation der Geschichte des Begriffs Politik im Frankreich des 20. Jahrhunderts*. Helsinki: Societas Scientiarum Fennica.
Palonen, Kari (1992): *Politik als Vereitelung. Die Politikkonzeption in Jean-Paul Sartres 'Critique de la raison dialectique'*. Münster: Westfälisches Dampfboot.
Palonen, Kari (1993): Introduction: From Policy and Polity to Politicking and Politicization. In *Reading the Political*, ed. Kari Palonen and Tuija Parvikko, Helsinki: The Finnish Political Science Association, 6–16.
Palonen, Kari (1998): *Das 'Webersche Moment'. Zur Kontingenz des Politischen*. Wiesbaden: Westdeutscher Verlag.
Palonen, Kari (1999a): Max Weber's Reconceptualization of Freedom. *Political Theory* 27, 523–44.
Palonen, Kari (1999b): Rhetorical and Temporal Perspectives on Conceptual Change. *Finnish Yearbook of Political Thought* 3, 41–9.
Palonen, Kari (2000a): Logic or Rhetoric in the History of Political Thought? Comments on Mark Bevir. *Rethinking History* 4, 301–10.
Palonen, Kari (2000b): Die Umstrittenheit der Begriffe bei Max Weber. In *Die Interdisziplinarität der Begriffsgeschichte*, ed. Gunter Scholtz, Hamburg: Meiner, 145–58.
Palonen, Kari (2001a): Politik statt Ordnung. Figuren der Kontingenz bei Max Weber. In *Moderne Politik. Politikverständnisse im 20. Jahrhundert*, ed. Hans J. Lietzmann, Opladen: Leske + Budrich, 9–22.

Palonen, Kari (2001b): Was Max Weber a 'Nationalist'? A Study on the Rhetoric of Conceptual Change. *Max Weber Studies* 1, 196–214.

Palonen, Kari (2002a): *Eine Lobrede für Politik. Kommentar zu Max Webers 'Politik als Beruf'.* Opladen: Leske + Budrich.

Palonen, Kari (2002b): Four Times of Politics. Forthcoming in *Alternatives.*

Palonen, Kari (2002c): The History of Concepts as a Style of Political Theorizing. Quentin Skinner's and Reinhart Koselleck's Subversion of Normative Political Theory. *European Journal of Political Theory* 1, 96–111.

Palonen, Kari (2002d): Rehabilitating the Politician. On a Neglected Genre in Political Theorizing. *Archives européennes de sociologie* 53, 132–53.

Palonen, Kari (forthcoming): *Conceptualizing the Activity of Politics. A History of the Construction of a Temporal Concept.*

Parekh, Bhikhu and Berki, R. N. (1973): The History of Political Ideas. A Critique of Q. Skinner's Methodology. *Journal for the History of Ideas* 34, 163–84.

Pateman, Carole (1988): *The Sexual Contract.* Cambridge: Polity.

Peltonen, Markku (1995): *Classical Humanism and Republicanism in English Political Thought 1570–1640.* Cambridge: CUP.

Perelman, Chaïm and Olbrechts-Tyteca, Lucie (1958): *Traité de l'argumentation. La nouvelle rhétorique.* Bruxelles: Editions de l'Université de Bruxelles 1983.

Pettit, Philip (1997): *Republicanism.* Oxford: OUP.

Pocock, J. G. A. (1957): *The Ancient Constitution and the Feudal Law. A Reissue with Retrospect.* Cambridge: CUP 1987.

Pocock, J. G. A. (1962): The History of Political Thought: a Methodological Enquiry. In *Philosophy, Politics and Society*, Second Series, ed. Peter Laslett and W. G. Runciman, Oxford: Blackwell, 183–202.

Pocock, J. G. A. (1971): *Politics, Language and Time.* Chicago: University of Chicago Press 1989.

Pocock, J. G. A. (1975): *The Machiavellian Moment.* Princeton: Princeton UP.

Pocock, J. G. A. (1979): Reconstructing the Traditions: Quentin Skinner's Historians' History of Political Thought, *Canadian Journal of Political and Social Theory* 3, 95–113.

Pocock, J. G. A. (1987): The Concept of a Language and the *Métier d'historien*: Some Considerations on Practice. In *Languages of Political Theory in Early-modern Europe*, ed. Anthony Pagden, Cambridge: CUP, 19–38.

Pocock, J. G. A. (1996): Concepts and Discourses: A Difference in Culture? In *The Meaning of Historical Terms and Concepts. New Studies on Begriffsgeschichte*, ed. Hartmut Lehmann and Melvin Richter, Washington: German Historical Institute, 47–58.

Rahe, Paul (2000): Situation Machiavelli. In *Renaissance Civic Humanism. Reappraisals and Reflections*, ed. James Hankins, Cambridge: CUP, 270–308.

Rawls, John (1971): *A Theory of Justice*. Oxford: OUP.

Rawls, John (1993): *Political Liberalism*. New York: Columbia UP.

Redlich, Josef (1905). *Recht und Technik des Englischen Parlamentarismus*. Leipzig: Duncker & Humblot.

Richter, Melvin (1990): Reconstructing the History of Political Languages: Pocock, Skinner and Geschichtliche Grundbegriffe. *History and Theory* 29, 38–70.

Richter, Melvin (1995): *The History of Political and Social Concepts*. Oxford: OUP.

Richter, Melvin (2000): Conceptualizing the Contestable. 'Begriffsgeschichte' and Political Concepts. In *Die Interdisziplinarität der Begriffsgeschichte*, ed. Gunter Scholtz, Hamburg: Meiner, 135–44.

Rorty, Richard (1979): *Philosophy and the Mirror of Nature*. Cambridge: CUP.

Rorty, Richard (1984): The Historiography of Philosophy. Four Genres. In *Philosophy in History*, ed. Richard Rorty, J. B. Schneewind and Quentin Skinner, Cambridge: CUP, 49–76.

Rorty, Richard (1989): *Contingency, Irony and Solidarity*. Cambridge: CUP.

Rosanvallon, Pierre (1985): *Le moment Guizot*. Paris: Gallimard.

Rousselier, Nicholas (1997): *Le parlement de l'éloquence*. Paris: Presses de Sciences Po.

Rowe, M. W. (1997): Review of *Reason and Rhetoric*. *Philosophy* 72, 471–6.

Runciman, David (1997): *Pluralism and the Personality of the State*. Cambridge: CUP.

Ryan, Alan (1979): The Past as Another Country, *New Society* 8 March.

Sartre, Jean-Paul (1943): *L'être et le néant*. Paris: Gallimard 1977.

Sartre, Jean-Paul (1948): Qu'est-ce que la littérature? In *Situations*, vol. II, Paris: Gallimard 1949, 55–330.

Sartre, Jean-Paul (1960): *Critique de la raison dialectique*, vol. I. Paris: Gallimard 1985.

Schmitt, Carl (1950): *Der Nomos der Erde*. Köln: Greven.

Schuhmann, Karl (1998): Hobbes. *British Journal for the History of Philosophy* 6, 115–25.

Shklar, Judith (1979): Review of *The Foundations of Modern Political Thought*. *Political Theory* 7, 549–52.

Simons, Herbert W. (1990): Preface. In *The Rhetorical Turn*, ed. Herbert W. Simons, Chicago: University of Chicago Press.

Springborg, Patricia (1997): The View from Diwell's Mountain. *History of Political Thought* 17, 614–22.

Springborg, Patricia (2001): Republicanism, Freedom from Domination and the Cambridge Contextual Historians. *Political Studies* 49, 851–76.

Stötzel, Georg and Wengeler, Martin, eds (1995): *Kontroverse Begriffe. Geschichte des öffentlichen Sprachgebrauchs in der Bundesrepublik*. Berlin: de Gruyter.

Struewer, Nancy S. (1998): Review of *Reason and Rhetoric*. *Quarterly Journal of Speech* 84, 247–50.

Tarcov, Nathan (1982): Political Thought in Early Modern Europe, I, The Reformation. *Journal of Modern History* 54, 56–65.

Thomas, Douglas (1999): *Reading Nietzsche Rhetorically*. New York: Guilford.

Thomas, Keith (1979): Politics Recaptured. *New York Review of Books* 17 May.

Toulmin, Stephen (1978): Introduction. In *An Autobiography*, ed. R. G. Collingwood, Oxford: Clarendon Press, x–xix.

Tuck, Richard (1991): Introduction. In *Hobbes, Leviathan*, ed. Richard Tuck, Cambridge: CUP, ix–xxvi.

Tuck, Richard (1993): *Philosophy and Government 1572–1651*. Cambridge: CUP.

Tully, James (1981/1988): The Pen is a Mighty Sword. Quentin Skinner's Analysis of Politics. In *Meaning and Context. Quentin Skinner and His Critics*, ed. James Tully, Cambridge: Polity 1988, 7–25.

Vaughan, G. M. (1997): Review of *Reason and Rhetoric*. *History of European Ideas* 23, 35–43.

Vickers, Brian (1989): *In Defence of Rhetoric*. Oxford: Clarendon Press.

Viroli, Maurizio (1992): *From Politics to Reason of State*. Cambridge: CUP.

Warrender, Howard (1957): *The Political Philosophy of Hobbes: His Theory of Obligation*. Oxford: Clarendon Press.

Weber, Max (1904): Die 'Objektivität' sozialwissenschaftlicher und sozialpolitischer Erkenntnis. In *Gesammelte Aufsätze zur Wissenschaftslehre*, Tübingen: Mohr 1973, 146–214.

Weber, Max (1906a): Kritische Studien auf dem Gebiet der kulturwissenschaftlichen Logik. In *Gesammelte Aufsätze zur Wissenschaftslehre*, Tübingen: Mohr 1973, 215–90.

Weber, Max (1906b): Zur Lage der bürgerlichen Demokratie in Rußland. In *Max-Weber-Studienausgabe* I/10, Tübingen: Mohr 1994, 1–104.

Weber, Max (1909): Agrarverhältnisse im Altertum. In *Gesammelte Aufsätze zur Sozial- und Wirtschaftsgeschichte*, Tübingen: Mohr 1988, 1–288.

Weber, Max (1915/1920): Zwischenbetrachtung. Theorie der Stufen und Richtungen religiöser Weltablehnung. In *Max-Weber-Studienausgabe* I/19, Tübingen: Mohr: 1991, 209–33.

Weber, Max (1917a): Der Sinn der 'Wertfreiheit' der soziologischen und ökonomischen Wissenschaften. In *Gesammelte Aufsätze zur Wissenschaftslehre*, Tübingen: Mohr 1973, 489–540.

Weber, Max (1917b): Wahlrecht und Demokratie in Deutschland. In *Max-Weber-Studienausgabe* I/15, Tübingen: Mohr 1988, 155–89.

Weber, Max (1918): Parlament und Regierung im neugeordneten Deutschland. *Max-Weber-Studienausgabe* I/15. Tübingen: Mohr 1988, 202–302.

Weber, Max (1919a): Politik als Beruf. In *Max-Weber-Studienausgabe* I/17, Tübingen: Mohr 1994, 35–88.

Weber, Max (1919b): Wissenschaft als Beruf. In *Max-Weber-Studienausgabe* I/17, Tübingen: Mohr 1994, 1–23.

Weber, Max (1922): *Wirtschaft und Gesellschaft*. Tübingen: Mohr 1980.

Weber, Max (1994): *Briefe 1909–1910*, ed. M. Rainer Lepsius and Wolfgang J. Mommsen. *Max-Weber-Gesamtausgabe* II/6. Tübingen: Mohr.

White, Hayden (1973): *Metahistory*. Baltimore: Johns Hopkins UP.

White, Hayden (1978): *Tropics of Discourse*. Baltimore: Johns Hopkins UP.

Wittgenstein, Ludwig (1953/1958): *Philosophische Untersuchungen*. Frankfurt/M: Suhrkamp 1971.

Wittgenstein, Ludwig (1970): *Über Gewissheit*. Frankfurt/M: Suhrkamp.

Zarka, Yves (2001): Yves Zarka on *Hobbes and Modern Political Thought*. In *Hobbes. The Amsterdam Debate*, ed. and introd. Hans Blum, Hildesheim: Olms, 7–16, further contribution to the debate with Quentin Skinner, 31–8.

Index of Concepts

Index of Names

www.ingramcontent.com/pod-product-compliance
Ingram Content Group UK Ltd.
Pitfield, Milton Keynes, MK11 3LW, UK
UKHW020929230426
470295UK00003B/32